Watching Human Rights

Mark A. Boyer and Shareen Hertel, Series Editors

International Studies Intensives (ISI) is a book series that springs from the desire to keep students engaged in the world around them. ISI books focus on innovative topics and approaches to study that cover popular and scholarly debates and employ new methods for presenting theories and concepts to students and scholars alike. ISI books pack a lot of information into a small space—they are meant to offer an intensive introduction to subjects often left out of the curriculum. ISI books are relatively short, visually attractive, and affordably priced.

Titles in the Series

The Rules of the Game: A Primer on International Relations
Mark R. Amstutz
Development Redefined: How the Market Met Its Match
Robin Broad and John Cavanagh
Protecting the Global Environment
Gary C. Bryner
A Tale of Two Quagmires: Iraq, Vietnam, and the Hard Lessons of War
Kenneth J. Campbell
Celebrity Diplomacy
Andrew F. Cooper
Global Health in the 21ˢᵗ Century: The Globalization of Disease and Wellness
Debra L. DeLaet and David E. DeLaet
Terminate Terrorism: Framing, Gaming, and Negotiating Conflicts
Karen A. Feste
Watching Human Rights: The 101 Best Films
Mark Gibney
The Global Classroom: An Essential Guide to Study Abroad
Jeffrey S. Lantis and Jessica DuPlaga
Sixteen Million One: Understanding Civil War
Patrick M. Regan
People Count! Networked Individuals in Global Politics
James N. Rosenau
Paradoxes of Power: U.S. Foreign Policy in a Changing World
David Skidmore
Global Democracy and the World Social Forums
Jackie Smith and Marina Karides, et al.

Forthcoming in the Series

Democratic Uprisings in the New Middle East: Youth, Technology, and Human Rights
Mahmood Monshipouri
The Stealth Pandemic: Violence Against Women
David L. Richards and Jillienne Haglund
Global Democracy and the World Social Forums, Second Edition
Jackie Smith and Marina Karides, et al.
The Global Political Economy of Food
Kimberly Weir
Spirits Talking: Conversations on Right and Wrong in the Affairs of States
Stephen D. Wrage

Watching Human Rights
THE 101 BEST FILMS

Mark Gibney

Paradigm Publishers
Boulder • London

Copyright © 2013 Paradigm Publishers

Published in the United States by Paradigm Publishers, 5589 Arapahoe Ave., Boulder, CO 80303 USA.

Paradigm Publishers is the trade name of Birkenkamp & Company, LLC, Dean Birkenkamp, President and Publisher.

Library of Congress Cataloging-in-Publication Data

Gibney, Mark.
    Watching human rights : the 101 best films / by Mark Gibney.
        p. cm. — (International studies intensives)
    Includes bibliographical references and index.
    ISBN 978-1-61205-141-3 (pbk : alk. paper)
    1. Human rights in motion pictures. 2. Motion pictures—Evaluation. I. Title.
    PN1995.9.H83G53 2012
    791.43'655—dc23

                                                                    2012029351

Printed and bound in the United States of America on acid-free paper that meets the standards of the American National Standard for Permanence of Paper for Printed Library Materials.

17 16 15 14 13   5 4 3 2 1

For My Mother: Recalled to Life

Contents

Part II   Documentaries

Preface

My brilliant colleague and friend Ken Betsalel first came up with the idea of bringing human rights and film together. Ken suggested that we approach *Human Rights Quarterly* and propose that there be a Film Review section much in the manner of the journal's Book Review. Bert Lockwood, the longtime Editor in Chief, was receptive to this idea, and over the past few years *HRQ* has published a number of our reviews, several of which have been adapted for this book. But anyone who publishes in *HRQ* knows full well how much of the heavy lifting Nancy Ent does, and our film reviews benefitted from her counsel and her great patience. I would also like to thank Andrea Holley of Human Rights Watch—she has been so generous in providing me with film.

The *HRQ* reviews have purposely been limited to newly released films; the present book is not. Teachers have told us that one of the great services we can bring to their students is an appreciation for historical films and the context in which they were made.

I have known Jennifer Knerr for nearly a quarter century and have worked with her in the past. When I asked her if Paradigm Publishers might be interested in a book such as this, she immediately displayed an enthusiasm that has never flagged. Initially, I was fearful of leaving some "important" film out, and the result was a never-ending, tiresome tome that analyzed hundreds and hundreds of films, many of which are anything but "great." It was Jennifer who convinced me that quality was much more important than quantity, and 101 seemed to be the perfect number.

Most readers will be familiar with most of the feature films. But I am guessing that most readers might be quite surprised to see some of their all-time favorite movies listed as a "human rights film." One of my goals in this project is to bring forward the human rights themes in these popular movies as a way to help people better understand the meaning of human rights. Thus, I've included several features beyond the film reviews themselves aimed at students of human rights from every walk of life:

- Introductions to each film drawing out the human rights themes and context
- Photos from films with human rights themes highlighted

- A matrix of films keyed to the Universal Declaration of Human Rights
- A link to the complete Universal Declaration of Human Rights on the web site for the book at http://www.paradigmpublishers.com/Books/BookDetail.aspx?productID=298816

We live in the Golden Age of documentary filmmaking. Still, only the most rabid movie watcher will be anywhere near as familiar with the 51 documentaries. But the more important point is that there is no drop off in quality. Instead, both feature films and documentaries can give us enormous insight into the human condition—which goes to the very core of human rights.

Films are released all the time, seemingly every day. In that way, it is impossible for a book such as this not to become "dated," at least to some extent. However, another of my goals in this project is to help start a conversation—or, better yet, a passionate argument—about the relationship between human rights and film. I hope this book will begin this conversation, but it will continue in other ways and by other means. Toward that end, there is a Facebook page "Watching Human Rights: The 101 Best Films" that will become active as soon as this book is published. A website with the domain name "WatchingHumanRights.org" will also be posted and continually updated. And, finally, my students are already working on creating Tumblr, Twitter, and other social media accounts for me. The point is that I will have more to say about the relationship between film and human rights, and I am just as confident that many readers and fellow film buffs will have and want to express their own views as well.

Let me close with two special acknowledgments. The first goes to my wife, Rita. It has now become a bit of a running joke in the house that whenever she would ask me what we were going to do that evening, I would excitedly tell her that I had a "wonderful" movie for us to watch—invariably something on torture, famine, genocide, and the like. But she patiently and lovingly acceded to my passion and watched film after film alongside me, and for this I am eternally grateful.

This book is dedicated to my mother. Those familiar with Charles Dickens's classic *A Tale of Two Cities*—either the book or the movie or, hopefully, both—will recognize the inscription from Book the First: Recalled to Life. A year ago my mother was an inch from death, but through sheer willpower and prayers she has been recalled to life. Those who know her and love her are deeply appreciative of this unexpected joy.

Introduction

At its core, human rights is about how human beings treat one another. Yet, the study of human rights has often had the unfortunate tendency of removing this essential human element, replacing it with such abstract things as statistical analysis or the provisions of various international human rights law treaties. When a human rights violation occurs, that person's humanity has been denied in some way. What film helps us to do, better than any other medium, is to see and understand this. Film puts a human face on terms such as *persecution, inequality,* and *oppression,* and in doing so it provides outsiders with vital information and meaning about the lives of "others." Certainly, books and photographs also serve this function (Linfield 2010). However, film increasingly serves as our universal reference point for many things, and human rights has become one of these.

For the past few years, my colleague Ken Betsalel and I have served as the film review editors for *Human Rights Quarterly* and the present book grew out of this work.[1] The *HRQ* reviews have purposely been limited to recently released films. However, there are many other movies—feature films and documentaries alike—that have a strong human rights component, and after watching (and re-watching) literally hundreds of these, I have selected what I consider to be the 101 best human rights films: 50 feature films and 51 documentaries, which I have divided into two main parts. In addition to those so recognized, I provide a brief analysis of some other noteworthy films on the same subject general matter, and here I pay less attention to the divide between feature films and documentary. Every one of these films is, in at least some way, about human dignity, compassion, empathy, and bravery. But these films are also about political and societal oppression, the denial of basic rights, and, most of all, the inability or unwillingness to see some other human beings as human beings.

What Are Human Rights?

Although there are various ways to explain the meaning of "human rights," my own favorite is one provided by the political philosopher Michael Perry, who sums up the essence of human rights this way: there are certain things that ought not to be done to people, and certain other things that should be done (Perry 1998). These "things" are human rights and they are best spelled out in a number of international human rights treaties, most notably the International Bill of Rights, which consists of the (1) Universal Declaration of Human Rights (UDHR), (2) the International Covenant on Economic, Social, and Cultural Rights (ICESCR), and finally (3) the International Covenant on Civil and Political Rights (ICCPR). In addition to these, there are a host of other major human rights treaties, including the Genocide Convention, the Refugee Convention, the Convention on the Elimination of Discrimination Against Women, and the Torture Convention.

What these treaties and conventions (these terms are interchangeable) do is to spell out certain human rights protections. Some treaties, including the International Bill of Rights, cover a fairly extensive set of rights, while others (such as the Torture Convention) focus on a particular right. What also has to be said is that there is a fair amount of overlap in international human rights law. Thus, torture is not only prohibited in the Torture Convention, but it is also prohibited in the UDHR as well as the ICCPR—not to mention regional human rights treaties, such as the European Convention on Human Rights. Of course, all this law notwithstanding, the ugly truth is that more countries engage in torture than those that do not.

Although this book makes no attempt to deal with every single human right, still, there is a wide range of coverage. Reflecting the two major international covenants, human rights is generally divided into two broad categories: economic, social, and cultural rights (ESCR) and civil and political rights (CPR). Both sets of rights are well represented here. Note, however, that human rights are indivisible and interdependent, and thus any categorization in this manner will miss much of the overlap between various rights. Listed below are some of the rights that are addressed (with references to articles in the UDHR) along with a brief discussion of the films that serve as the basis of analysis (note that FF refers to feature films and D to documentary).

Article 3: The Right to Life, Liberty, and the Security of the Person

Arguably, this represents the most basic right of all, and what it reflects is that the essence of human rights is protecting people. Needless to say, a good number of films deal with this human right.

Genocide

Genocide is defined as an act carried out with the intent to destroy, in whole or in part, a national, ethnical, racial, or religious group, and it is generally considered to be the most serious of all international crimes. Although genocides had occurred prior to the Holocaust, it was not until after this tragic period in history that genocide was formally recognized under international law. I provide analysis of four powerful and intelligent Holocaust feature films, each of which treats the subject in a different way: *Schindler's List* (FF-1), *The Pianist* (FF-12), *Sophie's Choice* (FF-27), and *Au Revoir, Les Enfants* (FF-42).

In the aftermath of the Holocaust, the international community collectively vowed "never again." One manifestation of this commitment was the creation of the United Nations, which is dedicated to the preservation of peace and the protection of human rights. Another was the Genocide Convention, the text of which was adopted by the United Nations on December 9, 1948—the day before the promulgation of the UDHR. Under this convention, states obligate themselves not only to not commit genocide but to prevent genocide and to punish those who carry out acts of genocide. The treaty has universally been interpreted as requiring states to take proactive measures to achieve these ends. Unfortunately, states have not carried out these legal obligations, and genocide has since occurred.

In terms of just sheer numbers, the worst case of genocide in the post-Holocaust period was in Cambodia (1975–1978), where between a third to a half of the country's population was eliminated. The excellent feature film *The Killing Fields* (FF-5) uses a true human interest story as a way of addressing these issues, while the chilling documentary *Enemies of the People* (D-21) takes the viewer forward several decades where we hear from both perpetrators and victims. More recently, the 1994 genocide in Rwanda resulted in more than 800,000 people being slaughtered in a brief hundred-day period. The complete insanity of this, and also the failure of outside states to act, is captured well in two feature films: *Sometimes in April* (FF-9) and *Hotel Rwanda* (FF-9). Finally, while there is some debate whether the conflict in the Darfur region in the Sudan in the first decade of this century constituted genocide or not, *The Devil Came on Horseback* (D-42) comes out squarely on the side that this was genocide and also shows the manner in which Darfur came to the attention of the international community.

Government Oppression

The good news is that most states do not commit genocide. The bad news is that there is no short supply of government oppression. Each year, I direct a project that produces the Political Terror Scale (PTS) (www.politicalterrorscale.org), which measures every country's level of political violence—measured through the number of incidents of torture, summary executions, political imprisonment, and disappearances. And one of the most startling (and depressing) things about this project is just how intractable human rights violations happen to be in so many countries.

Certainly one of the most brutal regimes has been the military dictatorship in Myanmar (Burma), which made every effort to restrict the amount of information coming out of that country, particularly that which shows off its atrocious record on human rights. Because of this, documentaries such as *Burma VJ* (D-46) and *Burma Soldier* (D-46) play a vital role in helping us see, and understand, what conditions have been like in this country.

Israel is a Western-style democracy within its own territorial borders. However, Israel is also an occupying power, and it is an enormous tragedy that the Palestinian-Israeli standoff remains unresolved. This conflict is repeatedly covered in both feature films and documentaries, and I have chosen the following as rising to the top of the class. *One Day in September* (D-48) focuses on the massacre at the 1972 Summer Olympic Games in Munich, where members of the Black September Movement kidnapped a group of Israeli athletes. Nearly all of this drama played out in front of a worldwide audience, and in many ways this event served as the advent of what is now commonly referred to as "international terrorism." *Arna's Children* (D-7) is an extraordinarily powerful documentary that introduces us to a group of young Palestinians. As adolescents, all had aspirations of becoming famous actors, but a decade later most are intent on becoming famous in another way: as Palestinian martyrs. How and why this transformation has occurred is the reason why *Arna's Children* is such an important and absorbing film. Terrorism is also the central issue in the feature film *Paradise Now* (FF-30), a thoroughly captivating and thought-provoking film, although this view is controversial and not always appreciated by viewers. Finally, the documentary *Budrus* (D-28) shows the viewer a burgeoning nonviolence movement in the Occupied Territories, something that has gotten almost no attention by the mainstream media.

Any study of human rights should not only examine instances where human rights have not been protected, but also situations where human rights protection has been achieved. Certainly one of the great success stories has been the dismantlement of the apartheid regime in South Africa. The feature film *A Dry White Season* (FF-21), starring Donald Sutherland and Marlon Brando, gives a wonderful account of the practices of the apartheid regime, but also the manifestations of white denial of those atrocities. *Amandla! A Revolution in Four Part Harmony* (D-41) is a sweet documentary that recounts the country's decades-long revolution and the importance that music played in this cause. Finally, *Long Night's Journey into Day* (D-9) presents an insightful analysis into the workings of the country's Truth and Reconciliation Commission (TRC), which accomplished nothing less than transforming South African society.

The "Troubles" refers to the battle between Catholics and Protestants in Northern Ireland. In *Hunger* (FF-7), Michael Fassbender essentially becomes Bobby Sands, who led a hunger strike in an attempt to have the government of Northern Ireland recognize imprisoned Irish Republican Army operatives as political prisoners. *Bloody Sunday* (FF-28) is a feature film that meticulously recounts the events of this now infamous day, when a peaceful civil rights march was turned into a bloodbath. Finally, *Omagh* (FF-29) is almost studiously apolitical in its depiction of a car bombing attack in this small town in Northern Ireland, which resulted in the single largest number of casualties during the Troubles. In addition to the film's quiet beauty, what it shows us is the universality of human suffering.

Throughout the 1980s, political violence gripped much of Latin America. In Chile, the day September 11 has special meaning because it was on this date in 1973 that the country's military overthrew the democratically elected president Salvador Allende, which in turn led to the brutal Pinochet dictatorship. The feature film *Missing* (FF-3), starring Jack Lemmon and Sissy Spacek, helps bring forth US complicity in this coup. *The Official Story* (FF-4) takes place in neighboring Argentina, which suffered under its own right-wing dictatorship. The film revolves around the government's practice of kidnapping young children from "subversives," who were subsequently disappeared or killed, and placing these children with other families.

Certainly the worst levels of political violence in Latin America occurred in Guatemala, where over the course of several decades approximately 200,000 civilians were killed, the great majority of whom were members of the country's indigenous population. *When the Mountains Tremble* (D-43), which was released in the mid-1980s when the killings reached epidemic levels, provides some of the only available film footage documenting the brutalities of the military regime. *Granito: How to Nail a Dictator* (D-43), which was released in 2011, shows how the past is never really the past by showing how outtakes from the earlier film were instrumental in establishing genocide in that country, as well as the government officials responsible for this. Finally, John Sayles's *Men with Guns* (FF-40) is a feature film revolving around a civil conflict in some unspecified Latin American country. Given the massive levels of human rights violations in this region during this period of time, perhaps it is only appropriate that no location is given in the film. The sad truth is that the movie's setting could be almost anywhere.

War Crimes

There has always been an uneasy relationship between human rights, on the one hand, and international human rights law, or the laws of war, on the other. What needs to be underscored is that the existence of war does not mean that human rights standards are no longer applicable, and this is all the more true with respect to the protection of civilian populations. Several noteworthy films explore this issue. The black-and-white feature film *City of Life and Death* (FF-49) is set against the backdrop of the "rape of Nanking," when, before the outbreak of World War II, Japanese troops invaded this Chinese city and then proceeded to commit unspeakable horrors against the civilian population, especially women. The documentary *White Light/Black Rain: The Destruction of Hiroshima and Nagasaki* (D-12) presents very graphic, but also very compelling, visual images of the terrible horrors brought about by the nuclear attacks on Hiroshima and Nagasaki.

Waltz with Bashir (FF-32) is an animated film that explores themes about war and memory, but what will certainly jolt any viewer is the one "real" scene in the film that shows civilians attempting to flee from atrocities being committed in the Lebanese refugee camp where they were living. Nicolas Cage plays the *Lord of War* (FF-46) in this equally amusing and horrifying look at the world's arms industry. But to close this part on a positive note, *Pray the Devil Back to Hell* (D-20) is an uplifting documentary about the Women of Liberia Mass Action for Peace, an organization that helped end the savage civil conflict in this country.

Non-State Actors

Under traditional international law, human rights standards only apply against states. However, states also have an obligation to protect people from harms caused by private actors, which includes individuals, nongovernmental entities, and corporations. Unfortunately, this obligation is seldom acknowledged, and several films address these types of private wrongs. *Crude* (D-25) is a controversial documentary that tells the story of the massive environmental destruction caused by oil drilling in the Amazonian forests in Ecuador. The issue raised in the film is whether this is the responsibility of the US companies Texaco/Chevron, which had operated in Ecuador for decades, or Ecuador, which later took over these operations. However, what is lost in all this is the issue whether both countries—the United States and Ecuador—failed to meet their obligation to protect these indigenous populations. *The Constant Gardener* (FF-44) tells us a great deal about the drug-testing practices of Western pharmaceutical companies in this political thriller with Ralph Fiennes and Rachel Weisz. Of course, not all corporate malfeasance occurs in developing countries. *The Insider* (FF-19), starring Russell Crowe and Al Pacino, looks at the deceptive practices of the tobacco industry, but also the unsettling relationship between corporate power and a press that holds itself out as being free, but which in some cases is not. A much different spin to all this is shown in the intriguing documentary *The Interrupters* (D-39), where ordinary citizens (of sorts) intervene in settings where there is impending violence. In this case, private individuals do not commit human rights violations but rather prevent them from taking place.

Article 5: Freedom from Torture

Torture is defined as "any act by which severe pain or suffering, whether physical or mental, is intentionally inflicted on a person for such purposes as obtaining from him, or a third person, information or a confession." The classic film *The Battle of Algiers* (FF-41) is in the nature of a faux documentary that revolves around the Algerian war for independence and the brutal French response to this. The vivid torture scenes certainly add to the realistic quality of this film, and modern-day audiences might be surprised at the manner in which they pull for those who today would be labeled as terrorists.

    The Road to Guantanamo (FF-48) offers a blend of documentary and feature film to explore the arrest and torture of the "Tipton Three." Alex Gibney (no relation) is one of the finest documentarians, and his Academy Award–winning film *Taxi to the Dark Side* (D-23) uses the murder of an Afghan taxi driver while in the custody of US security personnel to explore the brutality and the duplicity of the "war on terror." *Ghosts of Abu Ghraib* (D-23) focuses primarily on the now-infamous photos of the torture carried out by American military personnel at the Abu Ghraib prison in Iraq. Finally, *You Don't Like the Truth: 4 Days Inside Guantanamo* (D-15) is the only publicly available film footage of the interrogation practices at Guantanamo Bay, Cuba. What the viewer sees is the interrogation of Omar Khadr, a sixteen-year-old Canadian national, who painfully describes his previous physical torture while he was detained in Afghanistan. However, the viewer is also witnessing a form of mental torture of this young boy.

Article 7: Equal Protection and Nondiscrimination

Equality under the law and nondiscrimination are basic human rights principles. Yet, as many of the following films show, these standards are violated repeatedly.

Sexual Minorities

Sean Penn gives a magnificent performance in *Milk* (FF-17), a film that brings to life the story of Harvey Milk, the first openly gay public official in the United States. *We Were Here* (D-8) is a deeply moving documentary about the AIDS crisis in San Francisco in the 1980s. The film not only portrays the terrible ordeals of the people profiled in the film but also the various policy proposals that were seriously debated at that time, including a plan to quarantine those who were infected with the disease. *Philadelphia* (FF-22), starring Tom Hanks and Denzel Washington, is a deeply satisfying story of an attorney who sues his former law firm for unlawfully discharging him after he was suspected of having AIDS. Finally, *Out in the Silence* (D-34) shows the viewer the kind of everyday discrimination that gays suffer—in Oil City, Pennsylvania, but certainly in other areas of the United States as well.

Gender Discrimination

Discrimination against women remains rampant. Without question, Iran is a terribly repressive society, and this is explored in a rather novel way in *The Circle* (FF-35) but also the engaging animation *Persepolis* (FF-31). *Moolaadé* (FF-43) is an African feature film that achieves something quite rare: it provides an intelligent and insightful look at the practice of female genital mutilation (FGM). A woman's right to abortion services is denied to many. Oftentimes, the result of this will be abortions performed by nonprofessionals in less than sanitary conditions. Such is the case in two feature films. *4 Months, 3 Weeks and 2 Days* (FF-37) takes place in Romania and it is not for the faint of heart—although, I suppose, this could be said about a lot of films on this list. *Vera Drake* (FF-38) is a Mike Leigh film that is set in 1950 London before abortion became legal in that country. The title character cleans the homes of people of means, she cares for her aged mum, she serves as the gravitational pull for her nuclear family—and she helps girls who are in trouble. Finally, *Lilya 4-Ever* (FF-39) is a feature film that concerns a young Ukrainian teen who is induced (and seduced) into traveling to Sweden, where she is forced into prostitution.

Racial Discrimination

The first international human rights movement occurred nearly two centuries ago, and it involved the worldwide effort to eradicate slavery. The feature film *Amazing Grace* (FF-33) tells the story of how, against all odds, slavery came to be abolished in Great Britain, due in large part to the brave and tireless efforts of William Wilberforce. The raw racism of the American South is on full display in *Mississippi Burning* (FF-34), starring Gene Hackman as a former Mississippi sheriff now working for the FBI who is attempting to locate the whereabouts of several civil rights workers. Spike Lee's wonderful documentary *4 Little Girls* (D-6) also takes the viewer back to a time where blacks were expected to know their place in American society—and the exhilarating thing is that they did not.

Moving outside the context of the United States, indigenous or aboriginal populations have repeatedly been subjected to discrimination or worse. *Once Were Warriors* (FF-6) is a highly acclaimed film from New Zealand that offers a stark portrayal of life for a Maori family living in the white world. The effort to eliminate Australia's aboriginal population—clearly genocide, under today's standards—is shown in *Rabbit-Proof Fence* (FF-50).

Ethnic and Caste Discrimination

In addition to racial discrimination, there is also a disturbing amount of discrimination based on ethnicity, and caste in the case of India. To my mind, the largest and most obvious (or what should be obvious) case of ethnic discrimination involved European colonialism, when vast areas of the globe were under European domain. *Days of Glory (Indigènes)* (FF-25) is set in World War II when the fallen French government rushed out into "its" colonies in North Africa to press the native population into service to fight for the motherland—a land none of these men have ever stepped foot on before or otherwise would have. No surprise, but what they find is the same kind of second-class citizenship they had experienced before. *Even the Rain* (FF-45) ties together two strands of colonial oppression. The first involves a back story of the making of a movie about Columbus's arrival in the New World, followed by the genocide of the Spanish Conquest. The second deals with a modern-day fight against privatizing water, which is opposed by indigenous people, several of whom play "natives" in the Columbus film. Apparently, past oppression is much easier to see than our own practices.

Gandhi (FF-15) tells the life story of Mohandas K. Gandhi, who led the fight for Indian independence from British rule while advocating the principle of non-violence. Unfortunately, religious and caste differences still exist in Indian society, and these tensions serve as a focal point in the Academy Award–winning feature film *Slumdog Millionaire* (FF-16). Finally, *District 9* (FF-26) offers a beguiling story involving extraterrestrial visitors. The film can be interpreted in a number of different ways, but my own take is that we are much quicker to see the differences in others than we are to understand our shared commonalities.

Children

The Convention on the Rights of the Child is the most widely adopted international human rights treaty, with only two countries—Somalia and the United States—that are not state parties to it. One might thereby assume that children receive all kinds of human rights protection. Unfortunately, just the opposite of this is true, and a strong argument could be made that children are the single most oppressed group of people of all. A good number of the films analyzed here involve children. However, for purposes of this part, the one film I will specifically make mention of is *Children Underground* (D-31), a documentary that follows a group of desperate and incorrigible street children in Bucharest, Romania. Let the viewer be warned: this is an extraordinary difficult film to watch.

Article 8: The Right to an Effective Remedy

There is little question that the weakest aspect of the entire human rights enterprise is the lack of enforcement of these rights. The irony (or tragedy) of this is that most human rights treaties not only guarantee certain human rights but also detail that those whose rights have been violated must be given recourse to an "effective remedy." What so often occurs, then, is a double victimization. The first is the violation of the substantive right and the second is the denial of any form of effective remedy or any other form of accountability.

One of the odd things about this is that at the outset of the human rights revolution, accountability was a key component. The post–World War II Nuremberg trials against former Nazi leaders shown in *Judgment at Nuremberg* (FF-47) represented the first time in history that the international community prosecuted former political and military leaders. Unfortunately, this effort was short lived, and in the ensuing decades oppressive dictators ruled with impunity. All this seemed to change with the international effort to extradite and prosecute the former Chilean dictator Augusto Pinochet, which is shown in Patricio Guzmán's documentary *The Pinochet Case* (D-27). Although Pinochet was not extradited to Spain to face charges for his crimes, the more important issue, or so it was thought, was the establishment of the "Pinochet principle," which allows any country to prosecute those who directed or carried out the worst forms of human rights violations. Unfortunately, the reality has not come anywhere near the legal principle itself, as can be seen in *The Dictator Hunter* (D-50), a documentary about the effort to bring Hissène Habré, the former dictator of Chad, to justice.

Article 9: Freedom from Arbitrary Arrest
Article 10: The Right to a Fair Trial

Admittedly, a film where justice is served is not nearly as compelling as one where it is not, but even with this in mind, what is deeply unsettling are the number of films that cast the judicial system in a less-than-flattering light. Most of these films are from the United States, so I will begin instead with *Presumed Guilty* (D-22) an aptly named documentary showing the strange way in which the Mexican criminal justice system operates. In the United States, *To Kill a Mockingbird* (FF-24) remains one of the most compelling stories about racial inequity in American society and in the judicial system itself. Although some elements of the film have aged, it is still certainly not unknown for black criminal defendants to face all-white juries.

There are a host of outstanding documentaries that explore injustice. One of the most disturbing is *In the Land of the Free* (D-14), which tells the human story of the "Angola 3," three inmates at the infamous Angola state penitentiary who collectively have spent nearly a century in solitary confinement—for crimes that seem problematic at best. To stay with Angola, the inmates the viewer meets in *The Farm: Angola, USA* (D-49) may well be guilty. But what is shocking is the length of their imprisonments and the unwillingness of prison authorities, as well as political leaders, to consider even the possibility of rehabilitation. Equally disturbing are the domestic terrorism charges brought against University of South Florida professor Sami Al-Arian, which is examined in the documentary *USA vs. Al-Arian* (D-4). Finally, *Dead Man Walking* (FF-11) is a sensitive and insightful look at capital punishment that does not make the defendant (wonderfully played by Sean Penn) into anything but the mess of a human being that he is.

I will close by returning to injustices outside the United States. The first comes from the Chinese documentary *Petition (The Court of Complaints)* (D-45), where ordinary citizens travel to Beijing, at times for years on end, in an attempt to press their claims with government authorities. I am still not sure whether this film is a sign of hope or complete hopelessness. Finally, the most unique setting for a trial is on display in *Bamako* (FF-36), where the World Bank and the International Monetary Fund are in the dock in the middle of a sleepy African village for crimes committed against the people the two organizations were supposed to help.

Article 13: Freedom of Movement
Article 14: The Right to Apply for Asylum

Article 13 provides that there is freedom of movement within the borders of a state and also that there is a human right to leave one's country and return. However, there is no recognized human right to enter the territory of any other state other than one's own. What also must be said is that Western states are becoming increasingly restrictive in terms of who is allowed entry and are enforcing their own immigration regulations farther and farther away from their own national borders. *Journey of Hope* (FF-13) provides a dramatic and insightful view of the strong pull of European migration and of the cold reality that also goes along with it.

Article 14 of the UDHR provides that everyone has a right to seek and enjoy asylum in other countries. Once again, however, there is no correlative duty for states to provide asylum. States are obligated not to send a person back to a country where his life or well-being might be threatened, but there is no obligation to allow refugees to apply for asylum. Because of these limitations, states have taken a number of measures to prevent refugees (or would-be refugees) from leaving their country of origin in the first place. The documentary *Well-Founded Fear* (D-30) provides a revealing portrait of the asylum process in the United States, and one of the apparent lessons of the film is that success or failure is dependent on a number of factors, including which asylum officer hears a particular case and other matters of luck as well. Finally, one would be hard pressed to find a more successful refugee story than that involving Rose Mapendo, who fled from the Democratic Republic of the Congo with ten of her children and was eventually able to gain entrance into the United States as a refugee. The documentary *Pushing the Elephant* (D-19) tells the story of Rose's reunion with her eleventh child, who had been forced to stay behind, and also her remarkable efforts fighting for the weak and the oppressed.

Article 18: Freedom of Thought
Article 19: Freedom of Opinion and Expression

Human rights is not simply about having adequate food, housing, education, health care, or being free from physical harm. In addition, each individual enjoys a personal autonomy that is, or at least should be, beyond government influence and control. *The Lives of Others* (FF-2) offers great insight into East German society under communist rule where censorship was the rule. On the other side of the Cold War, the feature film *Good Night, and Good Luck* (FF-23) shows the insidious nature of McCarthyism in the United States. *Fahrenheit 9/11* (D-44) brings government-induced fear forward several decades to the present-day war on terror. *V for Vendetta* (FF-20) gives the viewer a glimpse of what society will look like when there is no free press and when the government is thereby able to keep its citizens in a constant state of fear. But not everyone can be cowered, even by the most brutal regimes. *The Agronomist* (D-5) is a joy to watch simply because the viewer gets to spend time with the outspoken and indefatigable Jean Dominique, the voice of Haiti's poor, who eventually paid for his political and social commitment with his life.

Article 22: The Right to Social Security
Article 25: The Realization of ESCR

The Political Terror Scale (PTS) is a ranking of countries in terms of their level of physical integrity violations. These violations are the most serious of all, but in sheer number they pale in comparison with violations of economic, social, and cultural rights (ESCR). Unfortunately, many people (and governments) continue to associate human rights only with physical integrity rights. In the United States, there are at least two reasons for this. The first is that there is no mention of ESCR in the American Constitution, which in large part simply reflects the period of time when it was drafted (Sunstein 2004). The second is that while the United States has signed and ratified a number of international human rights treaties, including the International Covenant on Civil and Political Rights, it has only signed (but not yet ratified) the International Covenant on Economic, Social, and Cultural Rights.

It is ironic, then, that there are so many great American films that deal with poverty and inequality. Still, even in these films there is an inability or unwillingness to associate any of this with "human rights." I spotlight two feature films: *Precious: Based on the Novel "Push" by Sapphire* (F-8) and *Midnight Cowboy* (F-14) starring Dustin Hoffman and Jon Voight. In terms of documentaries, *Roger & Me* (D-11), *Hoop Dreams* (D-3), *Public Housing* (D-35), and *When the Levees Broke* (D-29) stand out.

Article 23: The Right to Work and the Right to Form and Join Trade Unions

Article 23 is designed to protect workers from various forms of exploitation. The feature film *Norma Rae* (FF-18) and Barbara Kopple's two documentaries *Harlan County, USA* (D-36) and *American Dream* (D-36) deal with the issue of trade unions. In *Last Train Home* (D-17) and *Mardi Gras: Made in China* (D-38) the viewer gets a much fuller sense of the brutal working conditions that exist in China. There is no narrative theme in *The Inheritors* (D-33); rather, what the viewer is shown is a litany of stunning images of young children hard at work, enjoying only a few precious moments of what others would think of as childhood. Finally, consider how desperate a person would have to be to do a job where an average of one person a day is killed. This is the fate of *The Shipbreakers* (D-37).

Article 26: The Right to Education

Education is not only important in its own right, but the fulfillment of this right is vital in terms of protecting other human rights, such as freedom of opinion and conscience. *Waiting for "Superman"* (D-10) is a gripping account of a group of American children, nearly all from the lower strata of society, vying for a space in a decent school so they can have a fighting chance in life. There is a more subtle kind of desperation shown in *Where Soldiers Come From* (D-13), a documentary that follows a group of young men from the Upper Peninsula in Michigan who join the military in order to receive the signing bonus, which will then give them the means to go to college. However, standing squarely in the way of this plan is a dangerous stint in Afghanistan.

Article 28: The Right to a Social and International Order to Promote and Protect Human Rights

Human rights are declared to be "universal," yet there has been a strong tendency to view human rights in territorial terms, so that a state's human rights obligations begin—but also end—at its own territorial borders. This represents a fundamental misreading of human rights; while a state has certain human rights within its own territory, it has human rights obligations beyond its borders as well (Gibney and Skogly 2010). Thus, rather than seeing human rights protection as something that states engage in individually and that only apply to their own citizens, a better conceptualization of human rights is to see this as a shared endeavor—and directed at *all* people.

Unfortunately, as the following films show, the international order seems to be going in the opposite direction. *Darwin's Nightmare* (D-1) brings the viewer to a destitute fishing village on Lake Victoria in Tanzania. Here, fish from the lake are flown to European markets—at a time when Tanzania is experiencing massive famine. In addition, the planes that are flying into the town's dilapidated airport are not empty, as everyone keeps insisting. Instead, these planes are packed with arms headed to various civil conflicts in Africa. No Westerners in the film seem to see anything wrong with this; in their mind, the violations lie with the Africans directly involved in the conflict and not with those who deliver the arms. The reason for this is that under the dominant approach to human rights we attribute any and all human rights violations in this situation to Tanzania—but not to "us." Similarly, *Nero's Guests* (D-2) presents us with another way that Westerners impact the human rights of others, by presenting evidence of the manner in which Western agricultural policies, especially subsidies, are having an enormously negative effect on Indian famers, among others in the Third World.

Quite often, we are able to simply ignore the negative consequences of how our actions affect others. However, the one possible exception to this is global warming, although what also needs to be said is that Western states are in a vastly better position to deal with the tremendous dislocations that will arise from this than poorer countries will be. *An Inconvenient Truth* (D-16) offers a wonderful primer on how this grave situation has arisen and what can be done—what must be done—to address this issue. But if we do not, perhaps the more appropriate film is *The Age of Stupid* (D-40).

What Makes a Film a (Great) Human Rights Film?

I will close this introduction by explaining what, in my view at least, constitutes a human rights film and the standards I employed in choosing and ranking these movies. Many people would associate a "human rights film" with some clunky documentary produced by a well-meaning nongovernmental organization that lectures to the viewing audience.

It should already be obvious that I do not think like this, and I must also confess to having a strong aversion to being lectured to by anyone, let alone a film or a film director. To my mind, a "human rights film" is simply a film that brings forward issues that relate to human rights. This can be done directly or indirectly, although my general preference is the latter. What might surprise most readers is their familiarity with many of the films on this list, especially feature films. But human rights issues are all around us—or on the screen right in front of us. Thus, in addition to introducing many new films, I also hope to engage the readers to re-think movies they have already watched.

That said, no film gets a high mark simply for a well-intentioned effort alone or because it deals with a human rights issue in some fashion. To make the cut in this book, a film must score high on at least three criteria. One is *illumination*: Did the film made the viewer think significantly about human rights issues in a new and interesting way? A second is *complexity*: Did the film allow for the complexity of human rights to emerge, or was it didactic or even propagandistic?

A third criterion is *teachability* or *watchability*: Would the film work in a human rights course, and would it resonate with a general audience? On this last point, I tend to judge films on the basis of present-day standards and not the time when they were released. Thus, movies such as *All Quiet on the Western Front* (1930) and *The Grapes of Wrath* (1940) were great films in their era, but they would not necessarily play well with today's audiences, although I should also add that several classic films are included here.

My hope is that the viewer will find all the listed films "classic"—intelligent, challenging, entertaining, and deeply thought provoking—and that they will help each one of us understand and honor the human rights of all.

Notes

1. Parts of the reviews of films first appeared in the following articles: Ken Betsalel and Mark Gibney, "Human Rights Watch 2007 Traveling Film Festival," *Human Rights Quarterly* 30 (2008): 205–208; Ken Betsalel and Mark Gibney, "Can a Film End a War?" *Human Rights Quarterly* 30 (2008): 522–525; Mark Gibney and Ken Betsalel, "Human Rights Begins with Seeing: A Review of Human Rights Films," *Human Rights Quarterly* 33 (2011): 1186–1194.

References

Gibney, Mark, and Sigrun Skogly, eds. 2010. *Universal Human Rights and Extraterritorial Obligations*. Philadelphia: University of Pennsylvania Press.

Linfield, Susie. 2010. *The Cruel Radiance: Photography and Political Violence*. Chicago: University of Chicago Press.

Perry, Michael. 1998. *The Idea of Human Rights: Four Inquiries*. New York: Oxford University Press.

Sunstein, Cass. 2004. *The Second Bill of Rights: FDR's Unfinished Revolution and Why We Need It More than Ever*. New York: Basic Books.

Part I

Feature Films

1

Schindler's List
(Steven Spielberg, 1993)

It is only appropriate that the Holocaust serves as the backdrop for the top-rated feature film. For one thing, there is simply no historical parallel for the systematic slaughter of Europe's Jewish population. But the Holocaust is important to human rights for another reason: the international response to it set in motion the human rights revolution of the twentieth century. Before World War II, how a state treated its own citizens was viewed as a purely domestic matter and outside the purview of the international community. All this has now changed. Now international law mandates that states are obligated to protect the human rights of not only their own citizens but of individuals in other lands as well.

✳ ✳ ✳

Steven Spielberg's masterpiece *Schindler's List* tells the story of a German industrialist (Oskar Schindler) who goes to occupied Poland to make his fortune manufacturing war kits for the Nazi regime and ends up risking his life and his fortune in an effort to save his Jewish workers. What is so remarkable about Oskar Schindler is how unremarkable he is, at least at the outset of the film. Schindler is the ultimate capitalist who wines, dines, and bribes German officials in order to increase his business opportunities. There is no altruism involved in Schindler's decision to employ Jewish workers. He does so only because he does not have to pay them wages, thereby increasing his own profit as well as his ability to pay off Nazi officials. Like so many others, Schindler does not see—nor does he want to see—the enormous horrors and injustices going on all around him. Business is business, and business with the Nazis is particularly lucrative for Oskar Schindler.

Schindler's metamorphosis in the movie begins during the liquidation of the Krakow Ghetto, but not as one might imagine. As this scene develops, Schindler is out horseback riding with one of his young female lovers in the hills overlooking the city. Schindler is at first oblivious to the slaughter and mayhem going on directly below him. But a small child in a red dress—one of the very few times that color is used in the film—wandering the streets in search of safety catches his eye. As for so many of us, for Schindler the death of millions is incomprehensible, but the fate of one helpless young child is something that can be understood. And it is the reality of this fleeting image that begins the transformation of Oskar Schindler from an otherwise ordinary, self-serving business operative to a most remarkable and honorable person.

If Liam Neeson's portrayal of Oskar Schindler was the role of a lifetime, Ralph Fiennes was his equal as Amon Goeth, the commander of the Plaszow concentration camp. Goeth is a sadistic psychopath who finds great joy in randomly shooting camp inmates and severely beating his Jewish mistress. But Fiennes achieves the remarkable task of making Goeth into a human being—albeit an extraordinarily flawed one. Somewhat less effective is Ben Kingsley who plays Itzhak Stern, Schindler's Jewish assistant who runs his business and is in charge of hiring, and thus saving, his Jewish workers. Kingsley is a fine actor, but the character is a bit of a stock figure: the self-effacing but saintly Jew.

It might sound like a truism to talk about the ability of a single individual to change the world, but *Schindler's List* is no make-believe story. The real Oskar Schindler is buried in Jerusalem, and he has been honored as a hero to the Jewish people. The truth is that he is a hero for *all* people, and *Schindler's List* does a superb job of telling this story. In the final scene, now filmed in color, many of the surviving "Schindler Jews" honor him by walking up to his simple grave and placing upon it a single stone. *Schindler's List* is filmmaking at its very finest; and Oskar Schindler represents humanity at its finest as well.

Also of Note

The Last Days (James Moll, 1998)

The Holocaust has been portrayed in a number of movies, feature film and documentary alike, many of which are analyzed later on. However, special mention should be made of three outstanding documentaries that also deal with efforts to save Jews. *The Last Days* focuses on five Holocaust survivors from Hungary who now live in the United States. Two questions continue to haunt these five—and perhaps all Holocaust survivors: First, why did the genocide against the Jews occur, and second, why did I survive?

The best feature of this film involves the small and personal stories that the survivors tell. One relates using the latrine at the concentration camp as a place to sing Jewish songs with the other children. Another involves one of the survivors, who put on a bathing suit as a reminder of better times before her family was rounded up, and then realizing this when she found herself in the shower at Auschwitz—with the bathing suit still on. The five are all deeply conflicted when they return to Hungary, although all are accompanied by family members and all use this as an opportunity of trying to educate the younger generations. One of them, Tom Lantos, the only Holocaust survivor to serve in the US Congress, takes his young grandchildren to his old hiding places—where he hid when he was just a few years older than they are now. Toward the end of the film, notwithstanding all of the horrors he has been put through, Lantos seems to feel that he is a blessed man because he and his wife (whom he has known since childhood) have been given the greatest gift of all: children, grandchildren, and great-grandchildren. And watching them frolic on the family lawn, certainly no one could dispute this.

Into the Arms of Strangers: Stories of the Kindertransport (Mark Jonathan Harris, 2000)

Into the Arms of Strangers is an uplifting documentary about the Kindertransport program. This program, instituted a few days after Kristallnacht, transported some 10,000 Jewish children to the United Kingdom from Germany, Austria, Poland, and Czechoslovakia, until hostilities ended the program. Every child who was transported survived the war and nearly all lived happy and productive lives after that. Given the fact that the Nazis eliminated somewhere in the realm of 1.5 million Jewish children, in all likelihood most (if not all) of these survivors would have been killed if they had stayed back home with their families. At the end of the war, some of the children were reunited with their families, but in most instances they came to learn of the demise of their parents and other relatives. Thus, for many, what began as a temporary measure became a new life with a new family in a new country. Or as one survivor commented: "I ceased to be a child when I boarded the train."

Anne Frank Remembered (Jon Blair, 1995)

Tens of millions of people have read *The Diary of Anne Frank,* and yet few of us know much about this young girl who has almost singlehandedly come to symbolize the horrors of the Holocaust. Thus, one of the unexpected joys of this fine documentary is learning something that we thought we knew—but did not. The film has no shocking revelations, but the viewer gets to see Anne as a person and not just an icon or symbol.

2

The Lives of Others

(Florian Henckel von Donnersmarck, 2006)

Younger readers may not even be aware that at one time there were two Germanys: East Germany and West Germany. The decades-long separation was the result of the Cold War, which pitted the United States and its Western allies against the Soviet Union and the Eastern bloc countries it dominated, which included Poland, Hungary, Romania, and East Germany. Although Berlin was physically located within East Germany, West Berlin remained part of West Germany, and this section of the city served as a beacon of hope for the oppressed people of East Germany and an avenue of escape for a lucky (and brave) few.

All this ended with the fall of the Berlin Wall in 1989, which remains one of the signature moments in the human rights movement.

✳ ✳ ✳

It has become common to restrict our notion of what constitutes a human rights violation to such things as genocide, torture, and massive starvation. Yet what is portrayed in *The Lives of Others* is a much quieter, but equally insidious, form of oppression. The story centers around three central characters: Georg Dreyman (Sebastian Koch) is a successful East German playwright and one of the darlings of the communist government; Christa-Maria Sieland (Martina Gedeck) is his live-in actress girlfriend; and Gerd Wiesler (Ulrich Mühe) is the Stasi agent who has been assigned to spy on this couple. In addition, there is Grubitz (Ulrich Tukur), who is Wiesler's immediate superior, and Hempf (Thomas Thieme), a government minister who has compromised Sieland for sexual favors in exchange for illegal drugs and the acting roles she covets.

What *The Lives of Others* provides is a chilling account of a society that is this in name only. Although there are a few harsh interrogation scenes, the East German state usually did not have to operate in such a heavy handed fashion. Instead, government operatives were well aware—often because neighbor spied upon neighbor, and family members spied upon other family members—of each "citizen's" personal weaknesses, and it routinely used this information (or merely threatened to use it) as a means of maintaining its power and dominion. Thus, when Stasi agents break into Dreyman's apartment in order to install a bugging device, Wiesler knocks on the apartment next door and informs the frightened neighbor that if she makes any mention of this, her daughter will lose her treasured spot at the university. No physical threat is used—or needed.

As Wiesler goes about spying on the couple, he becomes aware that Hempf intends to have Dreyman imprisoned for acts against the state so that he can have Christa-Marie for himself. Although Wiesler is a staunch adherent to socialist values, this act of government overreaching, along with his growing attachment and even admiration for the couple, begins to change him. In response, Wiesler arranges to make Dreyman aware of Sieland's relationship with Hempf.

In one of the movie's most effective scenes, a short time later Sieland goes out for the evening, against Dreyman's vehement wishes, and she wanders into a nearly deserted bar where Wiesler also happens to be after his shift eavesdropping has ended. He knows Sieland, but she has no idea who he is. Wiesler pretends to be a fan of hers, and he tells her what a great actress she is. She in turn tells Wiesler what a "good man" he is, and she then returns to Dreyman, where she promises never to see Hempf again.

One central issue in the film is the state's attempt to control the country's artists and writers. One of Dreyman's friends, Albert Jerska, has been blackballed by the government and has not been able to direct a film for more than seven years. At a party, Jerska presents Dreyman with the sheet music for "Sonata for a Good Man" and shortly thereafter hangs himself. Shaken by this, Dreyman sets out to publish an article on the high suicide rates in East Germany. Because the government keeps tabs on all of the typewriters in the country as a means of ensuring censorship, a miniature one is smuggled in from the West and then hidden under the floorboard between two rooms in Dreyman's apartment. The conspirators operate under the belief that Dreyman is not being spied upon, but the reason for this (mistaken) belief is that Wiesler has started to censure his reports, and he purposely does not pass along certain pertinent information to his superiors. In that way, the location of a simple typewriter serves as the dramatic force of the film.

Wiesler's transformation as a person—one might even say to a person—lies at the heart of *The Lives of Others*. At the outset, his adherence to the socialist system is made to be quite understandable and even noble. Like many of his countrymen, he truly does believe that communism was an advance over capitalism, and that enemies would do everything in their power to destroy this more humane type of governance. Thus, what was needed was a state security system that would "guard" the people. It is interesting to note that Wiesler never totally rejects the system he was brought up on, but he does exert his own individual will by small acts of resistance. Certainly his bravest move comes after Sieland is arrested for obtaining drugs illegally, and she informs on Dreyman by confessing where the typewriter is hidden. However, before the other members of the secret police can conduct a search, Wiesler rushes to the apartment and removes it. Unaware of this, when Sieland returns home and sees government agents she becomes guilt-stricken and runs out into the street and into the path of an oncoming car, where she is killed.

Sensing Wiesler's involvement in all this, Grubitz demotes him to opening mail, where Wiesler toils until the day the Berlin Wall comes down. After reunification, Dreyman is informed by Hempf that his apartment had been bugged, and he also discovers that Sieland had not heroically removed the typewriter as he had thought. After reading his secret police file, Dreyman comes to the realization that Stasi Agent HGW XX/7 (Wiesler) had purposely filed inaccurate reports in order to protect him, and through the trace of red ink that is on a piece of paper in his file, he is also able to figure out that this same agent had removed the typewriter. Dreyman is able to track down Wiesler, now working distributing leaflets, although he does not approach him. However, two years later Dreyman publishes a novel titled "Sonata for a Good Man" and he dedicates the book: "To HGW XX/7, in gratitude." Likewise, we owe our own gratitude to director Florian Henckel von Donnersmarck for making this remarkable human rights film.

Also of Note

Fahrenheit 451 (François Truffaut, 1966)

A much earlier film that also deals with life under totalitarian rule is *Fahrenheit 451*, which is set in some indeterminate time in the future where books have been banned and firemen are termed this because their job is not to put out fires but to start them—by burning books. The problem, it seems, is that books have the ability to upset people and get them to think and to feel and to emote.

Passions are considered to be dangerous, so the (one) party line is that it is best if the people are never exposed to these things, and if someone is thought to have a book in his/her possession, the job of the fire department is to break in and destroy the likes of Shakespeare, Milton, and DeFoe.

3

Missing
(Costa-Gavras, 1982)

People the world over are familiar with September 11, 2001, the day that the United States was attacked by terrorists who had hijacked commercial airliners and flown them into the World Trade Center buildings and the Pentagon. However, there is another September 11 that serves as an important milestone in the field of human rights—September 11, 1973. It was on this date that the Chilean military overthrew the democratically elected government of Salvador Allende and installed Augusto Pinochet in power. Under Pinochet's authoritarian rule, thousands of Allende supporters were either killed or tortured and many more were driven into exile.

General Pinochet would eventually be voted out of office, although he retained considerable power as the head of the country's armed forces and a Senator for Life. However, his name once again came to world attention when he was arrested in 1998 while he was in Great Britain pursuant to an indictment issued by Spanish magistrate Baltasar Garzón for crimes committed during his dictatorship based on the principle of "universal jurisdiction": the notion being that there are some international crimes that are so heinous any country can prosecute them. After years of legal maneuvering, the British High Court agreed that Pinochet could be extradited—thereby establishing the "Pinochet principle"— but the country's home secretary allowed him to return to Chile based on "humanitarian considerations." These events have been told in several of Patricio Guzmán's films including The Pinochet Case (D-27).

***

Missing is based on a true story. The protagonist, at least at the beginning of the story, is Charles Horman (John Shea), a young American freelance writer who obtains some information from CIA operatives concerning the US involvement in the coup. Soon thereafter, Horman disappears. This then forces his deeply annoyed father (Jack Lemmon) to travel from the United States in order to straighten out the mess that his seemingly naïve son has gotten himself into once again.

Jack Lemmon had many great roles in his career but none that surpass his portrayal of Ed Horman. When the viewer is first introduced to Lemmon's character, he is the epitome of the American way of life. In his mind, his son's whereabouts is the result of a simple misunderstanding that will be undone by employing some political muscle, and he puts his full faith in the minions at the US Embassy who scurry all around him.

Yet, as the film progresses so does Ed Horman, and he slowly begins to realize that the Embassy is lying to him and has been so all along. But there is another transformation depicted in the film, and it involves the manner in which the senior Horman is able to understand the idealism that drives both his son and his daughter-in-law, magnificently played by Sissy Spacek. Because of this, although he is off the screen, Horman (junior) becomes a more fully developed person, not only to his father but to the audience as well.

Almost all great movies have particular scenes that remain indelibly etched in our consciousness and *Missing* has several of these. Perhaps the most telling moment comes during the course of a conversation between Ed Horman and the US ambassador. By this juncture, Horman has already developed a deep cynicism toward the Embassy and he begins to lecture the ambassador about the involvement of the United States in the Chilean coup. But the most devastating line is not delivered by Horman but by the ambassador, who astutely points out that the only reason why Horman cares about American misdeeds, here or any other place in the world, is because his son has become involved. Absent this, the ambassador lectures him, Horman would be at home championing the removal of a socialist government by whatever means necessary. Horman's silence speaks volumes.

There is some gore shown in the film, mainly in the form of dead bodies at the city morgue, but the most effective scenes have none of this. One of the most affecting of these comes about halfway through the film when Lemmon closes his hotel room door and collapses against it in total grief. He will soldier on and do everything in his power to find his son or to learn what has happened to him, but in that one single moment it is clear to the viewer, as it is to Horman, that his son is dead.

Another scene that is almost unbearable to watch occurs after the US Embassy is able to get Horman access to the soccer stadium where thousands of Chileans are being held captive. Horman scours the multitudes unsuccessfully, and he is then handed a microphone where he begs "Charlie" to come forward and make himself known. The scene works exquisitely on two different levels. The first is simply the depiction of the cruelty of the military regime in the form of countless numbers of detainees whose fate is still to be determined, although we now know that thousands were tortured and disappeared by the military regime. The second level involves the human consequences of those cruelties. As a US citizen, Horman certainly has much more political clout than the families of these other detainees, but the enormous pain of losing a loved one is universal.

Missing is based on real events. Would the film work as well if there was more of an attempt to focus on Chilean victims and not on one of the two Americans who were disappeared? For an American audience at least, this is by no means likely. But this also misses the major point of the film. The reason why *Missing* is such a great movie is not because it uncovers a tragedy visited on an American citizen and his family but because it is able to show that the way we have come to think of human rights—as atrocities carried out in far-away lands that have no connection with us and our own way of life—is simply wrong. And at the end of the film, Horman (senior) comes to understand that he, and not his son and his daughter-in-law, is the one who has been naïve about the manner in which the world operates.

4

The Official Story
(Luis Puenzo, 1985)

Chile was not the only Southern Cone country that was ruled by a brutal right wing dictatorship in the 1970s and 1980s. The same was also true of Paraguay, Uruguay, and Argentina, where the next film takes place. From 1976 to 1983 Argentina experienced what is generally referred to as the "Dirty War," as the country's various military juntas made war on leftists and all others considered to be subversive. Torture, disappearances, and summary executions became a part of everyday life. Yet, the only reason the dictatorship fell was because of Argentina's defeat in the Falkland Islands War with Great Britain. After this, however, a remarkable political phenomenon took place: the new democratic government carried out domestic trials against the country's former junta leaders. Not coincidentally, Argentina has been a democracy ever since. Still, one of the issues the country is still wrestling with involves the adoption of the children of some of those who had been "disappeared."

✳ ✳ ✳

At the outset, the viewer is introduced to a loving middle-class couple who dote on their adopted daughter, Gaby. The wife, Alicia (Norma Aleandro), is a high school history teacher and her husband, Roberto (Héctor Alterio), is a businessman with vague ties to the military government, at that time still in power. All is seemingly well in their lives until Alicia meets up with her old friend Ana (Chunchuna Villafañe), who has just returned from living in Europe. In one of the central scenes in the movie, Ana is invited to dinner, where Roberto alternates between flirting with Alicia's attractive friend and arguing with her about her leftist politics. Following the dinner, Roberto retires to bed and the two old friends reminisce on the couch. One of the things Ana and Alicia talk about is the government practice of placing the children of the "disappeared" up for adoption. Eventually, the conversation turns to the reason why Ana left Argentina, and in an extraordinarily moving scene she describes her previous arrest and repeated torture, which forced her to flee the country.

Alicia is stunned by this, and because of her new suspicions that Gaby might be the child of one of the "disappeared" she begins to investigate the circumstances of the adoption. At that point she meets Sara (Chela Ruíz), who may (but may not) be Gaby's grandmother. What also disrupts Alicia's life is the changing nature of the relationship with her students, who repeatedly resist her efforts to keep history at a very safe distance away from present-day realities. Roberto grows increasingly agitated with Alicia, and when she brings Sara to the house in order to talk about the circumstances of Gaby's adoption, he angrily tells her to leave and later proceeds to beat Alicia. At this point Gaby is already at her grandparents, and in the final scene Alicia leaves the house and presumably Roberto.

One reason why *The Official Story* works so well is the quality of the acting involved, particularly Norma Aleandro's natural and intelligent depiction of Alicia. Another is the manner in which the story unfolds. Although Alicia is the protagonist and generally positioned as a positive figure, it is clear that the events in the film would not have taken place but for her rather chance meeting with Ana. In that way, Alicia's willful ignorance of the atrocities carried out by the military junta serves as a proxy for Argentine society writ large. Yet, after being awakened, Alicia does not hesitate to go after the truth, even if this means destroying the family that she loves. In the same fashion, after the removal of the military junta from power, the new democratic government in Argentina took the nearly unprecedented step of prosecuting members of the old regime. However, subsequent proceedings against lower level officials eventually were halted. Thus, while a certain societal truth was established, this is by no means the entire truth. To this day, the Mothers and the Grandmothers of the Plaza de Mayo who march outside the presidential palace in Buenos Aires place diapers upon their heads as a symbol of the children they have lost. One would hope, and fully expect, that Alicia is among them.

5

The Killing Fields
(Roland Joffé, 1984)

Arguably the worst genocide in human history occurred in Cambodia after the Khmer Rouge came to power in 1975. Under the maniacal leadership of Pol Pot and Nuon Chea, it is estimated that anywhere from one half to one third of the population of the country was systematically eliminated. By way of further background, the Cambodian tragedy needs to be seen within the context of the larger Vietnam War. What helped to set off all these horrific events was Richard Nixon's decision to engage in a "secret war" in Cambodia, which in turn led to a weakening of the Cambodian government, and with that the eventual rise to power of the Khmer Rouge.

The documentary Enemies of the People *(D-21) tells much of this story, and that film closes just as the special UN tribunal for Cambodia is about to put Nuon Chea on trial for war crimes and genocide.*

* * *

The Killing Fields centers on the relationship between *New York Times* reporter Sydney Schanberg (Sam Waterson) and his Cambodia interpreter Dith Pran (Haing S. Ngor). As the Khmer Rouge approached the capitol Phnom Penh, Schanberg was able to have Pran's wife and four children flown out of the country. However, Pran refused to accompany them and much of the drama in the middle act of the movie is the effort to pass Pran off as a British subject so that he would not be arrested by Khmer authorities. This ruse is not successful and Pran is taken away, and what he experiences over the course of the next four years almost defies description. As an essential part of Pol Pot's "Year Zero" campaign, Phnom Penh is totally evacuated and much of the citizenry is taken to re-education camps. In order to survive this ordeal, Pran has to remove any vestiges of his past and assume the role of an uneducated peasant. In the film's most harrowing scene involving his attempt to escape, Pran falls into a wetland of dead bodies, all with plastic bags tied over their heads.

As this is going on, the movie shifts back and forth to Schanberg in the United States, who is making every attempt to get information about his colleague's whereabouts. In one scene, Schanberg is honored for his coverage of the Cambodian conflict, and in his acceptance speech he dedicates the award to Pran. Back in Cambodia, Pran has been assigned to work with a Khmer leader (Phat) and tend to his young son. Once again, Pran has to pose as an illiterate peasant, and the incredible drama that unfolds involves Phat's attempt to uncover Pran for being the intellectual he suspects he is. Larger political events then intercede in the form of a humanitarian intervention undertaken by Vietnam, and in the ensuing mayhem Pran is able to escape. As Phat is killed, Pran rescues the young boy, but then loses him in a landmine explosion. Almost miraculously, Pran is eventually able to find his way to the Thai border, where he receives medical attention from the Red Cross. Schanberg is immediately notified, and he flies to the camp where the two colleagues—and two great friends—are reunited in a deeply emotional meeting.

6

Once Were Warriors
(Lee Tamahori, 1994)

The term "indigenous people" refers to those who inhabited a land before it was conquered by colonial societies and who consider themselves distinct from the majority culture in that society. It is estimated that there are somewhere between 300 and 500 million indigenous people in the world. Almost without exception, indigenous people continue to suffer persecution and oppression, if not genocide as was the case in Guatemala in the 1980s. The following film gives us great insight into the lives of another indigenous group: the Maori people of New Zealand.

* * *

The two protagonists in this film, Beth Heke (Rena Owen) and her husband Jake "The Muss" Heke (Temuera Morrison), are from the indigenous Maori tribe of New Zealand. Apparently like many other Maori who are not able to find their place in the white-dominated world of modern New Zealand, the couple are on the dole and they spend much of their day (and seemingly most evenings) drinking and partying. Jake also has a propensity for beating up other people, although at the beginning of the movie this seems almost quaint, as he takes on a goon at his local watering hole, who insists on playing the jukebox while a family friend is singing.

The film has three horrific scenes. The first takes place during a late night party at the Heke household. There is loud music and good cheer, and although their five children are kept awake by the revelry, they seem content that Jake and Beth are enjoying themselves with friends. However, all of this shatters in a moment when Jake thinks that Beth has gotten "lippy" with him, and he savagely punches her in the face and proceeds to beat her unmercifully. Beth wakes up the next morning battered and bruised, and in this condition she is not able to accompany her second son (Mark) for his juvenile court proceeding, which results in him being taken away from the family.

The second disturbing scene, one that many viewers will not be able to sit through, involves one of Jake's drinking buddies, referred to as "Uncle Bully," who during the course of a party at the Heke house goes up to the bedroom of their thirteen-year-old daughter, Grace, and rapes her as she lies in bed in absolute terror. Grace tells no one—in this dysfunctional house, who can she tell?—and the bleeding brought on by the attack is later misinterpreted by her mother as an indication that Grace has become a "woman." In a later scene, Grace comes into the house where her father and his friends are drinking, and Jake orders her to kiss Uncle Bully—her rapist. She refuses to do so, and she flees from the house, which sets Jake off into an uncontrollable rage. This, in turn, leads to the third scene, which consists of Grace's dead body hanging from a noose tied to a tree outside their dilapidated public housing apartment.

As the storyline develops, the viewer learns more about the circumstances that first brought Jake and Beth together but also about the kind of discrimination that dominates New Zealand society, even among the Maori people themselves. Beth's family is from a higher social status, and in one of the few scenes where the viewer gets some glimpse into the basis of Jake's rage, we hear his complaint that her family did not think he was good enough for their daughter. While Jake has always been a low-life, it is Beth who has fallen into the gutter with him. However, Grace's suicide wakes her from her stupor, and she begins to reconnect with her family and with her heritage, as do her children, albeit in different ways. Their oldest son, Nig, joins a Maori gang, and he has his body and face tattooed as a manifestation of his devotion to his Maori brothers and sisters. Their second son, Mark, is sent away to a reform school, but one that is based on instilling indigenous values, and his turnaround is fueled by his desire to adopt the ways of his Maori heritage.

Despite the enormous family tragedies, the film ends on a high note. Beth takes in a friend of Grace who has been homeless. In addition, it is apparent that she will now begin to maintain much closer contact with her family and with her culture. Jake is a different matter altogether, and his situation prevents the film from falling into sentimentality. After Grace's death, Beth comes across her diary in which the young girl describes being raped by Uncle Bully. Beth then takes the diary to the bar where Jake is drinking with Bully, and she reads this entry to the gathered crowd. Jake beats and then stabs Uncle Bully, and in the last scene the police are arriving to take Jake away, presumably for a long period of time.

The meaning of the title only becomes clear at the end of the film. As Beth is about to leave Jake, she is able to reflect not only on her own fall but that of the Maori people. She informs Jake—and the viewing audience as well—that the Maori people "once were warriors"; and it is evident from all that preceded this that what makes a person a "warrior" is not the ability to fight—Jake could certainly do this—but something much deeper than this. As this fine film ends, the viewer is hopeful that Beth, and the rest of the Maori people, will once again become the warriors they once were.

7

Hunger

(Steve McQueen, 2008)

"The Troubles" refers to the bloody conflict between Catholics and Protestants in Northern Ireland starting in the 1960s and continuing to the "Good Friday" accord in 1998, which, by and large, has maintained peace and security. Three of my top-rated feature films take place during this time. In addition to Hunger, *there is also* Bloody Sunday *(FF-28) and* Omagh *(FF-29). For many readers, what is portrayed in these films might all seem like ancient history—and in some respects is ancient history. But what these films also show is how people can be taught to hate others on the basis of a single difference between them, in this case religion, and the horrible things they are capable of doing because of this.*

The next film deals with the imprisonment of Irish Republic Army operatives in Northern Ireland. The IRA insists that their members are fighting an occupying military force, and thus they are deserving of "political prisoner" status. What this would mean, among other things, is that they should be allowed to wear civilian clothes and not prison uniforms. For the British, these men are "terrorists."

✳ ✳ ✳

In one of the most astonishing film portrayals ever, Michael Fassbender plays Bobby Sands, the Irish Republican Army operative who became famous (or infamous, depending on one's point of view) by engaging in a hunger strike in the Maze prison in Northern Ireland, eventually taking his life in this manner. Initially, the film does not focus on Sands but on two other characters. One is Raymond Lohan (Stuart Graham), the warden at Maze, whose only response to the demands of the IRA inmates to be recognized as political prisoners is to apply brute force. The other is Davey (Brian Milligan), a new IRA prisoner who follows the party line and refuses to wear prison garb. Davey and the other IRA inmates stay wrapped up in blankets all day, and they smear feces on the walls and urinate in the hallways, which in turn sets off Lohan and his baton-wielding men.

One of the strengths of *Hunger* is that it does not glorify the Irish Republican Army, and one of the things that drives Sands to undertake a hunger strike is his dissatisfaction with the manner in which he and the other inmates are being used as pawns by the IRA. In a truly astonishing sequence that is filmed in a single shot, Sands meets with the prison priest (Rory Mullen) and explains to him why he has volunteered to be the first sacrificial lamb. This talk begins on a jocular note, as the two enjoy a few smokes and engage in small talk about Sands's health, the life of an Irish parish priest, and so on. However, the mood subtlety shifts to politics, and almost in the way of a biblical parable Sands relates a story from his youth when he was a cross-country runner. He and his teammates were taken from their home in Ulster (Northern Ireland) to a running meet in the countryside in the Republic of Ireland; he describes the lush surroundings as if he were describing somewhere in a distant galaxy.

The crux of the story involves finding a young doe that had broken one of its legs and was thrashing about in agony in a shallow stream. The boys go into the water to investigate, but one of the priests discovers them there, and he orders them to leave the stream immediately. Sands ignores this command, knowing full well the consequences that he will pay. He does so not only because he cannot stand to see the doe suffer like this but because he also knows that he is capable of acting in ways that others are not. And so he kills the doe—as he will now kill himself.

The last part of the film following Sands's physical decline is quite difficult to watch, but it does add some balance to the film. Most notably, Sands's primary caregiver is a prison official, who goes to great lengths to lessen the pain from the bedsores that his emaciated body is now covered with, although another caregiver who has UDA (Ulster Defence Association) tattooed on his knuckles revels in Sands's horrible suffering.

Did the sacrifice of Sands and the other prisoners who ended up killing themselves achieve anything? That much is not clear, and to its credit the film does not attempt to know the answer to this.

Also of Note

In the Name of the Father (Jim Sheridan, 1993)

This feature film stars the incomparable Daniel Day-Lewis as Gerry Conlon, who along with three other Catholics from Northern Ireland were wrongfully convicted of setting off a bomb in a British pub and were designated the "Guildford Four." The four are repeatedly tortured, and eventually each one signs a confession and is imprisoned. Fifteen long years go by before their newly appointed lawyer, Gareth Peirce (Emma Thompson), accidentally discovers that the government had hidden evidence in the case, including proof of Conlon's alibi. In addition to the political angle, there is also a moving story involving Gerry and his father, Giuseppe (Peter Postlethwaite), who himself was wrongfully convicted and eventually died in prison.

8
Precious: Based on the Novel "Push" by Sapphire (Lee Daniels, 2009)

It is common to limit our idea of human rights to civil and political rights (CPR) and to downplay violations of economic, social, and cultural rights (ESCR). In the American context, one reason for this is the Constitution itself, which, reflecting the era in which it was drafted, only protects CPR. Fortunately, many modern-day constitutions (most notably the post-apartheid South African Constitution) also have provisions protecting ESCR, such as the right to health care, education, housing, and so on.

❋ ❋ ❋

Precious is truly a disturbing film that deals with a host of human rights issues. In terms of ESCR, the viewer gets some important insight into the precarious nature of these rights in this country, especially education, housing, and adequate child care. With regard to CPR, the protagonist is repeatedly raped by her father and brutally assaulted by her mother—and yet there is no government mechanism in place to protect her. Some might claim that these are merely private wrongs. This is incorrect. Under international human rights law, the state is obligated not only to not cause harm itself but to ensure that private individuals do not cause harm. This film powerfully shows how this duty to protect has been ignored and violated.

As strange as it may seem, *Precious* is ultimately an uplifting story of an overweight, illiterate teenage girl of this name (wonderfully played by Gabourey Sidibe), who already has one child (with Down Syndrome) as the result of being raped by her father and who is pregnant with a second child by him as well. If this is not horrible enough, Precious is both physically and psychologically assaulted by her welfare-grabbing mother Mary (Mo'Nique), who she lives with in Section 8 housing. When school officials become aware of her pregnancy, Precious is expelled, but her life begins anew when she is placed in an alternative school, where she begins to learn to read and imagine a different life for herself.

Sidibe (Best Actress) and Mo'Nique (Best Supporting Actress) were both nominated for Academy Awards (Mo'Nique won) and deservedly so. It would have been quite easy for this story to have turned into a stereotypical never-say-die movie where the protagonist overcomes all kinds of obstacles on her way to glory. The problem with such stock characters is not only that they are inauthentic but that they can be used to deny the very existence of human rights violations in cases such as this. *Precious* avoids this trap in several ways. First, the movie avoids sentimentality altogether. Mary is a cruel and conniving psychopath at the outset of the film, and she remains as such throughout the film. There is no reconciliation and no transformation here. In addition,

Precious's triumphs are small but meaningful ones. She does not go on to become an intellectual beauty or class president or something on that grandiose order. Rather, she simply learns how to read and how to take care of herself and her children—and that is about it. Fortunately, this is more than enough to fuel this remarkable movie.

Also of Note

Love and Diane (Jennifer Dworkin, 2002)

Perhaps the best way to describe *Love and Diane* is that it is an unvarnished documentary version of *Precious*, with very similar mother-daughter dynamics. Diane is the mother, a former crack addict who eventually had all of her children taken away from her by the Department of Social Services. After years of use, Diane is now clean and attempting to get her life back together through perseverance and her religious faith. Love is her daughter, who after being removed from her mother when she was a child ran away from any number of foster parents and group homes during the lost years. The documentary begins when Diane's children (except for a brother who had been killed) are finally reunited with their mother, and it then follows the family for a number of years.

   Like her mother before her, Love is a single teenage mother, and to add yet another layer of complications, her child, Donyaeh, was born HIV positive. Love vows to love her child and to raise him considerably better than she was raised. However, as the film progresses it is evident that Love is certainly not a good parent, and in one of the most painful scenes, Diane feels obligated to report Love to Social Services, which results in Donyaeh being taken away and placed in a foster home. Will the circle be unbroken? *Love and Diane* could be seen by some social conservatives as proof of the notion of the cycle of poverty, but what prevents this label from being applied so readily is that these are real people making real human decisions, not theoretical abstractions. However, what the film does show is that the denial of basic human rights will invariably have devastating effects, not only on those who are the immediate victims, but on all those around them as well.

9 (tie)
Sometimes in April
(Raoul Peck, 2005)

Hotel Rwanda
(Terry George, 2004)

As mentioned earlier, after the Holocaust, the international community vowed "never again"— meaning that genocide would never take place again. The most visible and concrete manifestation of this was the 1948 Genocide Convention, which obligates states "to prevent and to punish" any and all acts of genocide. Unfortunately, this promise—but this legal obligation as well—has not been kept. An earlier film, The Killing Fields *(FF-5), is set against the backdrop of the Cambodian genocide (1975-1978). The next two movies involve the 1994 genocide in Rwanda where in a 100 day period more than 800,000 people were killed. Most of the victims were Tutsis, a minority ethnic group, although some moderate Hutus who refused to slaughter their Tutsi friends and family members were also killed.*

Although both of these films are set against the Rwandan genocide, they approach the subject matter in very different ways. Sometimes in April *is oftentimes described as the "African" version of the Rwandan genocide in the sense that nearly all of the lead roles are played by African actors, although Debra Winger does have a prominent part as Prudence Bushnell, a US State Department official.* Hotel Rwanda *presents more of a Hollywood version—isn't that Nick Nolte as a UN officer? Still, both films, individually and collectively, do a remarkable job of conveying the horror and insanity that prevailed during this period, and not only in Rwanda itself, and it is for this reason that I have decided to treat the two movies together.*

✳ ✳ ✳

Sometimes in April relates the story of two brothers—arguably Cain and Abel. Augustin (Idris Elba) is a Hutu soldier who is married to a Tutsi woman, and he remains in denial of the danger that his "mixed" family is in until it is too late. His brother Honoré works at a radio station that transmits the hatred that leads to the extermination of the Tutsi "cockroaches." The film goes back and forth from the 1994 genocide to 2004 and the trial proceedings against Honoré before the International Criminal Tribunal for Rwanda (ICTR) for his role in fomenting the genocide.

Perhaps the most memorable scene in *Sometimes in April* involves a group of female students at a French Catholic school who refuse to identify the ethnic identity of their classmates, resulting in all being killed together. Bushnell's role is also noteworthy and based on real-world events. Under the Genocide Convention, all state parties have a responsibility to prevent genocide no matter where this takes place. This provision has long been interpreted as demanding military intervention wherever and whenever genocide occurs. However, as Bushnell's character points out, Western states generally (and the United States in particular) actively resisted describing the genocide that was occurring in Rwanda as "genocide," thereby giving themselves license not to act.

Hotel Rwanda tells the true story of Paul Rusesabagina, a Hutu who manages the Hôtel des Milles Collines and who is married to a Tutsi woman. When the Rwandan genocide breaks out Rusesabagina, intelligently played by Don Cheadle, is desperate to save his wife, his guests, and a host of other beleaguered and frightened stragglers. Operating much in the manner of Oskar Schindler, Rusesabagina bribes, pleads, and threatens Hutu extremists in a brave attempt to save his compatriots' lives.

11

Dead Man Walking
(Tim Robbins, 1995)

In the United States there is still debate over whether the death penalty constitutes "cruel and unusual punishment," and thus violates the 8th Amendment to the Constitution. Abolitionists remain in the minority, although it must also be said that the number of death sentences handed down by juries and the number of executions that are actually carried out have both declined precipitously, in large part because of the rising public concern that innocent people have been sent to their death by the state. While the American people and their state representatives continue to wrangle with this issue, let it be said that all other Western democracies have already answered this question: by proscribing capital punishment—based on human rights principles.

✳ ✳ ✳

Perhaps the single best aspect of *Dead Man Walking* is that the "protagonist," Matthew Poncelet, is a cold-blooded killer. One might expect a Hollywood film dealing with the death penalty—especially one with a big name star like Sean Penn—to sidestep the issue and rely instead on some form of mistaken identity. To his credit, director and screenwriter Tim Robbins makes Poncelet into an absolutely heinous and pitiless figure, one who not only has raped and killed but who during the course of the film displays a rash of lesser transgressions including racism and misogyny.

Despite all this, what shines through is Poncelet's humanity, and it is this humanity—more accurately, the taking away of it—that is the central focus of *Dead Man Walking*. Penn is completely convincing as the condemned man, and this role is as good as any that he has played or that he ever will play. On the other hand, Susan Sarandon does not portray Sister Helen Prejean so much as she plays Saint Helen. More effective, and more believable, are members of the Poncelet family, although many viewers will be distracted by a young Jack Black with a god-awful redneck mullet.

Is the death penalty itself a human rights wrong? Robbins does not come right out and say this and one can fully understand the victims' need for closure and revenge. Rather, what the film does say is that there is humanity in everyone—even the vilest and cruelest among us.

Also of Note
Love Lived on Death Row (Linda Booker, 2007)

Even the most ardent supporter of the death penalty will be moved by this documentary, which tells the story of the four Syriani siblings who were youngsters when their father, Elias, murdered their mother and was sentenced to death. In the ensuing years there was no contact between the children and their father. However, in 2004, these young adults collectively decided to visit him and what they found was not the monster who had effectively made them orphans, but the father who had loved them dearly and whom they also had loved. Along with anti–death penalty activists, the four fight vainly to keep their father from being executed. In that way, then, it is really the state that has made the Syrianis orphans.

After Innocence (Jessica Sanders, 2005)

As this moving documentary notes right at the outset, at the time the film was made some 150 men had been released from prison after DNA testing cleared them of the crime they had been convicted of committing. This film is about some of these men, the kind of hell that they had to go through while in prison, in some cases for decades, and then the different kind of hell that all of them have had to go through to get their lives back, or at least in some coherent order.

Pierrepoint: The Last Hangman (Adrian Shergold, 2005)

From 1953 to 1955, Albert Pierrepoint (Timothy Spall) was considered to be England's "greatest" hangman. This was a person who prided himself on his preparation before each execution and the workmanlike way that instant death was achieved. However, as societal values begin to change, Pierrepoint is increasingly seen as the perpetrator of barbaric practices.

12

The Pianist
(Roman Polanski, 2002)

While Schindler's List *is the story of a remarkable man who helped save Jews' lives during the Holocaust,* The Pianist *is an equally moving story of an equally remarkable man who, against all odds, managed to survive, and survive with his humanity intact.*

✳ ✳ ✳

Adrien Brody's portrayal of Wladyslaw Szpilman, a Polish musician who somehow survived the "final solution," deservedly garnered him an Oscar for Best Actor. The film begins with some old archival film of Warsaw before the outbreak of World War II, but the peace and serenity is blasted away by the German blitzkrieg, which not only disrupts everyday life but any sense of normalcy or morality. Like the other Jews in the city, the Szpilman family is subjected to ever-tightening restrictions, culminating in their being herded into the Warsaw Ghetto. One of the most vivid scenes shows a group of German soldiers rushing into an apartment and ordering everyone in the room to stand up. A person in a wheelchair is not able to do so, and the soldiers respond to this affront by picking him up in his chair and dumping him over the balcony. The rest of the terrified family is then taken into the street and ordered to run, at which point they are gunned down. Yet perhaps the most poignant scenes are not the most violent ones. Rather, it is the dead Jewish bodies lying on the sidewalk that go from being an anomaly to being so commonplace that people don't react or even seem to notice anymore.

As bad as the cramped quarters, the repeated beatings and daily humiliations, the starvation, the forcible wearing the Star of David, and so on are, the viewer is fully aware that this is just the beginning. Szpilman ultimately survives, and there are several reasons for this. The first is that one of the capos, who is an old friend of his, yanks him out of the railway line that is being shipped off for "resettlement," which is in truth one of the concentration camps. In addition, as a healthy male Szpilman can be put to work for the German war machine. However, when this no longer provides him with safety, he relies on the assistance of a group of old friends, non-Jews, who are able to place him in various safehouses, although his life is constantly in peril. Finally, as the war is coming to an end and the devastation of Warsaw nearly complete, Szpilman is able to find a secure hiding space in, of all things, a building housing German military headquarters.

In the film's most moving scene, one cold evening when Szpilman is desperately looking for something—anything—to eat in this locale, he is discovered by Captain Hosenfeld, the head of German military operations. Hosenfeld is by himself, and he asks Szpilman if he is a Jew, which he does not deny. Hosenfeld then asks him what he does for a living, and Szpilman says that he is a pianist. Hosenfeld then points him to a piano that is situated (somewhat conveniently) in the next room and motions him to play. At this juncture, Szpilman is a shell of his former self, and he has not touched a key in years, although he is constantly playing music in his mind. Yet, after gathering up his strength, Szpilman plays a riveting Chopin. The music apparently serves as a human connection between Szpilman and Hosenfeld, who is instrumental in Szpilman's survival by providing him with food and clothing. In their final meeting, Hosenfeld asks Szpilman his name for the first time, and he tells him that he will listen for his music. He also gives Szpilman his military overcoat, which almost gets him killed by the advancing Soviet soldiers. When later asked why he had this jacket on, Szpilman replies that he was cold. But the most remarkable thing is that he is still alive.

After the war, Hosenfeld is shown in a prisoner of war camp, and he comes across another Jewish musician, and he asks him to see if Szpilman can now help him. However, Szpilman is not able to locate him, and the viewer learns at the end of the film that Hosenfeld died in a Soviet prisoner of war camp in 1952. For his part, Szpilman was able to return to the thing he loved most and which helped keep him alive: his music.

There are a number of indelible scenes in this film. In one, a starving Jew in the Ghetto attempts to steal food from an old woman and in the process spills the food on the ground. Rather than running away, he dives on the ground and starts to lick up the food like a starving animal. Another comes late in the film where Szpilman is desperately looking for any kind of shelter amidst the utter devastation that surrounds him. What is so stunning about this scene is how small and insignificant Szpilman seems to be. Yet, his humanity—and perhaps even our own—is reaffirmed by this outstanding film.

Also of Note

A Film Unfinished (Yael Hersonski, 2010)

Film can help us know the world and provide certain insight into it, but there are other times when it is used to perpetuate illusions and lies. *A Film Unfinished* deals with both of these issues and raises issues of what we know—or what we think we know. For nearly a half century, the Nazi propaganda film *Das Ghetto* was viewed, at least by some in East Germany and elsewhere, as providing an actual portrayal of life in a Jewish ghetto. What *Das Ghetto* shows is two vastly different worlds of ghetto life. For some, life was indeed splendid, with a surfeit of food and drink, fine clothing, and an unhurried lifestyle. In stark contrast to that were other Jews who roamed the streets dazed and unkempt, or simply dead. The message sought to be conveyed by the film is that Jews could live quite well under Nazi rule if they chose to do so, while those who did not fare well only had themselves (and other selfish Jews) to blame for this.

 Das Ghetto was filmed just two months before deportations to the Treblinka extermination camp began, and given the fact that six million Jews came to be eliminated under Nazi rule, the message of the film was indeed a difficult one to square with reality. However, what gave lie to this fiction was that another film was unearthed in 1998, this one containing outtakes from the making of *Das Ghetto*. Given the staged sets and repeated outtakes, what could now be established with certainly was that although some of the scenes, most notably those showing Jewish suffering and despair, were real, *Das Ghetto* was nothing like the documentary it pretended to be.

13

Journey of Hope
(Xavier Koller, 1990)

Human rights does not require equality between people. However, what it does demand is that all people have such things as housing, education, health care, and some means of social security. Unfortunately, literally billions of people are without at least some form of human rights protection, and when this occurs perhaps the most natural of all human responses is to move to a country where such human rights protections exist.

***

Journey of Hope is a film about the lure of migration, especially in a world marked by vast differences in wealth between the West—and then everybody else. At the outset, the viewer is introduced to a young Kurdish family from Turkey that is desperate to move to Switzerland in order to enjoy the great riches that they believe they will find there. Setting off on this journey of hope is the mother and father and one of their young children. One of the great strengths of this film is that it provides an extraordinarily vivid account of the trials and tribulations such a trip would entail.

Certainly the most horrifying scene involves an ill-fated trip through a mountain pass in a terrible blizzard that the would-be migrants are taken on. As the frostbitten stragglers approach a luxury resort, one gets a full sense of how close these two worlds are but how far apart they remain. For the desperate travelers, the warm, indoor pool right in front of them represents all the reasons why they left their home countries in the first place. For those on the other side of the glass, one gets a sense that they view these interlopers as some kind of exotic animal. They will feed and give warmth and comfort to them, but they will also deport them back home after this is done, while making every effort to prevent its reoccurrence.

Also of Note

In This World (Michael Winterbottom, 2002)

In this World is a feature film that nonetheless has many elements of a documentary. It tells the story of two young Afghan refugees, Jamal and Enayatullah, who at the beginning of the film leave a sparse refugee camp in Pakistan and set out for Great Britain. Since there is no lawful way for them to get there, this trip is marked by peril at virtually every turn, and certainly one of the most compelling scenes occurs when Enayatullah and several other desperate migrants die from suffocation after being stuffed into a small shipping container.

There are no professional actors used in this film, and the two leads are essentially playing fictionalized accounts of themselves. To its credit, the film does not moralize or judge. Rather, it shows us what will continue to happen in a world that remains deeply divided between haves and have-nots. Many of "them" want to get here—and who really could blame them? The only question is whether we do everything in our power to keep them out, which in the end we might not be able to do anyway, or we address why they would want to come here in the first place.

14

Midnight Cowboy
(John Schlesinger, 1969)

Many Americans do not readily recognize economic, social, and cultural rights as human rights in the same way they would something like torture or political imprisonment. Thus, there is an unfortunate tendency not to see such things as the lack of food, or safe and decent housing, or adequate health care as all constituting human rights violations. So it may seem strange to consider Midnight Cowboy *to be a "human rights film."*

✳ ✳ ✳

This is the first great film I ever saw, and I am still convinced that *Midnight Cowboy* is one of the greatest movies ever made. It tells the story of two losers—Enrico Salvatore Rizzo (Dustin Hoffman), known to all as "Ratso," and Joe Buck (Jon Voight), a transplant to New York City from a small town in Texas—who eventually form a deep friendship living with only a scant amount of food and no water or heat in an abandoned building in New York City. Ratso has a horrible cough and can no longer walk, but he also has no money to see a doctor. Joe Buck doesn't have any money either. He came to New York to hustle rich women and have them pay him for sex, but his cowboy outfit and sexual prowess notwithstanding, he is a complete failure at this, although he is able to rob one of his male patrons in order to get money so that he and Ratso can take a bus to Miami, where life will become much better for them, or so they have convinced themselves. However, this dream ends when Ratso dies just as the bus is approaching Miami. And in a most touching display of love, Joe then puts his arm around his friend until the bus reaches its destination.

Midnight Cowboy is a quintessentially American movie in the sense that it portrays how those at the bottom of the heap have no place to turn. They must survive—and this word is chosen advisedly—on their ability to hustle in whatever way they can. Ratso's father was a shoe-shine boy in the subways, but given what this did to his health, his son refuses to do this. But this society has little use for a cripple, so Ratso picks cigarettes off the streets and hustles whoever and however he can. For his part, Joe is the product of a broken home and was raised by his grandmother. Joe is not too smart, but if one can get past the Marlboro Man getup he is a likeable young man. But American society has no place for an uneducated social misfit like this—and no safety net either.

Also of Note

Winter's Bone (Debra Granik, 2010)

While *Midnight Cowboy* depicts urban poverty, *Winter's Bone* and *Frozen River* provide us with two stunning portrayals of rural poverty. The former is set in rural Arkansas, and Ree Dolly's (Jennifer Lawrence) life is as bleak as the landscape. Ree is a high school student whose mother is in a near-catatonic state and who is forced to raise and feed her younger brother and sister. This, however, is not the worst of things. The real problem is that Jessup, her father, has disappeared. This normally would be a good thing, but Ree finds out that Jessup has a bail hearing in a week, and he has put up the family home as collateral. If he does not show up—and it is by no means clear that he is even alive—the Dolly family will be forced to move from their house. So what ensues is Ree's desperate attempt to find her father, or at least his dead body.

Frozen River (Courtney Hunt, 2008)

Frozen River is set in upstate New York, and it is anything but your typical "buddy flick." For one thing, the two central female characters—a down-and-out white woman and a down-and-out Native American woman—are anything but friends, at least at the outset. They are more apt to pull a gun on one another, and the relationship that develops between them, which consists of running a human smuggling operation across the Canadian border, is one that arises out of sheer economic necessity.

15

Gandhi

(Richard Attenborough, 1982)

One of the great ironies of the genesis of the human rights revolution in the post–World War II period is the fact that Western political leaders could proclaim, as they did in the Universal Declaration of Human Rights (1948), that all men and women have human rights by the mere fact of their existence, while at the same time Western states were deeply intent on maintaining colonial empires the world over.

✳ ✳ ✳

Gandhi is an epic film that covers more than a half century of the life of Mohandas K. Gandhi, the "little brown man in the loincloth" to some, especially defenders of the British Empire. To all others, this proponent of the principle of nonviolence was one of the greatest political and spiritual leaders of all time. The film opens with Gandhi's assassination on January 30, 1948. The next scene shows his funeral, which not only attracted political leaders from around the globe, but more importantly and more consistent with his life, throngs of followers of all castes and religions.

The film then shifts back fifty-five years when Gandhi was a young lawyer who had just moved to South Africa. He is sitting on a train reading a book and minding his own business when he is accosted by the authorities for sitting in the first class section, which was reserved for whites only. When he is asked what he is doing there, he mentions that he is a member of the bar and he has come to this country to engage in the practice of law. One of the white passengers claims that there are no "colored" lawyers in South Africa. Gandhi answers, quite patiently but also quite logically, that if one were to assume that an Indian was a "colored" person, this man is wrong because there is at least one "colored" lawyer in South Africa, namely, him.

At the next stop Gandhi is summarily thrown from the train. In response to this injustice, he organizes a small demonstration where other Indians in South Africa protest the country's pass law by burning theirs. This enrages the security officials who have come to the event, and he is brutally attacked. But rather than fighting back, he simply, and beautifully, picks up each of the passes and gently places them in a fire. Thus, a brilliant and remarkable political career, and movement, is born.

The rest of the film is chronological. With news of his nonviolent protest spreading rapidly, Gandhi returns home. No doubt, his most obvious achievement is to lead the fight for Indian independence against the British. Yet an ever greater achievement is his insistence on pursuing his political ends by means of nonviolence. Most people will readily agree with this sentiment, at least in theory. But one of the most wrenching scenes in the film involves a march where two Indians, standing side by side, offer their bodies up to British soldiers, who, it is obvious, are anything but adherents of this same philosophy. Instead, the blows they deliver are as savage as they are sickening. And when two marchers have been dragged away, bloody and bruised, two more take their place.

Ben Kingsley's physical resemblance to Gandhi is almost uncanny, and this goes far in making this a moving and absorbing film. But what makes this a truly great film is his ability to capture Gandhi's inner soul, which attracted people the world over, not only during his own lifetime, but in ours as well.

Also of Note

1947: Earth (Deepa Mehta, 1998)

1947: Earth (1998) is one of Deepa Mehta's "trilogy" films—earth, water, and fire—all of which are analyzed here. The backdrop is the violent partition between India and Pakistan at the time of Indian independence in 1947. Lenny Baby is a young girl who lives with her wealthy parents in Lahore, which eventually became part of Pakistan. Lenny Baby is attended to by her nanny, a beautiful Hindu woman who has a wide circle of friends who seem to cover the spectrum of religions. However, each turns on the other as Hindus make war on Muslims, who make war on Sikhs, who make war on Hindus, and on and on. Eventually the circle of violence becomes endless, and, unfortunately it remains timeless as well.

16

Slumdog Millionaire
(Danny Boyle, 2008)

The next film also takes place in India, and many of the same issues that Gandhi fought against, especially the oppressive caste system and the great horrors committed in the name of religion, are on display here as well.

✳ ✳ ✳

The winner of eight Academy Awards including Best Picture, it would have been a stretch to claim that anyone could have predicted the enormous success of a film that tells the story of three Indian street children. The film opens in the present, with a young man, Jamal Malik (Dev Patel), enjoying an incredible run as a contestant on the Indian version of *Who Wants to Be a Millionaire?* Jamal's ability to answer these questions raises deep suspicions because no "slumdog" is thought capable of doing so. The authorities (naturally) torture him to find out his illegal methods.

The key is that each of the questions he has been asked has had some bearing on events in his past life, which are shown in a series of flashbacks. Jamal and his brother Salim became orphans after their mother was killed in a religious riot, and they then meet up with Latika, a young girl, and label themselves the Three Musketeers. The children are taken in by Maman, a Fagin-like character who forces his wards to serve as beggars for his own purposes. However, the three children come to realize that Maman is purposely blinding some of the children as a means of increasing donations. Jamal and Salim hatch an escape plan, but Latika refuses to join them. After running away, the two brothers become street hustlers on trains and at the Taj Mahal, but at Jamal's insistence, they return to fetch Latika. In the process, Salim kills Maman. This sends him into a life of crime from which he never escapes and in the process he enslaves Latika (Freida Pinto) for his boss, Javed.

Jamal leaves Salim and Latika, but years later he tracks both of them down. He works his way into Javed's home where he is reunited with Latika and professes his love for her, but their attempt to run away together is foiled by Salim. Knowing that Latika watches *Who Wants to Be a Millionaire?* Jamal is able to get on the show in order to make his presence known to Latika. One of the interesting dynamics of the program, and of Indian society itself, is offered in the form of the show's host, Prem Kumar (Anil Kapoor). Kumar was a former slumdog before achieving wealth and fame in his current capacity as the host of this wildly popular television drama. Kumar tells Jamal that he wants him to win, going so far at one point as secretly providing him with a "correct" answer. However, in the end Kumar is more interested in suffocating the prospects of someone else from his caste.

Slumdog Millionaire ends on an uplifting note, and the final scene consisting of a dance number at the train station where Jamal and Latika have found each other is surreal—and vastly entertaining. Would there be anywhere near the popular interest in a slumdog who never became a millionaire? The chances of this, of course, are slight.

Also of Note

Salaam Bombay (Mira Nair, 1988)

Salaam Bombay is an earlier feature film that has many of these same themes. The protagonist is a young man (Chaipau) who delivers tea to a brothel and who becomes captivated by a young virgin he nicknames "Sweet Sixteen" because of her age. Although the acting is oftentimes stiff, still, *Salaam Bombay* needs to be recognized as a trailblazer for its willingness to offer a glimpse into a subterranean world that most would like to pretend does not exist.

Born into Brothels (Zana Briski and Ross Kauffman, 2004)

One of the most troubling aspects of making a documentary is the concern that the subjects in the film may be exploited in the process. This charge has been made against *Born into Brothels* (2004), and while this is unfortunate it is also understandable. The story told by the film is about a documentary photographer (Briski) who befriends a group of children living in the red light district of Calcutta: outcasts even among outcasts. Briski decides to teach these children how to take photographs and this simple act—at least simple by Western standards—transforms the lives of these children. What follows is not only a growing self confidence but future prospects, something that was nowhere evident earlier. More than that, the children even become international celebrities of sorts, topped off by an auction of their work at Sotheby's. To the cynical, *Born into Brothels* could be interpreted as showing how the human rights of eight young children in India can be protected—but only when a Western journalist intervenes, and even then it is not certain that they would not fall back into the gutter. It could also be interpreted as focusing on these few lucky ones to the exclusion of the other countless millions who will have nowhere near these same opportunities. I am not nearly as cynical as this. The filmmakers are able to engage the viewer to consider the plight of children condemned to have no childhood, and not much of a future beyond that. What the viewer sees is that these children have talents and interests that otherwise would never have been discovered or used. Briski does her best to save eight of these children; it is up to the rest of us to tend to the rest.

17
Milk
(Gus Van Sant, 2008)

Although gays can now marry in at least some Western states and are no longer subjected to widespread societal discrimination, it is important to remember two things. The first is that such freedoms are relatively recent. The second is that there still are many countries in the world where being gay is virtually a death warrant. In the United States, where the following film takes place, it was less than a decade ago (2003) that the Supreme Court (finally) ruled that state anti-sodomy statutes violated the US Constitution. In addition, while gay marriage is now legal in a few states, in most parts of the country gay marriage remains illegal. The following film helps explain where we have come from and where we need to go in order to protect the human rights of gays and other sexual minorities.

✳ ✳ ✳

In this film, Sean Penn plays Harvey Milk, who as a member of the San Francisco Board of Supervisors was the first openly gay public official in the United States. Although the movie alternates between the personal and the political, it is clear that the heart of the film is the latter. And it is also no coincidence that *Milk* was released a short time before a statewide ballot proposal (Proposition 8) that would have recognized gay marriages in the state of California. And yet, even this moving film, culminating in Milk's assassination (along with San Francisco mayor George Moscone) at the hands of Dan White (Josh Brolin), a conservative member of the Board, could not get this initiative to pass. Apparently it is easier to be outraged by the prejudices of the past than those with which we now live.

The opening credits are shown against the backdrop of archival footage of gays being arrested and harassed by police. In the opening scene, Milk celebrates his 40th birthday by seducing Scott Smith (James Franco) at a subway stop in New York City, and Smith becomes the first of several lovers, although he remains in Milk's life until the end. Milk and Smith then move to the Castro area of San Francisco, which at that time was an Irish-American neighborhood, and the viewer sees Milk's growing recognition of the importance of political power and the need to organize to achieve this power. Milk is certainly persistent. He is unsuccessful in his first three attempts at elected office, twice running unsuccessfully for the Board of Supervisors and the third time for the California State Assembly, before he is finally able to secure a position on the city's Board of Supervisors.

The film becomes more interesting at this point, mainly because of the presence of Dan White, a former Vietnam veteran, who as an arch-conservative stands for practically everything that Milk opposes. To the film's credit, White is not made into a straw man of wrongheaded conservative views, but rather as someone who was born and raised by certain social values. In one of the more touching and personal scenes, Milk attends the baptism of White's son and the connection between these two individuals—not between a gay and a straight, or even between two politicians—is quite evident.

Yet the two remain polar opposites in the political arena, and White is the only member of the Board of Supervisors to vote against a city gay rights initiative. Later, White becomes one of the leading forces behind Proposition 6, a statewide initiative that had a national following behind the likes of Anita Bryant, to ban gays from working in California schools. However, due to effective political organizing, much of it directed by Harvey Milk, the initiative is defeated.

Although the viewer is fully aware at the outset of the film that Milk is assassinated, still, the murder is suspenseful and difficult to watch, and perhaps even more difficult to fathom. White becomes increasingly isolated from the other members of the Board as a number of his initiatives are voted down. When his proposal to increase the salary of Board members is defeated, White resigns his position from the Board, but then has a change of heart. However, despite Milk's entreaties, Mayor Moscone refuses to reinstate him. Seemingly in retaliation, but also as an indication of an inability or unwillingness to face a markedly different world than the one he was brought up in, White clandestinely gains entry into City Hall, where he shoots and kills both Moscone and Milk.

Milk works well on several levels. For one thing, there is no attempt to portray the protagonist as any kind of saint, and this is particularly true of his assortment of lovers, especially after the break-up with Smith. A central part of the film is Milk's devotion to Jack Lira, an obviously unstable young man who eventually kills himself. But as mentioned before, the essence of *Milk* is the message that equality for gays will not be easy, and it will never come without garnering considerable political support. Harvey Milk would certainly have been disappointed that today there are still only a handful of states where gays can marry, but he probably would not have been surprised. He, of all politicians, was fully aware of the prejudices and passions that were driving the other side.

Also of Note

The Times of Harvey Milk (Rob Epstein, 1984)

The Times of Harvey Milk serves as a nice complement to the feature film *Milk,* although it spends virtually no time on Harvey Milk's personal life, focusing instead on his many political battles. One might complain that *The Times of Harvey Milk* is formulaic in the sense that there are a series of interviews with friends and associates, but what this ignores is just how personal Harvey Milk's politics happened to be. Certainly, his primary reason for entering into politics was to promote the rights of gays, but what the film also shows is his strong dedication to all of those outside the mainstream of American political life: feminists, the elderly, Asians, and workers. A union member recalls thinking the first time he met Harvey Milk that he could never work with a "fruit" like this, but soon enough Milk won him over politically, as he would win him over personally, eventually creating a strong friendship.

Unlike the feature film, this documentary spends a good deal of time on the assassinations and the trial that followed. Many now know these legal proceedings for the so-called Twinkie defense that the defense lawyers presented—White claims that his judgment was impaired because of the stress that he was under, which was exacerbated by the amount of junk food he was eating. However, as the documentary shows, his slight sentence (he served five-and-a-half years for two cold-blooded murders) is much better explained as a way of minimizing the killing of a gay man. As one commentator points out, if White had only killed Mayor Moscone he would have received a life sentence. Killing a "fruit" was seen by many at that time as a socially positive thing to do. The candlelight vigil immediately following Milk's assassination showed one side of his political persona, but so did the violent rage that rocked San Francisco after White's verdict was rendered.

Brokeback Mountain (Ang Lee, 2005)

No doubt the most widely known film in this realm is Ang Lee's *Brokeback Mountain* (2005), the "gay cowboy" movie to many, which presents the decades-long love affair between Jack (Jake Gyllenhaal) and Ennis (Heath Ledger). The two first meet up as lonely ranch hands working during the summer months. They then go on and try to lead "straight" lives with only infrequent trysts, but find little success in doing so.

Before Night Falls (Julian Schnabel, 2000)

Javier Bardem is now an internationally recognized movie star. However, arguably his best acting performance is given in this feature film about the life of Reinaldo Arenas, a gay Cuban writer who faced constant harassment and imprisonment for his sexuality. Arenas was born in 1943 and brought up in what he describes as a "household of angry women" in the rural countryside. His political awakening comes with the Cuban Revolution when as a fifteen-year-old boy he set out to join Castro's forces. Although his sexual awakening comes a few years later, he makes the interesting observation that the new Cuban government was initially quite liberal in terms of its attitude towards sexual freedom and that it was only some time later that being gay was considered "subversive." Arenas was subversive, all right, not only because of his sexual preferences but also because of his art, which was something that, try as it might, the communist dictatorship was not able to control.

La Mission (Peter Bratt, 2009)

The super-macho world of the Mission district of San Francisco serves as the backdrop for *La Mission*, which not only explores issues relating to discrimination against gays but violence directed toward women. The film's protagonist is Che Rivera (Benjamin Bratt), a city bus driver who has served some time in prison for unspecified crimes, although, in all likelihood, his propensity toward physical violence is somehow related to this. Che is a widower who is raising his teenage son, Jesse (Jeremy Ray Valdez), who in many ways is the antithesis of Che: he is a dedicated student, a young man who seems to try to avoid physical confrontations—and he is gay. Che does not know about this, and he is devastated when he discovers pictures of Jesse and his boyfriend.

Although Che appears to be a monster, his character is more fully formed when we see his interaction with others. But what really forces Che to change is his complicated relationship with Lena (Erika Alexander), an attractive black woman who lives in the same building, works at a women's shelter, and who tries to help Che break free from violence. To its credit, the film documents the up-and-down relationship that Che has with both Jesse and Lena. Changing a person's values is not easy, and the film accurately depicts this.

Fire (Deepa Mehta, 1996)

Another of Deepa Mehta's trilogy is *Fire,* which depicts the growing attachment, and reciprocal sexual appeal, shared by two sisters-in-law who live in a male-dominated household in India. Given its taboo subject matter, the film caused an enormous stir when it was released.

18

Norma Rae
(Martin Ritt, 1979)

Labor rights are human rights. Article 23 of the Universal Declaration of Human Rights provides:

> *(1) Everyone has the right to work, to free choice of employment, to just and favourable conditions of work and to protection against unemployment.*

> *(2) Everyone, without any discrimination, has the right to equal pay for equal work.*

> *(3) Everyone who works has the right to just and favourable remuneration ensuring for himself and his family an existence worthy of human dignity, and supplemented, if necessary, by other means of social protection.*

> *(4) Everyone has the right to form and to join trade unions for the protection of his interests.*

✳ ✳ ✳

Norma Rae involves all of these issues, but especially the human right to establish and join a trade union. Several of the documentaries featured in the next section also deal with this issue, including Barbara Kopple's two wonderful films: *Harlan County, USA* and *American Dream* (D-36).

There are times when a single scene encapsulates an entire movie, and for many *Norma Rae* will be best remembered for the moment when security officials at the textile plant where Norma Rae Webster (Sally Field) is working are taking her away, and she grabs a magic marker and scrawls out UNION—and then stands on a table holding this sign for her fellow workers. One by one, they respond by turning off their noisy machines, and later they will heed her plea and vote for a union in this Alabama plant, where anti-union sentiment is not only practiced by the management but at the outset by the rank-and-file workers as well. Most of the acclaim for this film has been directed at Sally Field, who was awarded with an Oscar for Best Actress, and deservedly so. However, every performance in this film is outstanding, particularly Ron Leibman, who plays Reuben Warshowsky, a union organizer from New York—and the first Jew that Norma Rae (and probably most of her coworkers) has ever met.

Norma Rae has two children—one by her former husband who was killed before the girl was born, and a son who was the result of a tryst in the back seat of a Cadillac with one of the town's important people. At the outset of the film she lives with her parents, who are managing to hang on at the factory, although her mother has bouts where she loses hearing and her father is battling high stress and a bad heart. He is a protective father—and there is every reason he should be, as his daughter drinks too much and has sex with every Mr. Wrong who passes through this sleepy little town. Entering into their lives is Reuben, who despite his tireless effort initially makes no headway in getting any kind of support for a union. However, what gets Norma Rae's attention is when Reuben carries out an "inspection" of the plant, as mandated by federal law, and he finds out what he is up against in terms of the obstructions of plant management. Despite the intimidating manpower that surrounds him, he insists that union announcements be hung on the company's bulletin board at eye level—no higher and no lower—and it is his chutzpah that grabs Norma Rae's attention, even if she would have no idea what this word means. Norma Rae then attends a union organizing meeting at a small black church, where Reuben talks about his grandfather's funeral and how it was attended by members of his immediate family and also by his grandfather's other family, made up of hundreds of his union brothers and sisters.

Despite a sexual tension between Norma Rae and Reuben throughout the film, nothing ever happens between the two, although there is a deeply sensuous scene involving skinny dipping at an old swimming hole. Instead, Norma Rae marries Sonny Webster (Beau Bridges), who at one point expresses enormous anger because Norma Rae is never home, between her work and her tireless union organizing activities. Her response is classic Norma. She opens the refrigerator and takes out a cabbage and stuffs it into a pot on the stove; then spills washing detergent all over some dirty clothes she has dumped in the sink; and then finally, she starts to iron madly. Sonny (and certainly the viewer) is stunned by this angry display, but later in bed he tells her how much he loves her and admires her. And apparently this issue never comes up again, although he initially resists when Norma Rae brings some black folks to the house (after all, this is 1970s Alabama) for a union meeting.

In the end, the workers vote the union in. However, it is too late for her father, who died on the job when his supervisor would not let him take a break after he felt a sharp pain in his arm. In the final scene, Norma Rae walks Reuben to his car as he is about to leave town. One fully expects Reuben to express his love for her, and hers for him. The two truly are that close. But both are beyond this. For Reuben, there are a host of other plants in a host of other towns where he will fight the good fight against the same impossible odds. And for Norma Rae, victory means that she will now have a little bit more time to spend with her children and her devoted husband—and to raise as much hell as she can whenever there is any attempt to backtrack.

Also of Note

Matewan (John Sayles, 1987)

Matewan refers to the desolate West Virginia town that was the site of the "Matewan Massacre" of 1920, which is depicted in this feature film. Coal mine owners want to break the union and to do this they hire black and Italian workers, attempting to substitute racial and ethnic dynamics for economic strife. What prevents this from taking place is the intervention of Joe Kenehan (Chris Cooper), a union organizer, who is able to convince the white workers that a true union admits all workers, no matter a person's color, ethnicity, or creed. Also instrumental is Few Clothes, wonderfully played by James Earl Jones, who tells whites that while being called a "nigger" does not particularly bother him, calling him a "scab" will send him into a fighting rage. Kenehan is keenly aware that the owners want violence to break out, so they can bring the law in on their side. Notwithstanding his entreaties, the film ends with a dramatic standoff between the owner's men and the striking workers. People on both sides are killed, including Kenehan. But the battle goes on—and on.

Bread and Roses (Ken Loach, 2000)

The title for the feature film goes back to a strike by a group of immigrant women in Lawrence, Massachusetts, in the early part of the twentieth century. Aside from transporting the action all the way across the continent to Los Angeles, very little has changed for the group of immigrant janitors in one of the city's high-rise office buildings who are only getting paid $5.75 an hour (down from $8.50 twenty years before) and who have no medical or dental coverage. The building where they work has any number of rich and important businesses and tenants, but these people live a world apart from the immigrant cleaning staff. In one of the best lines from the film, one of the janitors comments that the Angels cleaning company uniforms they wear make them invisible.

The film's protagonist is Maya (Pilar Padilla), an undocumented worker from Mexico whose sister, Rosa (Elpidia Carrillo), has gotten her a job with Angels. Entering into the mix is Sam (Adrien Brody), a labor organizer, who devises a number of high-visibility publicity stunts intended to force the upper-crust tenants to pressure the owners of the Angels to meet their employees' demands.

19

The Insider
(Michael Mann, 1999)

Human rights violations generally involve the state. But states also have an obligation to protect its citizens from the harmful acts of both private individuals and corporate entities. When a corporation or group of individuals violate human rights, we tend to forget that it's a human rights violation on the part of the state, which is obligated to prevent such abuses. Thus, what almost always is missing in stories involving corporate misdeeds—including the following film—is the responsibility of the state itself to prevent or to eliminate such practices and to offer human rights protection to its citizens.

✳ ✳ ✳

There are two villains in *The Insider,* one that is obvious and the other that is anything but obvious. The first is the tobacco industry, and the first half of this outstanding film revolves around the story of Jeffrey Wigand (Russell Crowe), who had worked as a scientist at the tobacco giant Brown & Williamson but who is later let go by the company. When it becomes known that Wigand intends to tell the industry's secrets to the television show *Sixty Minutes,* the company comes after him with a vengeance. Given its overall record, there is no great surprise that the corporation reacts this way.

The second part of the story, and the second villain of sorts, involves the media. What is under discussion is not your local news channel, but CBS News itself and its flagship program *Sixty Minutes.* Lowell Bergman (Al Pacino) is a producer for the show and his bona fides are established at the outset of the film, when he is able to arrange an interview with the founder of Hezbollah. The other major player is Mike Wallace (Christopher Plummer), whose take-no-prisoners approach on the air puts him squarely on the side of the First Amendment and the public's right to know.

These two stories come together after Bergman approaches Wigand concerning some technical questions about a study conducted at Brown & Williamson. At that point Bergman realizes that there is a much bigger story out there that needs to be uncovered: the purposeful and systematic manipulation of nicotine levels that serves to hook people and make them cigarette addicts. The problem is that even if Bergman can convince the increasingly volatile Wigand to give an interview, Wigand is bound by a confidentiality agreement, one that the company is not only quite willing to enforce against him but against *Sixty Minutes* as well. Thus, the drama in the second half of the film revolves around whether CBS will cave in to the pressure of its corporate sponsors, and the sad truth is that they do.

In the film's most dramatic scene, Bergman explodes after learning that producer Don Hewitt (Philip Baker Hall) and Mike Wallace will not put their careers on the line to buck corporate interests:

> You pay me to go get guys like Wigand, to draw him out. To get him to trust us, to get him to go on television. I do. I deliver him. He sits. He talks. He violates his own fucking confidentiality agreement. And he's only the key witness in the biggest public health reform issue, maybe the biggest, most-expensive corporate-malfeasance case in US history. And Jeffrey Wigand, who's out on a limb, does he go on television and tell the truth? Yes. Is it newsworthy? Yes. Are we gonna air it? Of course not. Why? Because he's not telling the truth? No. Because he is telling the truth. That's why we're not going to air it. And the more truth he tells, the worse it gets!

The Insider is based on a true story. What is also true is that while *Sixty Minutes* originally did blink in the face of pressure from Brown & Williamson, the Wigand interview was eventually aired. And at the same time that CBS News was capitulating to corporate pressure, the *New York Times* carried a story on exactly this topic, documenting the manner in which CBS News had been cowed by corporate interests. Thus, while the First Amendment seems to take a severe hit, the free press and the public's right to know were ultimately honored—at least in this particular instance and for this particular story.

Also of Note

The China Syndrome (James Bridges, 1979)

The China Syndrome had the good fortune, as it were, to be released just twelve days before the Three Mile Island accident in Pennsylvania, which remains the most significant (and certainly the scariest) nuclear power episode to occur on American soil. The film makes good use of its three mega-stars. Jane Fonda (Kimberly Wells) is a daytime television reporter hired for her good looks, who, along with her cameraman Richard Adams (Michael Douglas), becomes a crusader for the public's right to know about the dangers from a nuclear power accident they both witness. Eventually joining them is Jack Godell (Jack Lemmon) after he discovers that the top management at California Gas & Electric, where he is employed and which owns the nuclear plant, insists that there had been no accident when Godell knows better. The film's climactic scene occurs after security officials storm the room where Godell had barricaded himself and they shoot and kill him. However, Wells carries the mantle by telling a live viewing audience of Godell's heroic efforts to avoid the "China syndrome"—meaning a nuclear meltdown.

Silkwood (Mike Nichols, 1983)

Silkwood also features three Hollywood stars, and it is also about the dangers of nuclear power. Meryl Streep plays Karen Silkwood, an employee at the Kerr-McGee nuclear power plant in Oklahoma, who died under what could best be described as suspicious circumstances when she was about to meet a reporter for the *New York Times* to divulge information about dangerous workplace practices at the plant. Karen lives with her boyfriend Drew (Kurt Russell) and her lesbian friend Dolly (Cher). The three spend their time smoking, drinking, screwing, and working at the Kerr-McGee nuclear power facility.

The dangerous conditions in which they work first come to light when a coworker gets "cooked"—exposed to radiation. In such cases, the company protocol is to first haul the person into a shower where the person is scrubbed within an inch of his or her life, followed by sending this person to the company doctor (although many claim he only has a veterinarian degree). The company doctor's prognosis is always a positive one: the exposure to plutonium was within "acceptable levels." No one seems to question any of this, but the heart of the film depicts Karen's slow awakening, brought on when she herself gets "cooked"—on three terrifying occasions—and also her growing involvement in union activities.

Erin Brockovich (Steven Soderbergh, 2000)

It is easy to understand why Julia Roberts was awarded an Oscar for Best Actress for her role in *Erin Brockovich* as a struggling single mother who through sheer determination and perseverance essentially wills at least a small amount of justice into the world for hundreds of residents in Hinkley, California, whose water supply had been poisoned by Pacific Gas and Electric. Erin had been represented by Edward Masry (Albert Finney) in a personal injury case (which she lost), and after he failed to return her phone calls she simply decides to go work for him. Although he and the others at the firm are initially put off by her *Pretty Woman* ways, they eventually are won over. It is Erin who comes to the realization that there is poison in the water of their clients' homes. In one of the best scenes, she meets with the Jensen family and explains to them that the family's health problems have been caused by the PG&E plant across a field. The mother looks out the window, sees her children swimming innocently enough (or so she had thought) in the family pool, and becomes hysterical in an attempt to get them out of there as quickly as possible.

The good guys win in the end after reaching a $333 million settlement with the company, with the first proceeds being paid out to the Jensens. Meanwhile, Erin and Masry have the opportunity for one more public spat, where she can insult the legal profession and he gets in a final dig about beauty queens not knowing how to apologize. But Erin certainly does not need to apologize for the work she has done on behalf of her poisoned clients.

20
V for Vendetta
(James McTeigue, 2005)

It is relatively easy to depict political oppression in film when it involves such things as torture or political imprisonment. A much more difficult task is to portray more subtle forms of oppression, including limitations on freedom of thought, conscience, and religion and the lack of a free press. In its own unique way, V for Vendetta *does all this.*

✳ ✳ ✳

Remember remember the fifth of November
Gunpowder, treason and plot.
I see no reason why gunpowder, treason
Should ever be forgot ...

A few years after the film's release, *V for Vendetta* experienced a resurgence in interest. Protesters participating in the Occupy Wall Street movement, which was then extended to other localities in the United States, began to don the Guy Fawkes mask worn by V (Hugo Weaving), the political crusader in the film. Guy Fawkes is famous—or infamous, depending on one's point of view—for his plot to blow up the Houses of Parliament in order to restore a Catholic monarchy to the throne of England. The plot was uncovered on November 5, 1605, and this day has been celebrated ever since, usually accompanied by bonfires, fireworks, and, of course, the recitation of the poem commemorating the event.

V is fighting political oppression on two fronts. The first relates to an act of state terrorism many years before that ended up taking the lives of 80,000 people. One person who was directly affected was Evey (Natalie Portman), the protagonist in the story, whose brother died from poison placed in drinking water, an event that also claimed the lives of her parents, who had been political activists at the time. V was also a victim; he was severely burned in an industrial fire, but able to escape. V has now turned himself into a superhero fighting machine—although only armed with knives—who most decidedly has vengeance on his mind.

But it is not only personal vengeance that V is after. Rather, what he wants to expose is the entirety of government oppression. This is difficult to do when the government, along with its media partners, keeps the population in a constant state of anxiety, all the while feeding it a pack of lies. At the outset of the film, Evey is out walking after the government-imposed curfew when she is set upon by two men who are either hoodlums, police officers, or both. V comes to her rescue and then invites her to a symphony on the top of a roof, which she reluctantly accepts. V has been able to hack into the government's security system, and on the government's omnipresent public address system he blares out Tchaikovsky's "1812 Overture," complete with fireworks—after all, the clock has just struck midnight, and it is now Guy Fawkes Day. British television report all this as something the government initiated on its own, but some citizens are not fooled. They do not know the whole truth, and it is V's job to bring it to them.

In this he is joined by Evey, although she is a reluctant revolutionary. She is kept as a prisoner in his luxurious dwelling, but escapes to the home of a colleague at the television station when the opportunity arises. Meanwhile, V is killing the most dangerous government officials, particularly those who were part of the government experimental program where V and others were used as human guinea pigs. One of his victims is a loudmouth political pundit on television (think Rush Limbaugh), who calls himself the Voice of London. This bombastic fascist meets his fate while in the shower—with televised images of himself displayed all around him. Another is a man of the cloth, who is decidedly a man of the flesh and who actively participated in these government experiments. The good father meets his demise when he is distracted by Evey, dressed up like the little girl the monsignor fancies, before V comes crashing through the window and kills him.

Most of the story relates to political awakening—Evey's, but also the political awakening of the British people. In the film's final act, V has hidden a massive amount of explosives in an abandoned train line that runs below the Houses of Parliament. But he tells Evey that it is her decision whether to go through with the bombing. V has a final showdown, and at this point he kills the Chancellor (John Hurt), who is the country's supreme ruler, and all those who would assume absolute power, although V is fatally wounded in the battle as well. Before Evey can push the lever that will start the train on its destination, she is confronted by the Inspector (Stephen Rea) who has been trailing her. But this is a man who also has developed both a personal and political conscience, and because of this he does not try to stop her.

The most exhilarating scene involves the mass of British citizens who at midnight on November 5 come marching through the streets, all dressed up as Guy Fawkes. The police do not know what to do, but the protestors do not give them much of a chance, walking right past them. They finally stop right outside the House of Parliament. At that point, the longstanding political oppression ends and the fireworks and "1812 Overture" begin. As Evey puts it just before releasing the train: this country needs more than a building right now, it needs hope. And hope she delivers.

21

A Dry White Season
(Euzhan Palcy, 1989)

Much in the manner of the Jim Crow laws that governed race relations in the American South for decades, apartheid was the official position of the South African government from 1948 until 1994, which coincided with Nelson Mandela's election as the country's president. As its name indicates, apartheid was based on the separation of races, but in truth the elevation of whites and the oppression of blacks and those considered to be "coloreds."

* * *

Reflecting the political blindness of most of South Africa's white population under apartheid, Ben du Toit (Donald Sutherland) refuses to believe that the country's security forces would commit a wrong against blacks without a valid reason. At the outset of the film, Gordon (Winston Ntshona), the gardener at the school where du Toit teaches, brings his son Jonathan to show him the caning he has suffered for demonstrating against apartheid rule. Ben du Toit advises that nothing be done and that the authorities must have acted for a reason. Gordon knows much better than this and a short time later Jonathan is killed along with a number of other children. The government won't even tell Gordon where his son's body is, although they assure him that at some point they will reveal the location. Gordon begins his own investigation, but soon he is arrested as well. At this point, du Toit still has faith in the country's security officials, and he pays a visit to this office in order to vouch for Gordon. The police are not the least bit interested in his testimonial and one laments how little the country's blacks appreciate all that the government does for them. Following this, there is a wonderful scene where du Toit is talking with some friends (all white, of course). Seemingly oblivious to the black servants waiting on them, all speak about the duplicity of blacks and the ways in which they all lead double lives.

It is Gordon's death that finally awakens du Toit. The authorities claim that he committed suicide, but du Toit convinces Stanley (Zakes Mokae), a black friend of Gordon's, to show him the body and the torture marks covering it. At this point, du Toit meets Melanie (Susan Sarandon), who is a reporter for the *Daily Mail* newspaper, but at first he refuses to speak to her. Ben decides to help Gordon's wife, Emily (Thoko Ntshinga), to pursue an inquest. He approaches civil rights attorney Ian Mckenzie (Marlon Brando), who at first turns him down because the case is unwinnable in the current regime but who finally relents, if for no other reason than to show du Toit how futile it is to fight the system.

The courtroom scenes with Brando are incredibly good, as he metaphorically twists the knife into each of the government witnesses, especially the chilling Lt. Stolz (Jürgen Prochnow). However, none of this matters. The court reaches the conclusion that Gordon died by committing suicide, joining a long list of activists who the apartheid government maintains decided to end their own life, either by throwing themselves out of government windows or by hanging themselves while in police custody.

At this point, Ben du Toit becomes persona non grata within the white community. His fellow teachers shun him, and his wife has had enough. She warns him that he has to choose sides, that he is not one of "them," and that blacks don't want him to be that either. These same sentiments are shared by his married daughter and her husband, but not by his younger son, Johan (Rowen Elmes), who is quite proud of his father's willingness to pursue the truth and is willing to fight those who would refer to him as a "kaffir-lover."

Ben will not be dissuaded, and his wife soon leaves the house. However, the authorities clamp down ever harder, and they kill Gordon's wife, Emily, when she resists being evicted from her township home. Ben is also subjected to police harassment, and his home office is blown up in an attempt to burn the affidavits that he and others have been collecting regarding the deaths of Jonathan and Gordon. These affidavits are delivered to the *Daily Mail* by Johan on his bicycle, after du Toit uses his daughter's betrayal to lead Stolz astray. However, Lt. Stolz responds to this traitor to his race by running over du Toit with his car and killing him. But the bloodshed is not yet over. In the film's final scene, Stanley (who somehow evades the authorities throughout the film) drives up to Stolz's house and kills him as he is about to get into his car. The film ends by noting that more than 50,000 blacks have been locked up, for at least some period of time, for their political activities. However, what we now know is that these efforts were not in vain.

Also of Note
Cry Freedom (Richard Attenborough, 1987)

Cry Freedom is two movies in one. One depicts the life of Steven Biko (Denzel Washington), a leader of the anti-apartheid movement in South Africa who eventually is tortured and killed by security officials. This part of the film chronicles the friendship that forms between Biko and Donald Woods (Kevin Kline), a liberal newspaper editor who comes to understand that in South Africa, a white "liberal" is someone who wants to keep blacks in their place, but to do so more gently than the apartheid regime has been operating under.

The best parts of the film involve Biko's commentaries and insights on racism. He tells Woods that blacks know how whites live, especially because so many serve as domestic servants, but few whites know how blacks live. He then invites Woods to visit a black township, and the abject poverty is appalling to him. Biko tells Woods that in your world what is white is normal, but that the genius of whites is their ability to convince blacks of their own inferiority. What Biko wants to change is not only the apartheid system itself but, more importantly, the way blacks think about themselves. In fact, he holds the belief that no change can occur without this transformation in black consciousness.

The second part of the film does not work nearly as well as it chronicles Woods's attempt to flee the country with his family. Sad to say, but what is missing here—and what we are missing now—is Steven Biko's electrifying presence and his role as conscience for the South African people, both black and white.

22
Philadelphia
(Jonathan Demme, 1993)

Today, it is difficult to fathom the combination of despair and cruelty that responded to the AIDS epidemic in the United States during the 1980s. The following film provides great insight into this, as does the documentary We Were Here *(D-8), which is presented in Part*

II. Although HIV/AIDS is no longer front page news as it was at that time, let it also be said that the number of cases of infection worldwide continues to increase, as does the number who die from being infected with AIDS.

＊ ＊ ＊

From the opening strains of Bruce Springsteen's haunting song "Philadelphia," this deeply moving film fully captures the HIV/AIDS panic of the 1980s and the deep-seated prejudices against gays. The film stars Tom Hanks as Andy Beckett, a hotshot lawyer at the largest corporate law firm in the city who is fired after one of the senior partners notices a lesion on his forehead, soon after he was assigned an important case. Equally compelling is Denzel Washington, who plays Joe Miller, an ambulance chaser who ends up representing Andy in a wrongful termination suit. In many ways Washington's character is the more fully developed one. Originally, Miller not only declines to take Andy's case but is deeply worried that he will be infected just by Andy sitting in his office. Thus, the film is not only about Andy's quest in his dying days to achieve a measure of justice but about Miller's struggle to recognize and overcome his own prejudices. Miller makes remarkable progress, but he is no saint, best exhibited in a scene late in the film when he becomes outraged when a male law student tries to pick him up in a drug store, assuming that he is gay because of his representation of Andy.

Much of the drama in *Philadelphia* takes place in the courtroom. Miller does not have the same pedigree as Andy or the firm's senior partners, who are the defendants in this case, but his street-wise performance is more than their equal. At one point, Miller asks a defense witness whether he is gay or not, which brings forth a collective gasp in the room and an immediate objection as well. In doing this, Miller is not only trying to put Andy's law firm on trial but societal prejudices more broadly.

The main heavy in the film is Charles Wheeler (Jason Robards), a senior partner who originally serves as a father figure for Andy but who quickly turns against him when he learns that he is suspected of having AIDS. The problem is that Wheeler is a one-dimensional character. He loves Andy and then he detests him, and all this can only be explained by the fact that Andy has AIDS. Similarly, Antonio Banderas, who plays Andy's lover Miguel, is not asked to do much beside attend to Andy in his dying moments. What the film leaves unexplored is how Miguel feels about Andy's betrayal of him, which led to his infection in the first place.

The best scenes occur at the end of the film. Andy is struggling mightily to stay alive to see the case through, but he collapses in the courtroom and is on life support in the hospital when the jury comes back with a judgment of more than $4 million in punitive damages alone. Miller arrives at the hospital with food to nibble on and champagne to celebrate with, but of course his real reason for being there is to pay his respects to his fellow attorney and friend. A desperately weak Andy motions him to sit next to him on the bed, and for just a split second Miller hesitates—old prejudices die hard. But he is soon sitting there beside him and the two share the great pleasure of seeing justice served.

Also of Note

Yesterday (Darrell Roodt, 2004)

The ravages of AIDS and the discrimination suffered by those with the disease in South Africa are shown in the next two films. Yesterday (Leleti Khumalo) is the title character, who nurses her estranged and infected husband through his last terrible weeks, albeit in a makeshift "hospital" she has built for him outside the confines of the village—and away from prejudiced townspeople. Yesterday is also infected (by her husband), but the hope here is that, when her time comes, her friend who has promised to take care of her young daughter Beauty (Lihle Mvelase) and the other village residents will see to it that she be allowed to die at home.

Life, Above All (Oliver Schmitz, 2010)

The protagonist in this movie is Chanda (Khomotso Manyaka), a young South African girl who struggles after her mother Lillian (Lerato Mvelase) contracts AIDS. Once again, the viewer gets a sense of the deep societal shame, to the point where Mrs. Tafa, a neighbor friend, arranges it so that Lillian is sent away to die alone. However, Chanda will have none of this, and she goes off to bring her mother home.

The dramatic highpoint occurs when neighbors balk at Lillian's return. But at this point Mrs. Tafa comes marching out of her house next door, and she tells the assembled crowd to leave Chanda and Lillian alone. It seems that her own son had also died of AIDS, although she had long denied this. The only false note in this otherwise fine film occurs right after this, when these previously threatening neighbors break into gospel music. Someone should have shouted "Amen!" before allowing such hokum into this otherwise gritty film.

23

Good Night, and Good Luck
(George Clooney, 2005)

Freedom of opinion and freedom of the press are two pillars of human rights protection. Not only are these two important in their own right, but they serve to protect other human rights as well. Yet, in times of crisis, or perhaps more accurately, perceived crisis, these rights can be swept aside in favor of conformity and censorship—whether official censorship or self-censorship.

✳ ✳ ✳

The title of this absorbing film is the sendoff line of Edward R. Murrow, the former World War II correspondent who later became the face of *CBS News* and the conscience for those who were abhorred by the "Red Scare" tactics of Senator Joseph McCarthy. In the role of a lifetime, David Strathairn is the epitome of Murrow. The viewer sees and understands Murrow's courage in the face of McCarthy's onslaught, but also the manner in which he is able to withstand enormous corporate pressure from Bill Paley, the owner of CBS. As played by Strathairn, Murrow always remains human. He smokes incessantly, has bouts of nervousness and insecurity, and later in the film informs his colleague Don Hollenbeck (Ray Wise) that he will not back him after Hollenbeck was ruthlessly attacked by Hearst publishing, rationalizing that he already had enough on his plate. Under the enormous strain of these attacks, Hollenbeck later commits suicide.

Although he is the central player in this drama, Murrow does not act alone. Heading the rest of the ensemble cast is George Clooney (who also directs the film) as Fred Friendly, one of the producers for *CBS News* and Murrow's comrade in arms, ideas, and principles. Frank Langella plays Paley, a large man who is used to always having his way. Paley is a proponent of the First Amendment but also a man who likes advertising dollars coming his way. In his view, the best way to deal with Joseph McCarthy is simply to let his sad act play itself out. He goes along with Murrow, who believes it is essential to address the chilling effect of McCarthyism head on, but it is clear that Paley is a man of limited patience. On the other hand, while *CBS News* is losing money, Murrow does quite well for the larger company by subjecting himself to hosting *See It Now,* where he interviews entertainment lightweights such as Liberace and Zsa Zsa Gabor. Although he does not have a lot of screen time, Jeff Daniels plays a CBS lawyer whose presence is always unsettling to those in the newsroom. Finally, Robert Downey Jr. and Patricia Clarkson play a married couple who have to pretend they are not married because CBS (like a lot of other corporations at that time) does not allow its employees to be married to one another. So, before they would go into work in the morning (separately), they would have to remember to remove their wedding bands.

The film begins and ends with a speech that Murrow gave to the Radio and Television News Directors Association in 1958. In the speech he excoriates the networks for giving the viewing public what they want, rather than what they need. His deep concern is that television will be relegated solely to entertaining the masses. Few can now doubt the prescience of his message.

24

To Kill a Mockingbird
(Robert Mulligan, 1962)

One of the central features of a democracy is the right to a fair trial. In criminal proceedings this entails nothing less than the following: the presumption of innocence, an unbiased judge, a fair and representative jury of one's peers, and legal representation for those who cannot afford counsel. In Part II, several documentaries provide stark evidence of how the human right to a fair trial has been violated. So does the following classic film.

✳ ✳ ✳

Like a lot of other young people of my generation, I wanted to be Atticus Finch when I grew up, the courageous white southern lawyer who is the protagonist of Harper Lee's book of this name and this outstanding film. Atticus is a widower raising two young children when he is called upon to represent Tom Robinson (Brock Peters), a black laborer accused of raping Mayella Ewell (Collin Wilcox Paxton), an unstable white woman. It is virtually impossible to imagine anyone playing Atticus Finch other than Gregory Peck, in this career-defining role. Who else could convey the same quiet dignity and controlled rage as Peck? Here is a person who in his devotion to the law knowingly transgresses the societal mores of southern life. Perhaps even more impressive is the manner in which Atticus camps out in front of the local jail and single-handedly (with the unintended help of his daughter) turns away an armed lynch mob. One of the neighbors points out that some men are on earth to do the unpleasant things that no one else is willing to do, and that this is what Atticus does.

The story is told through the adult eyes of his then young daughter. I would refer to her as Jean Louise but I am afraid she might smack me for doing so, so let me call her what everyone else does: Scout (Mary Badham). The summer months are spent mainly with her older brother Jem (Phillip Alford), who is as kind and considerate and protective as one might ask for in an older brother, but he is still her older brother. They play games with one another and a visiting friend from next door, and all three children are fascinated with the mysterious Boo Radley, who lives in a spooky house a few doors down and who is a recluse, if not a ghost.

The film's drama picks up mightily in the trial of Tom Robinson. This being the South in the 1930s, the jury is all white and all male. During the trial, the courtroom is packed, with whites taking the best seats and blacks relegated to the balcony. Mayella and her papa both testify that Tom Robinson attempted to strangle her and beat her on the right side of her face. The problem with this testimony, as Atticus shows quite cleverly and quite convincingly, is that Tom has no use of his left arm. During his own testimony, Tom describes a woman who was constantly asking him to do favors for her and his great hesitancy to do so, on the one hand, but his fear of retribution if he did not accede to the wishes of a white woman. Being accused of raping a white woman is damning enough, but Tom goes even further than this when he describes his pity—a black man's pity!—for a white woman. Tom painfully describes the manner in which Mayella came on to him and how, against his strong objections, she kissed him.

The die is cast and certainly Atticus and Tom both know this better than anyone. Atticus implores the jury to set aside their prejudices and decide the case on its merits, but this is not to be. One of the most touching scenes occurs after the jury has convicted Tom and the courtroom has cleared out—except for the black folks sitting in the balcony, along with Scout and Jem. A black minister softly instructs Jean Louise to stand up because her father is passing.

After the verdict, anticipating his fate, Tom Robinson makes a run for it and is shot and killed. Bob Ewell, Mayella's father, is not content with the verdict and Robinson's death however. Although the jury found in favor of him and his daughter, he was made to look like a fool at trial and plots revenge. In the film's last scenes he tries to stab the Finch children as they are returning from a pageant at school, where Scout was dressed in a ridiculous-looking ham outfit. Ewell knocks out Jem, who is trying to protect his little sister, but before Ewell can get to Scout someone intercedes and stabs and kills him. Jem is then carried home by this stranger. And it is then that Scout finally comes face to face with the mysterious Boo Radley (Robert Duvall).

Earlier in the film, Atticus had told a story to his children about getting a gun when he was thirteen and his father telling him that he could shoot bluebirds because they were a nuisance, but he was not to shoot mockingbirds because they added great joy to the world. Atticus's first instinct in this situation is to bring the law in. But young Scout convinces him that subjecting Boo to public scrutiny in that fashion would be akin to shooting mockingbirds. In the end, he agrees to allow Ewell's killing to remain unsolved.

Also of Note

12 Angry Men (Sidney Lumet, 1957)

12 Angry Men provides a fly-on-the-wall depiction of jury deliberations in a murder case brought against a young Hispanic in New York City. The film is time-bound in the sense that you would no longer find an all-male jury—although all-white juries are certainly still not unknown. In addition, people do not wear their prejudices on their sleeves the way that some of the jurors do here. But Henry Fonda, who plays the one juror who initially holds out and who is later able to convince the other eleven that there is not enough evidence to convict the boy, is every bit the equal of Atticus Finch.

The Verdict (Sidney Lumet, 1982)

Paul Newman plays Frank Galvin, an alcoholic ambulance chaser from Boston, who at the outset of the movie is physically thrown out of a wake as he tries to solicit business from the deceased's bereaved widow. Galvin is on a downward spiral, both personally and professionally, when he is handed a case by Mickey (Jack Warden), his former partner and friend, who ominously tells him that this is the last time he will help him. Frank seems intent on blowing off this case as he has so many others until he visits the comatose young woman who is the victim in this medical malpractice case, and he understands the terrible situation she and her family are in. Galvin's opponent is Ed Concannon (James Mason), a senior partner in a powerful Boston law firm who will resort to any practice to win the case, going so far as paying off an attractive woman (Charlotte Rampling) to get intimate with Galvin in order to learn how he will proceed with the case.

The dramatic high point comes after Galvin locates a nurse who was on duty the night of the malpractice incident. She testifies that the doctor who performed the operation subsequently ordered her to change the medical chart so that it would look as if the patient had eaten nine hours before the operation and not one. A ruffled Concannon stands up and objects to this testimony, citing some obscure Iowa case, and the presiding judge, who has repeatedly ruled in favor of the defense, instructs the jury to disregard this testimony—which, of course, they do not.

Although the story of the movie is fictional, Galvin's closing argument goes to the heart of the civil justice system. Exhausted but doggedly determined, Galvin reminds the jury that they—not the judge and not the attorneys—are the law, and legal niceties and technicalities aside, the essential role of the legal system is to do justice. And at least in this one case, this is exactly what the jury delivers.

A Time to Kill (Joel Schumacher, 1996)

A Time to Kill is based on John Grisham's novel of the same name. The backdrop is the rape and murder of a ten-year-old black girl by two white men in the heart of Klan territory and their subsequent killing by her outraged father, Carl Lee Hailey (Samuel L. Jackson). Murder charges are brought against Hailey, who is represented by Jack Brigance (Matthew McConaughey), an inexperienced lawyer who goes through all matter of financial and personal suffering during the course of the trial. The high point of the film comes in Brigance's closing argument when he puts aside his prepared remarks and he walks the jurors through the young girl's terrible suffering—and then asks them to imagine that she is white, the assumption being that any aggrieved white father would never be held to account for murdering those who had raped and murdered his daughter.

25
Days of Glory (Indigènes) .
(Rachid Bouchareb, 2006)

The key to colonialism was not so much forced oppression or military might but the manner in which the European powers were able to convince the colonized people to buy into the project themselves. This is one of the reasons why decolonialization has proceeded on such an uncertain path; it is also the reason why the former colonial powers continue to have enormous problems understanding their own role in all of this. As shown in Days of Glory, *their collective attitude still seems to smack of the attitude that "these people" should be grateful for having been colonized.*

✳ ✳ ✳

The setting for this film is World War II. France has fallen to the Germans, and in an attempt to reverse this state of affairs and to save the "motherland," the Free French government recruits young men from its North African colonies. Few of those who enlist have ever set foot on French soil or otherwise would do so absent these exigent circumstances. Still, many are moved by the promise of Charles de Gaulle, the leader of the French Resistance, of Liberté, Egalité, and Fraternité. However, all too soon, the colonial soldiers will come to realize how hollow this slogan actually is.

Their story is told through the experiences of four soldiers who serve in the same company. Said (Jamel Debbouze) is a one-armed peasant from Algeria who ignores the entreaties from his mother to stay with her and instead enlists. Said eventually serves as an aide-de-camp to the company commander, Martinez (Bernard Blancan), and in many ways Said best displays the conflicting feelings of these colonial soldiers. On the one hand, he hates Martinez with a passion, especially after the latter turns on him when Said innocently mentions that both have Arab mothers, a fact that Martinez is desperately attempting to hide. After this, Said tells a severely wounded Martinez that he hopes that he dies. Yet, in the film's climatic battle scene, he sacrifices his own life in an effort to save Martinez.

Yassir (Samy Naceri) is Moroccan. He and his brother enlist so that they can loot the fallen enemy and thus have the money to get married back home. Messaoud (Roschdy Zem) is the company's marksman who after the liberation of southern France meets and falls in love with Irene, a French woman, an interracial relationship that the French authorities work to prevent. Finally, there is Corporal Abdelkader (Sami Bouajila), the leader of the North African troops and the only one to make it through the various ordeals that these brave soldiers are called upon to fight.

The relationship between the regular French army and the colonial soldiers is established early on. Martinez castigates Abdelkader for saluting him, saying this will tip the other men off in terms of his commanding officer status, and it soon becomes clear why such officers would be targeted for "fragging," as the colonial troops are repeatedly sent on the most dangerous missions and essentially used as cannon fodder. Patriotic songs and invocations of protecting the motherland from the rape of the Krauts will only go so far, and the colonial soldiers experience such daily indignities as not being given the same amount of food as the regular French forces and are routinely denied leave.

One of the best features of the film is watching the awakening of the colonial soldiers. The breaking point comes when they are subjected to a ballet performance that was meant to entertain the (French) soldiers. The cultural divide between French and colonial culture could not be drawn any clearer. In disgust, the colonial soldiers walk out of the performance and a mutiny breaks out. Martinez and Abdelkader get into a fight and the latter is placed in detention. Meanwhile, Messaoud is arrested for going AWOL in a desperate attempt to see Irene. As a way out of this situation, the colonial troops are given the option of being the first "French" troops to liberate Alsace, and the stirring conclusion of the film depicts the enormous bravery exhibited, once again, by these men. During the fierce fighting all but Abdelkader are killed. However, when regular French forces finally do make it to the scene of the fighting, the French media portrays them as the liberators, ignoring the fact that all the fighting had been carried out by the colonial troops. However, the town's residents know better, and in a simple display of gratitude they applaud Abdelkader for what he and his fallen comrades have done to save them.

The film closes when an elderly Abdelkader goes to visit the graves of the others. He lives in a humble apartment, and the viewer learns during the closing credits that the pensions of the colonial soldiers were frozen just before the independence of these French colonies. However, by this juncture the viewer can no longer be surprised by any further indignity that the French government throws their way, and it is perhaps an even greater surprise that the colonial soldiers were given any kind of pension at all. Vive La France!—but this is only for those considered to be truly French. Notwithstanding their incredible allegiance and loyalty to the "motherland," this is something denied to those who remain colonial soldiers.

26

District 9

(Neill Blomkamp, 2009)

Everyone has human rights by the mere fact of his/her existence. We know this and we proclaim this, yet we continue to focus on our religious, gender, ethnic, and political differences as the basis for denying certain people human rights. District 9 *takes this one step further and asks what it means to be a "human" and whether only humans should have "human rights."*

✳ ✳ ✳

At first, it might seem strange to label a movie about extraterrestrial visitors as one of the top human rights films, but *District 9* works exquisitely on several levels. One is simply as a political thriller. The story line is that a hovering spacecraft over Johannesburg, South Africa, has on board a horde of sick extraterrestrial beings—"prawns" to humans—who are rescued and taken to Earth. At first, the prawns are given a warm welcome and are provided shelter, food (they have a particular fondness for cat food), and clothing, albeit of the rag-tag variety. However, soon the welcome mat is taken away, and as the film opens we see a group of employees from Multinational United, which operates District 9 where the prawns are held, about to effectuate a relocation to a distant concentration camp. Leading this operation is Wikus van de Merwe (Sharlto Copley) a dweeb of the highest order who seems to owe a great deal to nepotism, as his father-in-law, Piet Smit (Louis Minnaar), is the CEO of MNU.

The prawns offer resistance, and in a skirmish with one of them, Wikus is wounded and becomes infected. As the film progresses, he slowly becomes one of "them," and he soon becomes the most hunted (and hated) man in all South Africa. The drama that unfolds involves whether Wikus and Christopher, the head prawn, can locate a liquid fuel in the MNU headquarters that will enable the prawns to fly back to their mother ship. In exchange for his help, Christopher has promised to make Wikus into a human being once again.

Notwithstanding this unusual (but captivating) premise, there are a host of human rights themes in the film. The most obvious is the apartheid-like treatment of the prawns, as they are segregated from the rest of South African society and forced to live in abject conditions. In addition to this, the film deals with the treatment of refugees. In many cases, there is an initial rush to welcome dispossessed people, but this is invariably followed by efforts to segregate them and eventually repatriate these individuals from our midst.

Multinational United could easily stand in for a host of multinational corporations. In addition to running District 9 and the relocation effort, MNU is one of the leading arms manufacturers in the world. What Smit and others are trying to determine is how the prawns' weapons operate, and in Wikus they have the perfect candidate for understanding this. MNU is also involved in some gruesome genetic testing of the prawns, and in one of the most touching scenes Christopher grieves over the mutilated remains of his life-partner. But MNU does not have a monopoly on evil, and everything is not black and white; the prawns are also exploited and oppressed by a group of Nigerians, who sell weapons and meat products to them.

Although the prawns are at first totally repulsive creatures—I suppose, it is difficult for anyone to look good eating cat food—by the end it is clear that they are more human than any of the humans shown on the screen. In the end, the transformation of Wikus to a "prawn" is complete, although he still has Christopher's promise that he will return to Earth and transform him back to a human being within three years. Let us hope that in that period of time he comes to his senses and stays exactly as he is now.

27

Sophie's Choice
(Alan J. Pakula, 1982)

As in the case with genocide, sometimes the enormity of the level of human rights violations tends to overwhelm our capacity to understand the meaning of these events. Instead, as we see in the next film, what sometimes gives us a better understanding is the fate of a single individual.

✳ ✳ ✳

Sophie's Choice is a film about two impossible choices that Sophie Zawistowski (Meryl Streep) has been forced to make in her life. The story is narrated by Stingo (Peter MacNicol), an innocent and aspiring writer from Virginia who moves to Brooklyn in order to write the Great American Novel. The day he moves into the large pink Victorian house he meets two of the other tenants: Sophie and her boyfriend Nathan (Kevin Kline). The introduction is marred when Nathan physically and verbally assaults Sophie, before turning his venom on Stingo.

However, the following day, Sophie and Nathan are back together again and deeply in love. Nathan apologizes profusely to Stingo and the latter cannot resist, describing him later in the film as "utterly and fatally glamorous." And this he is. Soon the three form a deep friendship, but one that is severely tested with each of Nathan's outbursts. After one such episode, Stingo asks Sophie about her life. She was raised as a good Catholic girl in Poland, the daughter of a famous international law professor who in the 1930s became one of the country's most vocal anti-Semites. Sophie married one of her father's assistants, but she continued to work as a secretary for her father, transcribing his speeches. Sophie became increasingly distressed with his calls to exterminate the country's Jewish population, and she relates to Stingo a trip she took to the Jewish ghetto where she realized that if her father and his kind had their way, all of these people around her would be dead.

In reaction to this, Sophie carried out an affair with a Resistance leader, and a week after he was shot she was arrested and sent to Auschwitz with her two young children. At the camp, a sadistic concentration camp guard (is there any other kind?) tells her that because she is not a Jew, one of her children will be allowed to live. But there is one catch: she is the one who has to decide which child will be spared. After repeatedly saying that she cannot do this, the guard informs her that both will be killed—at which point she chooses for her son, Jan, to live. While her young daughter is being led away, the pain and horror in Sophie's face is overwhelming.

Sophie survives the war by working as a secretary for the concentration camp commander, who also has an eye on her. She then uses this to beg Commander Hoess to save her son from the disease that is ravaging the children's camp and send him to Berlin in the Lebensborn program, so that he can be raised as a devoted young Nazi. Hoess promises her this, but never follows up, and as the war ends Jan's fate remains unknown. An anemic and exhausted Sophie then makes her way to the United States at the end of the war, and it is here that she meets Nathan, who, she believes, has saved her.

As the story progresses Nathan's behavior becomes even more frightening, and Stingo and Sophie learn that he is not a pharmaceutical scientist on the verge of winning a Nobel Prize, as he said, but rather a paranoid schizophrenic who has nothing but a menial job at Pfizer. A short time after this, Stingo and Sophie flee Brooklyn after Nathan shoots off a gun and threatens to kill both of them. Stingo's plan is to marry Sophie and to live with her in Virginia. They spend an evening together in a Washington, DC, hotel, and Stingo tells her he wants to have children with her. She responds that "you should have another mother for your children," and she then relates the story of being forced to sacrifice her daughter. The next morning Sophie leaves and goes back to Nathan, where she makes her second fatal choice. Rather than seeing him disintegrate even further, Sophie and Nathan both take cyanide, and they die lying next to each other in bed.

I have never seen Meryl Streep in a better role. Still, her performance is matched by Kevin Kline, who is absolutely mesmerizing as the mercurial Nathan, and Peter MacNicol, who plays Stingo. *Sophie's Choice* is stunningly good movie that shows us a much different, but equally horrifying, depiction of the Holocaust.

28

Bloody Sunday
(Paul Greengrass, 2002)

The next two films are set against "the Troubles"—the conflict between Catholics and Protestants in Northern Ireland—but they both transcend time and place. What these movies do so effectively and so wonderfully is to give us a human face to the countless number of innocent victims who are invariably swept up in any conflict.

✳ ✳ ✳

If there is one tragic event that has come to symbolize the Troubles in Northern Ireland it would be in the town of Derry on January 30, 1972, a day that has come to be called

Bloody Sunday. This captivating film brings you there. The viewer sees the excitement in the air that morning for the planned civil rights demonstration, bringing together old and young alike, mainly Catholics but led by Ivan Cooper (James Nesbitt), a Protestant member of Parliament. The hyperactive camera then switches to the British troops, an elite and aggressive contingent with its war paint on preparing to do battle.

The camera goes back and forth between those who will lead the march and those who will do everything in their power to prevent it from taking place. Invoking the nonviolent resistance of Martin Luther King, Jr., "We Shall Overcome" is sung often. The Brits live a universe apart. We see what almost looks like a war room with maps and coordinates and constant radio chatter, and angry soldiers armed to the teeth—for a puny march following Sunday mass. Cooper and the other organizers talk about crowd control and not instigating any trouble; the army commanders speak of pincer movements.

The march begins innocently enough. The political leadership is at the head of the parade on a flatbed truck that winds slowly down the hill into the city itself. The original destination was to be the Guildhall, but the British soldiers have blocked this off, so a contingency plan is made to stay on the Catholic side of town. However, although the truck makes the necessary turn, a small group of marchers go on the original parade route, almost all young teens relishing a confrontation. Seeing this, Cooper jumps from the truck and tries to get these kids to rejoin the march, but he has little success. The march continues to its new destination where speeches are made about civil rights and nonviolence. Meanwhile, the street hooligans continue to throw rocks at the British soldiers, when the order to attack is given, and attack unarmed civilians they do, killing thirteen demonstrators and wounding the same number. And watching this mayhem and violence is not easy.

After the killing is over, we see the Brits go into immediate damage control. They maintain that they saw men shooting at them, and only then did they shoot back. As panic sets in amidst the growing list of fatalities, the stories grow even wilder, and some soldiers now report that they were hit by nail bombs and firebombs. A shocked press contingent asks the arrogant commander whether he had any regrets how his troops had acted, and he reports none at all; rather, in his view, his boys displayed enormous restraint. For their part, the Catholics are grieving at the dead bodies of their friends, neighbors, and sons strewn all around. But as Cooper elegantly states in a hastily assembled press announcement, the civil rights movement in Northern Ireland has been killed, and the British have now provided the Irish Republican Army its greatest victory imaginable. Subsequent events would show Cooper to be prophetic.

The follow up to this tragedy is interesting to note. Although an initial inquiry absolved the British troops of any wrongdoing, another was created in 1998. Twelve years later it issued its report—the Saville Report, named after Lord Saville who headed the commission—concluding that the demonstrators were unarmed and that the troops had no grounds for firing as they did. Moreover, the report also found that several civilians were shot in the back while they were seeking to flee from the violence. Finally, the Saville Report excoriated the leadership for fabricating false reports and for planting evidence. In June 2010, British Prime Minister David Cameron described the actions of the troops as "unjustified and unjustifiable," and on behalf of the British government and its people he issued a state apology, saying that he was "deeply, deeply sorry."

29

Omagh

(Pete Travis, 2004)

Omagh is another outstanding film about the Troubles in Northern Ireland. The film tenderly relates the human consequences after an IRA car bomb attack killed thirty-one people.

✳ ✳ ✳

In the opening, the viewer sees men working in secret making a bomb and then placing the device in a car, which they park on one of the city's main streets. As this is being shown, we also see cutting images of daily life in Omagh, as children set off for school, shops open up, and people greet one another as they walk the downtown streets of this charming village. The viewer is introduced to the Gallagher family, but only indirectly at first. Michael Gallagher (Gerard McSorley) is a car mechanic, and his son, Aiden, works alongside him while Patsy Gallagher (Michele Forbes) is seen busily getting her family off for the day.

The car is parked, and a telephone call is made informing the authorities that a bomb will be going off in thirty minutes. There is great confusion, and the police respond not by evacuating people from the area but directing them almost to the exact spot where the car is parked. The effect here is reminiscent of a Hitchcock thriller. The terrible blast goes off. At first, there is complete quiet. But then the silence is broken by the sound of screaming, crying, and overall panic. There are dead and wounded bodies everywhere. Michael knows that two of his children were planning on meeting downtown. He races home and sees that his daughter is safe, but Aiden is nowhere to be found. Michael rushes downtown, but he and others are turned away. So he first heads for the hospital, but he has no success there and ends up at some makeshift headquarters. Michael waits and waits and finally he is taken into a tent. The viewer never sees the mangled body, but there is no need. We see Michael's crushed face. He then drives home to tell the news to the girls and the outpouring of grief is horrible.

The film then moves to a second act. A short time after the bomb attack, the Gallagher family is invited to a meeting of victims. Venting their hurt and anger that no one has been arrested, people are literally screaming at one another. Michael stands up to talk, and he proves to be the (only) voice of reason there, and he is chosen as the spokesperson for the group. Initially, his involvement has a positive effect on him and his family, but quite soon the demands for media interviews and organizational meetings take their toll, and a fissure develops between him and the rest of his family, especially Patsy, who grows increasingly depressed and distant from him. In one scene, Michael approaches her and he tries to explain how and why he is doing what he is doing. He says to her that it is essential to know what happened. Her devastating reply is this: I know what happened. Someone killed Aiden. That's what happened. I don't care about why or who killed him.

But Michael and the others in the support group press on, although they get virtually no answers from the police, except to say that they are doing their best to solve the case. Meanwhile, Michael is called out of the blue one day and given a list of names of those involved, which then gets him involved with some shady characters. One is Gerry Adams, the head of Sein Finn, who says at the outset of the meeting that he is not going to talk to the group like a politician would—and then proceeds to talk to the group exactly like a politician would. Michael also has a secret meeting with Kevin Fulton, a member of the IRA and a police informant, who tells him that the authorities were tipped off about the possibility of a bomb attack more than forty-eight hours in advance, but that they did nothing to try to prevent it.

After yet another futile meeting with the authorities, Michael decides that he has to stop this and go back to his life. He goes back to his garage, and reestablishes a relationship with Patsy and his daughters. However, the day the police ombudsman report is to come out, Michael tells Patsy that he thinks he will be attending the proceedings. Soon thereafter, Patsy decides that, for Aiden, she and her daughters also need to be there. The ombudsman's report is devastating, detailing both police malfeasance and nonfeasance. Afterward, the support group turns to Michael to issue a statement to the press, and he delivers some beautiful yet powerful remarks. During the epilogue the viewer learns that there still have been no arrests in this case.

This film was a joint venture between Irish and British state television and shown on television in both countries in 2004. All of the acting is superb, but special mention has to be made of McSorley, who serves as the conscience of the Omagh victims support group.

30

Paradise Now

(Hany Abu-Assad, 2005)

There is a common expression that one person's terrorist is another person's freedom fighter. This, of course, is not meant to equate all acts of terrorism with the fight for political freedom. Instead it captures the idea that we are quick to label those who oppose us politically and who employ violent means on behalf of their cause to be nothing more than "terrorists," which then gives us license not to address the claims—legitimate or otherwise—that they are making on us.

✳ ✳ ✳

Paradise Now is one of the most thought-provoking films I have ever seen and it explores this very idea. It tells the story of Said (Kais Nashif) and Khaled (Ali Suliman), two Palestinian men living in the city of Nablus in the Occupied Territories who have been recruited as suicide bombers and given a few days to get their affairs in order before setting off on their assigned mission.

Khaled says his farewells, but Said has picked a terrible time to fall in love after he meets up with Suha (Lubna Azabal), an absolutely fetching woman who thinks that all this terrorism and suicide bombing stuff is a load of childish crap. She is distressingly baffled that Said (or anyone else, for that matter) would ever think about killing himself and innocent civilians, and there is no question but that she makes a convincing case to the viewer, if not to Said. But what she and the viewer eventually also learn is that Said's father collaborated with the Israelis, and thus his son's mission has as much to do with family dynamics as it does with international politics.

One of the funniest scenes in the movie involves the making of the final video where the martyrdom of Khaled and Said is to be established. However, what ensues is something out of *The Keystone Kops* meets *This Is Spinal Tap*, as repeated takes are required in order to create the "appropriate" terrorist tone.

Khaled eventually decides to abandon his mission, but Said presses forward. In his black suit and shaved face, he is able to pass himself off as a Jew—who also happens to have a bomb strapped to his body. At one point Said is on a bus carrying civilians and it is apparent that he is seriously contemplating detonating the bomb, but he decides not to when he spots a young child. However, he gets on another bus, this one filled with both civilians and soldiers, when the film suddenly cuts to white—and ends. Thus, it is left up the viewer to determine whether he explodes the bomb or not.

The reason this is such a thought-provoking film lies not in whether Said pulls the chord but whether he should do so. The easiest answer is simply to condemn all violence. Whether or not this is the appropriate response, this film shows why someone would consider violence in the first place. Khaled and Said are anything but monsters. They are probably no different from many of those watching the film. Regardless of one's nationality, political affiliation, or beliefs, they want what all people want, but they are denied many of these things due to the Israeli occupation. The question raised by the film is what they should do about this.

Also of Note

The Terrorist (Santosh Sivan, 1998)

The Terrorist in the title of this feature film is Malli (Ayesha Dharkar) a nineteen-year-old girl who seemingly has been training her entire life to make the ultimate sacrifice. The story takes place in the

Indian subcontinent, but other than this the political background is quite vague. Does this involve the conflict between Pakistan and India? Is Malli a member of the Tamil Tigers fighting a guerrilla battle against the government of Sri Lanka?

Perhaps on one level these questions do not matter. The film is much less interested in politics than it is in exploring how a "terrorist" becomes such. There is not much dialogue in the film, but maybe it is because Malli does not have much to say. Instead, she is a blank slate and, for the most part, she is what others have wanted her to become. There is, however, one major complication: right before her mission, she meets a young man and, in what seems like the only moment of passion or even humanness in her life, she becomes pregnant. Thus, the suspense for the audience, and perhaps for her as well, is whether she will still carry out her suicide bombing mission as the targeted political leader is walking past her, or whether, now that there is another person involved, she will back off and give birth to the child, who might grow up to be just like his or her mother.

Miral (Julian Schnabel, 2010)

Miral caused a minor stir when it was released in 2010 because of the advertisement which read: "Is this the face of a terrorist?" In this instance, the face of the "terrorist" is the stunning Freida Pinto, one of the stars of *Slumdog Millionaire,* pictured rather provocatively in her schoolgirl's uniform. The question is whether Miral, who is a young student at a school for Palestinian orphans and who has had a political awakening due to the Intifada, will heed the advice of her school's master to follow the path of nonviolence or whether she will follow the example of her aunt and her friends and take up arms on behalf of the Palestinian cause.

The Baader Meinhof Complex (Uli Edel, 2008)

As difficult as it is to believe now, but there was a time when international terrorism was considered "cool," although "sexy" might be an even better term in the case of Germany's Baader-Meinhof group, which took its name from its two leaders: Andreas Baader (Moritz Bleibtreu) and Ulrike Meinhof (Martina Gedeck). This feature film opens in 1967 with the Shah of Iran visiting Berlin as a guest of the German government. A small group of young Germans who strongly object to the presence of this brutal dictator stage a protest. Initially, the Shah's Iranian bodyguards turn on them, but they are soon joined by their German counterparts, one of whom kills an unarmed demonstrator. The point is that, all appearances aside, Germany has not been able to escape its violent, fascist past, and what adds to this is the close political relationship the country has with the United States, which at the time was engaged in the bloody conflict in Vietnam.

The group comes to believe that they cannot oppose these policies by working within the system, and they turn to violence that is both random and senseless. Depressed by all this, Meinhof commits suicide in prison. Baader eventually shoots himself, and many of the other members of the organization also die violent deaths—and this is not to mention all those killed in the bombings and shooting sprees that the organization and those pursuing them carried out. Although the film shows how romanticized the Baader-Meinhof group was, at least at the outset, it makes no attempt to romanticize them. Peel back a layer, and it is easy to see these self-styled "revolutionaries" for what they really are: spoiled middle-class folks acting out. Yet it is much too easy to condemn the group outright. On one essential point they were absolutely correct: their own government *was* in league with some awful characters.

31
Persepolis
(Marjane Satrapi and Vincent Paronnaud, 2007)

For most people, the term "feature film" conjures up images of "real actors" and stage sets. Certainly, most of the films under discussion in this part fit this bill, but the next two films are animated. Persepolis *deals with women's rights, a subject that is explored in several other feature films and documentaries. One of the major human rights treaties is the Convention on the Elimination of Discrimination Against Women (CEDAW). As the Preamble to the Convention points out, notwithstanding previous international efforts to improve the situation of women, "extensive discrimination" continues to exist—thereby violating international human rights standards.*

✳ ✳ ✳

Persepolis is funny, sad, educational, outrageous, and personal. It tells the coming-of-age story of a young girl, Marjane, growing up in Iran in the period immediately before and after the 1979 Revolution. Marjane is brought up in a liberal family and this high-spirited young girl enjoys the freedoms that Iranian society allowed at that time. Life is not perfect, especially with the brutal Shah in power. However, life gets much worse, especially for Iranian women, after the 1979 revolution that brought the conservative religious ayatollahs into power.

One of the more joyful aspects of *Persepolis* is that, although the film always has a political edge to it, it is not all politics all the time. Instead, this is a story of a young person trying to find herself and oftentimes using rebellion—against her family and also against the autocratic political system—as a means of doing so. In seeming desperation, her family decides to send her out of the country for her education, and she enrolls in a French Lycée in Vienna. However, she grows increasingly dissatisfied with the shallowness of many of the young people around her, particularly those who have made her feel ashamed to think of herself as Iranian. Marjane eventually returns home, but the country's religious fanatics now control virtually all aspects of life. After a series of harrowing close calls, her family sends her abroad once again. The film ends as it begins, at the Charles de Gaulle airport in Paris, where Marjane is not able to return to the country she loves.

32
Waltz with Bashir
(Ari Folman, 2008)

There has been an unfortunate tendency to remove human rights considerations from situations of war, perhaps because there are two distinct legal regimes: international human rights law, on the one hand, and humanitarian law, or the laws of war, on the other. However, human rights principles continue to operate even in times of conflict. Thus, those who engage in fighting must attempt to kill the enemy while at the same time seek to ensure that they protect the lives and well-being of civilian populations.

✱ ✱ ✱

Waltz with Bashir is a brilliant animated film about Israel's invasion of Lebanon in the early 1980s and the horrors that took place during the course of this conflict. It is also about war more generally and the simultaneous need to remember and strong desire to forget about these experiences. The plot device in this film is that it is the year 2006 and because of a series of frightening nightmares a veteran of the Israeli military is now trying to reconstruct his role in the 1982 invasion of Lebanon. Except for one scene near the end, the film is done entirely in animation, and rather than being a distraction, the animation makes the story easier to tell and to comprehend.

As the film progresses, the protagonist (director Ari Folman) remembers more and more of his wartime experiences. There is a surreal and dreamlike quality to these memories, and the viewer is not sure whether the memories appear this way in his own mind or whether he simply chose to use this technique in making this movie. However, the one time where animation is not used is simply staggering. The scene begins with a group of Israeli soldiers approaching the Sabra and Shatila refugee camps, which the Israeli military had turned over to its Christian Lebanese allies. As the soldiers are moving forward we see Palestinians running toward them in great distress. It is at that moment that the animation turns "real," and all of the abstractness of the situation vanishes completely. What Folman and the viewer now can see, and understand, is the massive slaughter of the civilian population in these camps.

Also of Note
Lebanon (Samuel Maoz, 2009)

Lebanon is set entirely inside an Israeli tank in the 1982 war in that country. Claustrophobic is the only way to describe *Lebanon*, and one could imagine that the film would work well (and arguably much better) as a stage production. The crew is heaped on top of one another along with a captured Syrian prisoner who is being transported with them. War films have a habit of going over the top and despite its purposeful depiction of the drudgery of war, *Lebanon* is no exception. Despite all the time spent with the tank crew, there is no real connection with the viewer, and the death of one of them (Yigal) seems more in the nature of a plot device than anything else. If *Waltz with Bashir* raises the issue of how one is able to get through the horrors of war—not only at the time these occur but afterwards as well—*Lebanon* provides no comparable insights. You cannot see much of what is going on in the world when you are walled up inside a tank. Unfortunately, oftentimes you cannot see very much of what is going on outside of it either.

33

Amazing Grace
(Michael Apted, 2006)

Although the human rights revolution is often pegged to the post–World War II period, arguably the real genesis for the human rights movement occurred over a century earlier with the international effort to eliminate slavery. What the following film depicts is the effort to abolish slavery in Great Britain—something that seemed absolutely preposterous when it was first proposed.

✳ ✳ ✳

Amazing Grace is a difficult film not to like. For one thing, there is the story line involving the dashingly handsome British abolitionist William Wilberforce (Ioan Gruffudd), who fought for decades in Parliament to eliminate the slave trade in Great Britain. Add to this some wonderful English scenery, especially Wilberforce's manor, which he shares with a trove of animals that would put Noah to shame. The cut and thrust of legislative debate is also fun to watch, especially when someone is as clever and as quick-witted as Wilberforce. If this is not enough, throw in an inspirational love story where Wilberforce meets cute with Barbara Spooner (Romola Garai), the strong-willed (and drop-dead gorgeous) woman who becomes his wife and, along with William Pitt (Benedict Cumberbatch), convinces him to do battle once again—this time successfully. The last but certainly not the least thing that should be mentioned is the song itself, which is heard at various junctures in the film. The hymn was written by Wilberforce's mentor John Newton (Albert Finney), who had been the commander of a slave ship and is now spending the rest of his time on earth trying to make amends to the 20,000 "slave ghosts" he transported.

The film is notable for its restraint. The viewer is not exposed to vivid images of enslaved black men, women, and children being beaten within an inch of their lives.

Instead, the abolitionists who first make their case to Wilberforce do so by simply showing the bevy of chains that are used on slave ships. They explain that the chains were used not so much to prevent a revolt or to keep the slaves from escaping but to keep them from throwing themselves overboard because of the rancid and inhuman conditions.

The films depicts the impossible odds that Wilberforce had to overcome. At the outset of his quest, he is scorned and derided. His opponents, who comprise virtually the entirety of the House of Commons, simply cannot conceive that slavery is wrong or even that blacks are human beings. And besides, slavery is quite lucrative for so many members of Parliament, and for the British empire at large. But as we know, Wilberforce was on the side of the angels. His story is an inspiring one and so is the song, as is the film that goes with it.

Also of Note

Amistad (Steven Spielberg, 1997)

Amistad tells the true story of a slave rebellion aboard a Spanish vessel, which eventually turned into a long legal battle that ended up being decided by the US Supreme Court. The opening scene is simply riveting. The slave, Cinque (Djimon Hounsou), in full body chains and with an ocean storm howling all around him, is somehow able to extricate a small nail from the slave ship's hull, which he then uses to free himself and his fellow slaves. Blood revenge follows, but the slaves decide to keep two members of the crew alive so that they can steer the ship back to Africa. However, they are tricked by the whites, as the ship sails into New Haven harbor instead, where the slaves are once again placed in chains. Years of legal wrangling ensue, eventually culminating in a case that makes its way to the US Supreme Court, where the slaves are represented by John Quincy Adams (Anthony Hopkins). History is made, and the downfall of slavery in the United States begins.

Roots (Marvin Chomsky, John Erman, David Greene, and Gilbert Moses, 1977)

Roots was a national phenomenon when it first aired in January 1977, and its finale remains one of the most watched shows in the United States. This made-for-television movie is based on Alex Haley's book of that name, which chronicles his family's history going back to its African roots. Several of Haley's ancestors depicted in the movie—Kunta Kinte (LeVar Burton), Kizzy (Leslie Uggams), and Chicken George (Ben Vereen), in particular—became household names. The great importance of *Roots* is that it gave a human dimension to slavery and its aftermath that had been so long missing from historical accounts of the "peculiar institution."

34

Mississippi Burning
(Alan Parker, 1988)

Although the United States was one of the major players in establishing human rights institutions and standards, the United States began to remove itself from these processes when these same international standards were then used to challenge forced racial segregation in this country. There is no question that the raw racism depicted in Mississippi Burning *violates the US Constitution, but it also violates a host of international human rights standards as well.*

✳ ✳ ✳

Mississippi Burning presents a fairly realistic portrayal of the real-life disappearance of three civil rights workers in that state in 1964, which prompted a federal investigation that ended with many of the principals, including local law enforcement agents, being convicted on federal charges of denying civil rights. Gene Hackman plays FBI agent Rupert Anderson, while Willem Dafoe plays FBI agent Alan Ward. Their mismatched backgrounds and personalities are established right at the outset as they are driving down to Mississippi. Anderson had previously been a Mississippi sheriff, and he is almost too familiar with southern culture and mores, including the way that "colored" people are held in sheer terror by the white population. For his part, Ward is all about following FBI procedure. The two clash as they pursue the case, but most of the film focuses on the fascinating character of Anderson.

Just after the two take rooms at the local motel, the Ku Klux Klan attempts to kill both of them. Against Anderson's advice, Ward's response is to call in hundreds of federal agents, who spend most of their time (and much of the film) looking for the three bodies. Whites certainly won't talk to these federal agents, but neither will the local black population. In a wonderful scene, Anderson and Ward go into a local eatery where they are told they will have to wait for a table. However, there is some space in the "colored" section, and Ward strides across the restaurant to take the available seating. The diner goes completely silent, and when Ward attempts to talk with the blacks seated there he is repeatedly told that they have nothing to tell the FBI.

Meanwhile, Anderson knows that in a small southern town like Jessup County, Mississippi, much more can be gleaned simply by listening and observing, and one of the things that he quickly picks up on is the deputy sheriff Clinton Pell (Brad Dourif) and his wife (Frances McDormand) do not get along very well. What he also slowly learns is that she has a conscience regarding racial matters, which seems to put her in a minority of one, at least in this area of the state, and eventually she informs Anderson where the bodies can be located. Word gets out about her involvement, and Pell arrives home, accompanied by some of his fellow Klan members, and he beats her severely. She is hospitalized, and it is there that Ward and Anderson come to blows, before Ward vows that he wants justice—and he is willing to do things Anderson's way.

Anderson's way, it should be said, violates most federal law. The mayor of the town is kidnapped and he is threatened with the loss of his sexual organ unless he tells what he knows about the killing of the civil rights workers, which, it turns out, is quite a lot. Anderson also devises a scheme where Lester, one of the more nervous Klan members, believes he is about to be lynched for talking with the FBI. The reality is that those pretending to string him up are FBI agents, but the plan works like a charm and Lester spills the beans on his fellow Klan members. As a result, most of them (although not the corrupt sheriff) are sent to prison for some period of years.

As good as this film is in terms of depicting the terror that whites practiced against blacks, there are times when the plot line strains credibility. For one thing, although firebombings of houses and churches were widely practiced in the South at this time, the film gives the impression that this was a daily affair and that half the buildings in this small, sleepy town were set ablaze. The degree of federal involvement is also exaggerated, which based on the film seems to involve only slightly fewer men than took part in the invasion of Normandy.

One last thing is the political message of the film. What the film seems to be saying, albeit through the enormous charm and charisma of Gene Hackman, is that the only way to defeat the forces of segregation and evil is to adopt their practices. A lot of people would take issue with this, and rightly so.

35

The Circle
(Jafar Panahi, 2000)

We tend to think of human rights as having an upward progression, where ever-increasing numbers of people receive human rights protection. However, retrogression can also occur. Certainly this has been the case for women in Iran following the 1979 Iranian Revolution. This theme is explored in Persepolis *(FF-31) and in the haunting film* The Circle.

✳ ✳ ✳

There really is no plot to *The Circle*, but this is not intended as criticism. Rather, in a tag-team fashion, the film follows various Iranian women, all of whom have been detained by the authorities at some point in their lives, as they go about trying to construct something resembling a normal life. This point is poignantly made in the opening scene. The setting is a hospital delivery waiting room where a grandmother learns, to her complete horror, that her newborn grandchild is a girl. Terribly distraught, she flees from the hospital. The camera follows her out, but then it picks up on some women who happened to have been released from prison that day. One immediately gets arrested by some Iranian police officers (it is by no means clear what she might have done—if she has done anything at all). The camera then follows the other two who are trying to find money for bus tickets to go to the countryside. The viewer is then introduced to Pari, who has been thrown out of her house by her family. Pari meets up with a woman who is in the process of trying to abandon her pretty young daughter so that she might have some possible prospects in her life. After painfully carrying out this plan, she is offered a ride by a man who, unbeknownst to her, is a member of the Iranian vice squad (although all men in the film appear to play such a role) who accuses her of soliciting sex. This in turn leads us to a woman who really is a prostitute, who is arrested and taken to a detention facility. The final scene takes place in the holding cell, and we see at least one face that we had seen earlier, and we also learn that the woman who gave birth in the opening scene is also in detention. And in that way we have come full circle.

The women in the film are not fully developed characters and many go nameless. The suffocating burkas also obscure each woman's identify. Yet each of the characters has a story to tell, although there is a common theme to all, namely that life for Iranian women is a living hell. One cannot help but admire the courage of these women. They are certainly oppressed, and there is the constant fear of crossing the omnipresent "authorities." Yet, sad as their lives might be, these women are willing and able to fight for themselves and their sisters.

Also of Note

Kandahar (Mohsen Makhmalbaf, 2001)

This feature film that revolves around the story of Nafas (Nelofer Pazira), a Canadian-Afghan woman who goes back to Afghanistan because her sister there has declared that she will commit suicide. The film blends together a number of bizarre and wonderful images along with a litany of the abuses suffered by women in that country. The mood is established in the opening scene, as prosthetic legs are being parachuted to the ground to a group of desperate amputees. This is bookended by the closing scene, when the protagonist hides out among a wedding party consisting of women in gorgeously colored burkas who are crossing the desert. Whether she will ever get to her sister remains unclear, but what the film does above all else is to portray the reasons for this desperation.

The Stoning of Soraya M. (Cyrus Nowrasteh, 2008)

In terms of building suspense, a different title would certainly have helped in not telegraphing the plot line about this story of Soraya (Mozhan Marnò), a young Iranian mother of four who is unjustly and savagely stoned to death for allegedly committing adultery. What is her crime? It is nothing more than her refusal to agree to allow her husband to take another bride—a fourteen-year-old girl at that. Women have been stoned in Iran and elsewhere, and there should be an international concern for this. But it is important to remember that most human rights violations that women suffer are nowhere near as dramatic as this—and they happen every single day.

Silent Waters (Sabiha Sumar, 2003)

The protagonist of the story is Ayesha (Kiron Kher), a widow with an aimless and spoiled son, Saleem (Aamir Ali Malik). Ayesha is known as the woman in the village who never goes to the well to fetch water, and as the movie progresses the viewer learns the reason for this. At the time that Pakistan was created in 1947, there was a group of Sikhs living in this village. To keep Muslim men away from "their" women, all female Sikhs sacrificed themselves by drowning in the village well. The one exception is Ayesha, who had changed her name from Veero and who has come to live a comfortable existence in this village—until two Muslim fundamentalists come to town and expose the "heathen" in their midst.

Water (Deepa Mehta, 2005)

The setting is rural India in 1938, although its central theme—the horrendous treatment of widows in India—is, unfortunately, seemingly timeless, something that is also touched upon at the closing. The central "widow" in this case is an eight-year-old girl whose husband died. At the outset of the film her father is seen delivering her to a home for widows, a place women are expected to lead chaste lives, as scripture dutifully requires. What ensues is a political and personal awakening for some, but death and cruelty for others.

36

Bamako

(Abderrahmane Sissako, 2006)

As mentioned earlier, the most serious deficiency in human rights is the lack of enforcement mechanisms. Where are victims to go to enforce their human rights? What judicial body, if any, can they turn to for protection? The following film provides a unique answer to these questions.

✳ ✳ ✳

It is safe to say that *Bamako* will not be for all audiences. The film does two different things. One is that it provides a sliver of life in a small village compound within the capital city of Bamako, Mali. Much like *Moolaadé* (FF-43), *Bamako* makes viewers aware that not all of Africa is a cesspool of violence and poverty. One of the most beautiful features of *Bamako* is that is shows a tidy little community and shares with viewers the rhythms and shared intimacies of everyday life there.

But this is only one aspect of *Bamako*. The more revolutionary and challenging part of the film is that in the village courtyard itself two international organizations—the World Bank and the International Monetary Fund—are being put on trial, amidst the roaming chickens, goats, and children and as daily chores are being carried out. Despite these highly unusual circumstances, the charge against the two defendants is a deadly serious one: rather than helping the people of Africa to escape backwardness, poverty, illiteracy, disease, and so on, these international institutions have actually made matters worse.

The viewer is treated to the spectacle—and make no mistake, it is a spectacle—of representatives of the World Bank and the IMF attempting to defend their record before the assembled judges, lawyers, witnesses, and, most important, community members they are supposed to be protecting. The main character, Melé, believes that these charges are true and that the IMF and the World Bank are guilty as charged. Yet what makes the trial, and also the film, so effective is that there is nothing that is over the top. The charges are eloquently and intelligently made, and the truth is that there is a great deal of evidence supporting these charges. Thus, perhaps the only thing that truly is odd about *Bamako* is that these institutions have finally been held to account—if only in a feature film.

Also of Note

The End of Poverty? (Philippe Diaz, 2008)

World poverty is not an easy subject to capture on film. Where did world poverty begin? According to the filmmakers, we need to go back to the year 1492 and the European invasion of the Americas, which eventually extended European hegemony over all other parts of the globe. After this, there was the colonial domination of the nineteenth and twentieth centuries and then the neocolonial policies of more recent times, especially the structural adjustment programs imposed by the World Bank and the International Monetary Fund, the two defendants in our previous film.

This tale is told, over and over again, by a visual of a poor family followed by a white Western talking head spouting off in the nature of a graduate student, followed by a screeching voiceover by the ever-earnest Martin Sheen. True believers will certainly be moved by this, but it is not clear that anyone else would be. Although the filmmaker is to be applauded for asking big and important questions, what the documentary is in desperate need of is more subtle and sophisticated analysis, and much less mindless ideology.

Life and Debt (Stephanie Black, 2001)

Life and Debt covers some of the same ground as *The End of Poverty?* but focuses on one country: Jamaica. The film shows that the tourist view of the country—the gorgeous beaches, stunning sunsets, and drinks on the veranda served by smiling black faces—is not the true Jamaica. Former Prime Minister Michael Manley somberly and eloquently relates his longstanding battles and deep-seated frustrations with the IMF and the World Bank. Perhaps after their trial in *Bamako* is completed, these two institutions need to be shipped to Jamaica, and elsewhere, in order to answer for their crimes.

37

4 Months, 3 Weeks and 2 Days (Cristian Mungiu, 2007)

The next two films deal with the issue of abortion. For some, abortion itself constitutes the ultimate human rights violation visited on the unborn. However, for others, there is a human right to a safe and legal abortion, which is something that women in many countries are still denied.

✳ ✳ ✳

The title refers to the length of the pregnancy of Gabita (Laura Vasiliu), a young college student who is attempting to get an abortion. Gabita lives in a small town in Romania, a country where abortion has been criminalized under the old communist regime (a theme also touched upon in *Children Underground*). There to assist her is Otila (Anamaria Marinca), who is her roommate. The abortion is to be performed by a "Mr. Bebe" (Vlad Ivanov), and the hotel scenes involving the two young women and the rapacious Mr. Bebe are extraordinarily difficult to watch. Bebe not only employs crude and dangerous methods in the abortion but he also demands that the two girls have sex with him, adding to their discomfort, defenselessness, and humiliation.

Another part of the story involves Otilia and her boyfriend, Adi (Alexandru Potocean). After the events in the hotel, she goes off to a birthday party at Adi's parents' house, where she has to endure the trivial talk of the guests, many of whom are medical doctors. Otilia later tells Adi about the abortion, and they have a disagreement over whether she would have one if the situation involved her and not Gabita. Otilia then tries to call Gabita, but there is no answer. She then goes back to the hotel. Gabita tells her that the aborted fetus is in the bathroom. Otilia goes in there and wraps it up and takes the dead thing outside and throws it into a trashbin and walks away. This is abortion in Romania and, unfortunately, many other places in the world.

38

Vera Drake
(Mike Leigh, 2004)

The second film on this list that deals with abortion is Mike Leigh's Vera Drake.

✳ ✳ ✳

Vera Drake is a middle-aged woman living in an industrial town in England where she cleans the houses of wealthy people. Vera (Imelda Staunton) lives with her devoted husband, Stanley (Philip Davis), a car mechanic, and her two adult children: the mousy Ethel (Alex Kelly), who works in a light bulb factory, and Sid (Daniel Mays), who tailors men's clothing. She also takes care of her ailing mother and another elderly man (possibly her father) who is confined to a wheelchair. Her generosity and kindness are also exhibited by her insistence that Reg (Eddie Marsan), a droopy young man without family in the area, come round for dinner. He does and he eventually becomes her son-in-law. But there is another, hidden type of work that Vera engages in: she performs abortions, although she never utters the word. She sees this as a matter of helping young girls in trouble. She takes no money for her efforts and is quite efficient about matters.

The strength of the movie is the depiction of the Drake family. There is a naturalness to the acting that takes the viewer into the household, tea and biscuit in hand, thank you. In one of the small side plots, the daughter of one of Vera's clients, a Mrs. Wells, is raped by her drunk boyfriend and gets pregnant. We witness the ordeal that she is put through, first during her visit to a doctor who charges an exorbitant amount of money and then during her appointment with an arrogant psychiatrist who needs for her to say that there is some mental illness in her family so that an abortion can be performed for her mental health. After this charade, the abortion can then be lawfully performed.

Meanwhile, Vera gets her clients from Lily (Ruth Sheen), an old friend, who herself charges a fee for Vera's services—although Vera has no knowledge of this. Rather, Vera believes that Lily wants to help young girls in trouble just like she does. Things go well until one abortion results in complications, and the young woman is taken to the hospital and operated on. The doctor knows that the story of a miscarriage is a false one, and he calls the police. Soon Vera is implicated, and in a scene that is excruciating to see develop, the police arrive at Vera's house right in the middle of the family's Christmas dinner. The authorities take her into another room, while her family, who know nothing about this, sit baffled in the tiny living room.

Vera is incapable of lying, and in a halting voice she explains everything to the police. They then take her to the station where she is placed under arrest, and she spends the night in jail, before making bail the next morning. However, before all this, her husband Stanley is brought into the interrogation room, still unaware of why his wife is at the police station, and with deep and moving sobs she whispers to him why she is there. He is shocked, but he never wavers in his support for her. Neither does his brother, who owns the car repair business and who is married to a nagging and upwardly mobile young wife. True to course, Ethel does not say much, but she becomes quite attentive to Vera when she returns home. Sid initially condemns her, but after a discussion with his father he apologizes to his mother for his response. And in one of the nicest twists, her future son-in-law becomes one of her strongest supporters, telling her that the awkward Christmas "celebration" is the nicest one he has ever been to—and he might be telling the truth.

Vera gets legal representation, but her case is weakened because none of the families she cleans for (including the Wells family) will testify to her trustworthiness. She pleads guilty, and in the last third of the film Vera says little, a far cry from the person we were introduced to at the beginning of the film. She also cries constantly.

We never learn how and why Vera started doing abortions. At one point, one of the interrogating police officers asks her whether she had had an abortion when she was younger, but her response is indeterminate. Her explanation that she is simply helping young girls seems simplistic, but it also seems to offer the best explanation, although at least one of her clients would not fit this bill.

Notwithstanding this, *Vera Drake* is an outstanding film that shows what women oftentimes had to (and have to) go through to procure an abortion and the risk involved for those who carried them out.

39

Lilya 4-Ever

(Lukas Moodysson, 2002)

All too often sex trafficking has not been treated as a human rights violation. Many see it as a private choice that involves no state involvement or responsibility. But what invariably drives women into prostitution is the denial of certain human rights protections, and when sex trafficking involves crossing state borders, there are at least two states that are violating their own duty to protect those being victimized.

✳ ✳ ✳

The Western conception of human rights invariably involves atrocities in distant lands. But sex trafficking belies that assumption and is the focus of the disturbing feature film *Lilya 4-Ever*. The eponymous protagonist (Oksana Akinshina) is an attractive young girl who lives with her mother in a shabby public housing complex in the former Soviet Union. Lilya's mother leaves with her boyfriend to go the United States, but she refuses to take Lilya with her. Lilya's aunt moves into the apartment to take care of her, but what she does instead is throw her out. Lilya is left to fend for herself, aided in at least some small way by a young neighborhood boy (Volodya), who has as little emotional and financial support at home as she does.

Lilya jumps at a chance to travel to Sweden, where she thinks she will join a young man who has shown romantic interest in her. However, as desperate as her life has been before this, it gets considerably worse in Sweden. After arriving, she is immediately taken to a housing unit that is only a small step up from where she had been living in Russia. Lilya's passport is confiscated, and she is quickly forced into performing tricks for her handlers.

In terms of human rights protection, there is almost none to be found in the squalor back home in Russia, but there is no evidence of this in Sweden either. Like millions of other boys and girls in a similar situation, Lily is forced to fend for herself. The results, as this powerful film shows, will be nothing less than a living nightmare.

Also of Note
The Price of Sex (Mimi Chakarova, 2011)

In this documentary, filmmaker Mimi Chakarova sets out to show how and why so many young women from Bulgaria and Moldova turn to prostitution in foreign lands. Much of this has to do with the removal of any form of societal safety net after the fall of communism, but another reason is that corrupt governments look the other way. The film gives a voice to those who previously had been voiceless: the victimized women, who are quite lucky to be able to tell their story.

40
Men with Guns
(John Sayles, 1997)

Political violence in Central America and South America in the 1980s was epidemic. In Guatemala an estimated 200,000 people were killed, the vast majority indigenous people, while in El Salvador this number was approximately 75,000. The Southern Cone countries in South America experienced massive levels of political violence as well. Given this, perhaps it is only appropriate that the location of the following film is indeterminate. All the viewer can figure out is that it is set in a Latin American country that is engulfed in a brutal civil war.

* * *

Men with Guns received a lot of favorable attention when it was released in the late 1990s. Directed by the always-political John Sayles, it is set in an unnamed Latin American country experiencing civil conflict, although the people in the capital city seem completely unaware of this, including (or especially) Dr. Humberto Fuentes (Federico Luppi), a recent widower whose practice includes the powerful and those with too much time and money on their hands.

For his vacation this year, Dr. Fuentes decides that, rather than going to the beach as he and his wife had done for years, he will go into the mountains and visit his old students who participated in a project that was aimed at treating tapeworm and other maladies in the country's indigenous population. What confirms this decision is when Fuentes sees Bravo, who was in this class, at the market dealing in stolen goods. When Dr. Fuentes confronts him, Bravo answers that he trades stolen goods to buy drugs for those who have nothing. He chides Fuentes for sending the group into the mountains, where they were viewed by government forces as the enemy, and he says that while Dr. Fuentes is the most learned man he has ever met, he is also the most ignorant. Much of what follows is evidence of this latter point.

So Fuentes exchanges his shiny black Mercedes for a jeep, and he sets off (with a nice pair of loafers on!) to visit his students in the mountains. However, whenever he arrives at a village and asks to see the local doctor, everyone scurries away, and for a long while Fuentes interprets this simply as indigenous people not understanding Spanish. However, he eventually learns (much later than the viewer) that his former students have been viewed as guerrilla sympathizers and gunned down. Fuentes continues to press on in hopes of finding at least one alive, and during the course of his journey he meets some fellow travelers: a young orphan (Conejo), a military deserter (Domingo), Padre Portillo, and a young girl (Graciela).

Although Fuentes was totally unaware of the massive violence in his own country, these other travelers have been scarred by it. Both of Conejo's parents had been killed, and for a few years he acted as a gopher for some of the soldiers. Domingo is a deserter who now is appalled by the atrocities he carried out, which are shown in flashbacks. Padre Portillo had tended to the sick and the poor, but the military viewed his liberation theology as a direct threat and sought to have him and a few other "communists" killed. Portillo was able to run away, but in doing so he consigned the village to total death and destruction. And, finally, Gabriela had been gang raped by a group of soldiers two years previous and has not spoken since.

At the close of the film, Fuentes and his traveling companions (minus Padre Portillo, who was taken away by soldiers) are trying to find Cerca del Cielo, the place where he believes his last remaining student is now living. At this point, Fuentes finally understands the violence that has beset his country, and also the role that willful ignorance has played in perpetuating it. Fuentes has also seen this medical training program, which he had considered as his legacy, come completely undone, as one former student after another was gunned down by the oppressive regime. He dies thinking that his life and his work has been a failure, but Domingo picks up his medical bag intent on carrying on the doctor's work.

The great strength of the film is its unflinching look at political violence. Fuentes keeps crossing paths with an American couple who are fascinated by the violence in ancient times but completely (and perhaps purposely) ignorant of the violence that their own government is currently supporting. The weakness of the film is how unreal such a "realistic" film seems to be. Fuentes and Domingo travel for days on end, sleeping in cars and on the ground, and yet no one ever needs a shave and their shirts always remain clean and pressed.

Also of Note

Salvador (Oliver Stone, 1986)

Salvador is a feature film that provides some insight into El Salvador's civil war in the 1980s. Although the country's violence is alluded to more than shown, there are three scenes that bear mentioning. The first takes place when Richard Boyle (James Woods), a fast-talking American journalist and the film's protagonist, comes upon hundreds of dead bodies that had been dumped in a mass grave. The second scene involves the assassination of Archbishop Romero, who serves as a beacon of hope for the country's oppressed. The third scene involves the four American churchwomen who were raped and killed during the early days of the Reagan administration—at a time when American support for the rightist elements in El Salvador escalated greatly. Boyle is friends with one of the nuns, and he is deeply moved when the bodies are exhumed. He then has a confrontation with gung-ho types from the US Embassy, which is Stone's vehicle for questioning US foreign policy in this region.

Romero (John Duigan, 1989)

Oscar Romero (Raul Julia) served as the Archbishop of El Salvador until he was assassinated in 1980 while celebrating mass in the National Cathedral. The film traces his evolution from a neutral observer in the country's civil war, if not an outright apologist for the various right-wing governments, to being an ardent supporter of liberation theology and the right of the common people to be free from savage military rule.

The problem is that there is practically a halo around Romero's head, and he often speaks in holy man platitudes, including the always useful expression "it is God's will." Archbishop Romero, the real one, deserves better than this. He was a staunch opponent of the right-wing governments in El Salvador and a powerful voice for human rights. While he was Christlike in his beliefs and in his actions, there is no reason to make him cartoonishly Christlike on the big screen.

41

The Battle of Algiers
(Gillo Pontecorvo, 1966)

In addition to animated films such as Persepolis *and* Waltz with Bashir, *another vehicle for exploring human rights is the pseudo-documentary, where a film gives every appearance of being a documentary but in reality is a feature film with at least some professional actors. Present-day directors such as Michael Winterbottom (*The Road to Guantanamo *and* In This World*) and Errol Morris (*Standard Operating Procedure, The Fog of War, *and* The Thin Blue Line*) have used this technique in many of their films. However, the standard was set in the following film, which even many modern viewers think is a documentary.*

✳ ✳ ✳

The Battle of Algiers tells the story of the fight for Algerian independence from French colonial rule. It is filmed in black and white and makes use of a voiceover—thus giving the very strong impression of being a documentary. In fact, *The Battle of Algiers* is fictional, although based closely on real-world events. During the period depicted in the film (1954–1962), there were decolonization efforts in large parts of Africa and Asia, including Algeria. However, what makes *The Battle of Algiers* such an important film is that it is able to depict the colonial experience from the perspective of native people. Although there is a popular perception that the European powers readily acceded to de-colonization, this film shows how desperate and cruel the colonial powers were in trying to hold on to "their" rightful possessions.

Still, *The Battle of Algiers* is by no means one-sided. The film shows cruelties carried out on both sides. The scenes involving torture by the French forces rival our own present-day images of Abu Ghraib. For their part, the Algerians would be considered terrorists by today's standards, particularly for their practice of bombing places frequented by French civilians.

What adds tremendously to the film's effectiveness is its documentary technique. This raises the question whether there is something inherently "authentic" about documentaries—or simply those films that look like documentaries.

42

Au Revoir Les Enfants
(Louis Malle, 1987)

Nearly all Holocaust films will resort to showing emaciated bodies or display scenes of Jews being slaughtered. What is so beautiful about the following film is that there is not a drop of blood and not an ounce of suffering—yet the terror of being Jewish during that time has perhaps never been more effectively depicted.

* * *

The setting for *Au Revoir Les Enfants* is an all-boys Catholic boarding school in occupied France during World War II. In many ways the film has a timeless quality to it as we see young boys horsing around with one another and learning literature, math, Greek, and other subjects—just like countless others before them and countless others since. However, what breaks these daily rhythms is the war itself, at first manifested in heating and food hardships, but later on when three new students are brought to the school.

The central story involves the relationship between the most popular student in the school, Julien Quentin (Gaspard Manesse), and one of the new students, Jean Bonnet (Raphael Fejtö), who is later exposed as Jean Kippelstein—a Jew. Despite his social awkwardness, Bonnet displays a great talent in music and math and at first Julien's position in the school hierarchy is threatened by his new classmate. However, the two bond when they get lost in the woods together during a scouting trip and they are rescued by some German soldiers, who are not aware of Jean's religious identity.

In addition to the scouting rescue, there are several other scenes where it seems certain that Kippelstein's identify will become known. One involves a trip to the local baths where a group of German soldiers are hanging out in the locker room as the young French students are brought in to bathe. Julien's own discovery comes when he awakens one night, and he sees Jean praying in Hebrew. He further investigates and finds the name Kippelstein in a book in Bonnet's locker. In another scene, the two start to fight and Julien calls Jean a "heathen." However, all is forgotten in a moment, and Julien has his mother invite Jean to eat dinner with them in a fancy restaurant—which is populated with German soldiers.

At one point Julien asks Jean if he is ever afraid, and Jean answers, quite simply, that he is always afraid. Yet the film is anything but morose. The viewer revels in the way that boys will be boys. In one of the most eloquent scenes in the film, Julien and Jean skip out of an air raid, and the two have the school grounds all to themselves to do whatever they wish, including playing a wonderful jazz duet and having great fun in doing so.

But the noose tightens when the Gestapo are tipped off about the presence of Jewish students by one of the helpers in the school's kitchen who has been fired for stealing. When the Germans come into the classroom and demand to be told who the Jews are, Julien reflexively looks toward Jean and unintentionally identifies him. The Jewish students are then led out along with Father Jean, the principal who arranged for their protection. As they leave, all of the students in the courtyard stand up to the Nazis by yelling "au revoir, mon pere." At the end of the film we learn that the boys were all killed at Auschwitz and that Fr. Jean was also killed for being an enemy of the people. What the viewer also learns from Julien's voiceover—but presumably the voice of the director Louis Malle—is that there is not a day that goes by that he does not remember that fateful January day when his best friend was taken from him and led off to be killed.

Au Revoir Les Enfants is a hauntingly beautiful film. It not only humanizes victims of the Holocaust, such as Jean, but also those too young or naïve to understand what was going on. At one point Julien asks his brother to tell him what Jews are like, and his brother explains that they are smarter than non-Jews and they killed Christ. Julien seems stunned by the latter response and says that everyone knows that the Romans killed Christ. Later at the dinner with his family that Jean has been invited to attend, Julien asks his mother—not so innocently—whether they also have Jewish blood in them. Her horrified look has less to do with all the Nazis sitting around them than the truth to the answer to that question.

43

Moolaadé
(Ousmane Sembène, 2004)

For many Westerners the human rights issue they most associate with Africa is female genital mutilation—in a continent where there are massive violations of economic, social, and cultural rights but also civil and political rights. Because of this widespread assumption, I initially hesitated to include Moolaadé *on this list, but this film treats the subject of FGM in an intelligent manner, and the film also does a nice job of challenging the viewer's expectations in other ways.*

✳ ✳ ✳

The action in this film occurs in a remote Muslim village in Burkina Faso. The protagonist of the story is Collé, the second wife of one of the village elders, who has already lost two daughters in childbirth due to her own mutilation. Collé decides that she has had enough, and she has already refused to allow her surviving daughter, Amasatou, to face this ordeal. However, the issue comes to a head when four other girls come to her and she declares Moolaadé, or protection. Collé is then subject to tremendous political and social pressure. However, there are other women who support her, as do two men who have experienced life outside the village.

There is no patronizing tone to be found in *Moolaadé*, although it is obvious where the filmmaker's sympathies lie on this issue. Along these same lines, Sembène allows real people to tell this story and not one-dimensional characters or characterizations. In that way, perhaps one of the great achievements of this film is its overall portrayal of an African village. Unlike nearly all Western perceptions (and misperceptions) of life in Africa, there are no starving children, and the various residents of the village are probably not much different from what one might find in your own home town. Ultimately this is a story about ordinary people trying to do the right thing—although it isn't always clear to them what this is.

Also of Note

Mrs. Goundo's Daughter (Barbara Attie and Janet Goldwater, 2009)

The daughter in this documentary's title is only two years old, and she does not say a single word in the film—or at least none that could be understood. Speaking on her behalf, or at least attempting to do so, is her mother. Mrs. Goundo is from Mali, and as a child she was subjected to FGM. Mrs. Goundo has filed for asylum in the United States, and the basis of her claim is that she does not want her daughter to face what she experienced. The "experts" in this film are not human rights professionals or government officials but women—both those who carry out the procedure and those have been subjected to these practices.

44

The Constant Gardener
(Fernando Meirelles, 2005)

Multinational corporations (MNCs) have an odd standing in human rights. On the one hand, there is no question that MNCs have promoted trade and foreign investment in developing countries and in that way have promoted the cause of human rights. On the other hand, it is certainly not unknown for MNCs to engage in what is commonly referred to as a "race to the bottom," which means that these corporations will go to any lengths to exploit foreign workers and engage in practices that would clearly be illegal if engaged in back at home. Unfortunately, many host states are too weak (or too corrupt) to regulate offending corporate behavior, while the MNCs' home countries, such as the United States, Canada, and other Western countries, do not see such protection as their legal responsibility. The Constant Gardener *explores another way in which MNCs have been given license to do things in developing states that which they would be prohibited from doing at home.*

✳ ✳ ✳

The unethical testing practices of the world's pharmaceutical industry operating in developing countries serves as the backdrop for this feature film thriller starring Ralph Fiennes and the enchanting Rachel Weisz. Justin Quayle (Fiennes) is a career midlevel diplomat for the British government, while Tessa (Weisz) is a graduate student in London. They meet after she publicly chastises him for a guest lecture he has given at her school. Perhaps dull lectures are an aphrodisiac because within minutes the two are back at her studio apartment making love. Soon enough he is taking his new bride with him to his posting in Kenya. While there, she refuses to play the mindless wife of a career diplomat, preferring to spend her days attempting to do some good in Kenya's worst slums.

While this might otherwise be written off as bad manners or youthful enthusiasm, Tessa teams up with Arnold (Hubert Koundé), a handsome young African public health specialist, and the two go about investigating the Three Bees multinational corporation and the company's drug dypraxa, which is being tested for treatment of tuberculosis. The two are investigating deaths related to this testing, although this information is being repressed by the company. Quayle is not told any of this, and it is only after Tessa and Arnold are murdered that he begins to put the pieces of the story together. At this point Quayle is stirred to life.

It should be noted that the testing practices depicted in the film continue to this day, not only in Africa but in other underdeveloped areas of the world. One could say that poor Africans and Asians serve as human guinea pigs for Western consumers. In addition, as shown in this film, Western states actively promote and protect the business practices of the multinational corporations who carry out such tests, although one would at least hope that these governments would not involve themselves in such things as murder, torture, kidnapping, and the systematic cover-up of scientific data, as we see here.

The final scene is beautifully developed. After Quayle is able to get a copy of Tessa and Arnold's incriminating report, he has it sent to her cousin in London. He then has a UN relief flight crew drop him off at the site where Tessa was killed. He patiently awaits his approaching murderers by imagining wonderful moments with Tessa, and this is juxtaposed with funeral ceremonies in London where his diplomatic colleagues deliver the usual bromides about how much Tessa will be missed—until her cousin stands up to read a letter that incriminates the British government in these unethical and illegal practices.

45

Even the Rain
(Icíar Bollaín, 2010)

There are not many outstanding films about European colonialism, which helps to explain our collective amnesia about this important part of European and world history. The one, true exception, I would argue, is Even the Rain.

✳ ✳ ✳

Even the Rain is an intelligent and at times a mesmerizing account of the clash between the Old World and the New World—500 years ago, but at the present time as well. The premise places a Spanish film crew in the backwaters of Bolivia where a movie about the Spanish invasion is being shot. The producer, Costa (Luis Tosar), and director, Sebastián (Gael García Bernal), are in need of some local indigenous color, but they get much more than they bargained for when a drove of desperate locals come out for the small stipend being offered. Daniel (Juan Carlos Aduviri) is an indigenous leader who refuses to be sent away when he and the others are informed that there is no need for any more extras, and he and his daughter Belén end up getting speaking roles in the film.

The film under production shows the devastation and the cruelty of the Spanish. In one remarkable scene, Columbus's landing is reenacted during a script read-through done on a shady lawn with an umbrella serving as the Spanish flag. Columbus informs the two locals who are innocently tending bar at the resort that he comes in peace and as an emissary of God. However, all this changes when he spots the woman's small earrings, and he demands to know from her, and eventually from all the indigenous people who would suffer under Spanish yoke, where this gold can be found.

Although Spanish savagery was the rule, there were two exceptions. One involves Bartolomé de las Casas, a Spanish priest whose book *A Short Account of the Destruction of the Indies* documented and condemned the Spanish abuses. A second exception was Fr. Montesinos, a Dominican priest who asked his parishioners, week after week: Are we not obliged to love them [the indigenous people] as ourselves? The answer came in the form of Montesinos's dismissal from his post. Both men were light years ahead of their time, but what the film also shows is that they are ahead of our time as well.

The story of the Spanish invasion being filmed is interspersed with a present-day fight against the privatization of water. Daniel is one of the leaders in this effort, and the filmmakers' biggest concern, at least initially, is that he not be arrested or that his face not be smashed in, which would result in production being delayed or halted altogether. In one of the best scenes, the filmmakers are being feted by the dignitaries of the city and Sebastián asks the mayor, rather delicately, why the water rates have to be raised by some 300 percent. The mayor coolly responds by saying that there are tight financial constraints, and he then asks Sebastián why the film company is paying the locals a pittance for appearing in the film, while the European stars are making vastly more than this. Of course, the answer to both of these questions is exactly the same: these people do not matter as much as white people do.

In the end, at least some of the Europeans come to understand that they are not nearly as different from the original Spanish invaders as they used to be certain that they were. Costa in particular has a complete change of heart, and he places his own life in danger in an attempt to save Belén's life. In the end, it is not clear whether the film about Columbus and the exploitation of Spanish rule will ever be completed. However, what we do know from this fine film is that this same story continues uninterrupted to this day.

Also of Note

Indochine (Régis Wargnier, 1992)

Although *Indochine* sometimes drifts into soap opera territory, particularly during its various romantic scenes, this feature film does provide important insight into French colonial practices in Vietnam. The story centers around Eliane Devries (Catherine Deneuve) a Frenchwoman who owns a rubber tree plantation. Eliane loves the Vietnamese people, especially Camille, the young Vietnamese girl she is raising as her own daughter. But it is a love on her terms, not theirs. What eventually ensues is both a political and personal break between mother and daughter. The film closes with Eliane leaving the country with Camille's son while peace negotiations are being carried out. Unfortunately, it would take two horrible wars—one with the French and then a second one with the Americans—before Camille and the rest of the Vietnamese people would become free from colonial rule.

Chocolat (Claire Denis, 1988)

One might describe *Chocolat* as a combination of a PG version of *Mandigo* (that not-so-great 1960s flick on interracial sexual relations in the antebellum South) and a damning indictment of the racism that was at the heart of the colonial enterprise. The story is told through an extended flashback of France (Cécile Ducasse), the young daughter of the French District Governor in Cameroon. France spends most of her days hanging out with Protée (Isaach De Bankolé), the family's manservant.

Everything changes when an airplane with French colonialists aboard is forced to make an emergency landing near their outback home, and Marc (François Cluzet) and Aimée (Guilia Boschi), France's parents, take them in. Weeks pass and the company becomes more and more unbearable—and more and more racist. The dramatic high point comes when Aimée touches Protée's foot. She might not be fully aware of racial borders but he certainly is, and he stalks off. The next day Aimée has Protée transferred out of the house and into the garage. France does not see much of Protée after he is sent out, but one evening she goes out to the garage, and she points to a pipe and asks him whether it is hot or not. He puts his hand on it as a way of indicating that it is safe. However, when she puts her own hand on it she finds that it is scalding, leaving a permanent burn mark. Protée then walks away, exacting at least some small measure of revenge for the unfair treatment accorded to him. The film then returns to the present. France offers to buy a drink for a black man who has given her a ride in his car, but the she is rebuffed. It seems that the natives are fully aware that even the kindest and most benign gesture could get them sent off to the garage, or worse.

46

Lord of War

(Andrew Niccol, 2005)

I have done a fair amount of work on political apologies, and when I give talks on the subject one of the things that I try to get audiences to think about is what future generations will be apologizing for in terms of our own current policies and behavior. One of these, I am sure, is the manner in which arms are sold to states that carry out gross and systematic human rights violations.

✳ ✳ ✳

Nicolas Cage has such a good time playing the role of Yuri Orlov, a Ukrainian-born immigrant to the United States who goes into the gun-selling business and eventually becomes the largest private arms dealer in the world, that it becomes difficult to root against him notwithstanding all the blood he has on his hands. The film starts with Yuri in a black suit standing in a sea of gun shells. He turns to the camera and announces, in a matter-of-fact way, that there are over 550 million firearms in circulation in the world—which comes out to something like one firearm for every twelve people. And then he coolly asks: how do we get to arm the other eleven? I certainly do not like how Yuri makes his living, but at least I can appreciate his honesty. But the real action, as he points out at the closing of the film, is not private arms dealers like him but governments. And leading the pack, by quite a wide margin, is Yuri's adopted home country.

Yuri's family came to the United States by pretending to be Jews, a role that his father adopted with such relish that this lapsed Catholic (of sorts) is now more religiously observant than even the rabbi. His two sons are anything but observant. Yuri witnesses a gangland-style shooting in a restaurant and from that moment on decides he wants to run guns. He convinces his bother Vitaly (Jared Leto) to join him, but the partnership is dependent on Vitaly staying away from cocaine, something he has enormous problems doing.

Business is very good, and it becomes even better after the fall of communism and the dissolution of the Soviet Union. Conveniently enough, Yuri has an uncle who is a high-ranking military officer in the Ukraine. What the two do together—one working for money and ego, the other because of family loyalty—is to sell off the enormous cache of weapons now just lying around the Ukraine. They have never been fired in anger, and what Yuri does is to make sure that these weapons are in fact fired in anger, invariably in some poor and desperate African state, such as Liberia. The level of civilian carnage this brings about simply does not matter to him. It is all in a day's work, and if Yuri doesn't do it someone else will.

Life is good for Yuri. He is able to marry Ava Fontaine (Bridget Moynahan), the woman of his dreams, and they have a child. He is able to keep his business secret from his family, referring obliquely to being involved in some form of generic "international trade." However, Yuri has his own Inspector Javert in the form of Jack Valentine (Ethan Hawke), who is finally able to convince Yuri's wife that her husband's business is killing an awful lot of people.

Near the end of the movie, Yuri and Vitaly are in the process of finalizing yet another sale to yet another warlord in Africa when Vitaly comes to the realization that as soon as the weapons are sold they will be turned on the refugees living on the other side of the hill from where the transaction is taking place. Vitaly, who has been trying to go straight, has pangs of conscience and attempts to blow the deal up (literally), but he is shot and killed. One of the bullets is still in the carcass after the body is returned to the United States, and, finally, Valentine thinks he has enough evidence to prosecute Yuri. However, Yuri informs him what will ensue. He tells him (correctly) that Valentine will soon be called out of the interrogation room by one of his Interpol superiors; he will be complimented on the fine work that he has done; but he will also be informed that Yuri is to be let go.

The point is that Yuri understands that governments need people like him to do the dirty work. As he points out to Valentine, the US government sells more arms in a day than Yuri does in a year, but they need the pretense of only selling to human rights–respecting states. How, then, to get arms and equipment to the brutal dictators with whom they are secretly aligned? This is where Yuri comes in. The film ends by pointing out something that people should be outraged by but are not: the five permanent members of the UN Security Council constitute the five largest arms dealers in the world. And some day, perhaps soon, these states will stop such practices—and also apologize for the enormous harm they helped bring about.

Also of Note

Blood Diamond (Edward Zwick, 2006)

As its title indicates, this feature film concerns itself with the world's diamond trade and the manner in which money from these sales has been used to buy weapons to fuel civil conflicts, in this case, the civil war in Sierra Leone from 1991 to 2002. Danny Archer (Leonardo DiCaprio) is a soulless gun runner from Zimbabwe who develops a conscience after falling in love with Maddy Bowen (Jennifer Connelly), an idealist reporter. Solomon (Djimon Hounsou) is a fisherman who lives peacefully with his family, until he and his son are captured by Revolutionary United Front (RUF) troops. Solomon is sent to work digging for diamonds, while Dia is indoctrinated into becoming a child soldier.

In the end, Archer becomes one of the good guys, and after rescuing Solomon and Dia he dies a hero's death on the African soil he claims he loves but which he has helped soak in blood by trading diamonds for weapons. The Western demand for diamonds can kill. And certainly Western weapons can as well.

47

Judgment at Nuremberg
(Stanley Kramer, 1961)

A strong argument can be made that the present-day human rights revolution began with the Nuremberg trials of former German political and military leaders following World War II. For the first time in human history, those who directed or carried out war crimes were held to account by an international tribunal. One of the essential elements in protecting human rights is establishing accountability for wrongdoing, and the Nuremberg proceedings remain the gold standard in this regard. Unfortunately, following these trials, decades would pass before the international community would attempt to do this again.

✳ ✳ ✳

Judgment at Nuremberg is a fictionalized account of an actual trial brought against a group of German judges based on their role in supporting the Nazi regime by upholding Aryan supremacy laws. The chief justice presiding over this case is an American judge, Dan Haywood, played by the great Spencer Tracy. Although the film has all manners of cameo appearances by famous Hollywood actors—Judy Garland, Montgomery Clift, and Marlene Dietrich, to name a few—certainly the most riveting performance (Academy Award for Best Actor) is turned in by Maximilian Schell as a defense lawyer who repeatedly turns the knife on both the prosecution and the presiding judges by pointing out how the occupying powers have their own history and practice of racist and even genocidal policies.

Although there are times when Spencer Tracy seems to be bored with his character, what makes his overall performance so effective is that he serves as a kind of Everyman who is seeking an answer to this question: how could all these horrible things take place in a "civilized" country like Germany? In an important scene in a restaurant, Haywood is dining with the wife (Marlene Dietrich) of a German general, who professes not only her own personal innocence but that all "good" Germans were simply not aware of the genocidal crimes of the Nazi regime. Being the careful judge that he is, Haywood gives her and the German people the benefit of the doubt. However, the problem is that the contrary evidence is simply overwhelming.

Not only are the crimes of the Nazi regime horrible enough, but what made them even more incomprehensible to Judge Haywood is the zeal with which German judges applied such unjust laws as "race defilement," which had resulted in a Jew (Feldenstein) being put to death based on his innocent-enough relationship with an Aryan. Although there are four judges on trial, much of the action focuses on Ernst Janning (Burt Lancaster). What Haywood and Janning represent are two fundamentally opposed models of justice. Janning applies the law as written—no matter how far removed it is from any principles of human dignity and respect.

As the trial and the film wind down there is a great deal of political pressure put upon Haywood to do the "right thing" and to recognize the importance of having the Germans on "our" side in the upcoming Cold War with the Soviet Union and thus to hand down lenient sentences. Haywood will have none of this. He is fully aware of the political realities in the world, and he is equally cognizant that at some point, perhaps quite soon, the punishments that he has handed down will be severely reduced. This, however, is not his role, and the viewer is also convinced that, for someone like Haywood, human rights principles really do matter. The denouement comes when Haywood issues his verdict, and his words are every bit as relevant today as they were at that time:

This trial has shown that under the stress of a national crisis, ordinary men— even able and extraordinary men—can delude themselves into the commission of crimes and atrocities so vast and heinous as to stagger the imagination. No one who has sat through this trial can ever forget. The sterilization of men because of their political beliefs ... The murder of children ... How easily that can happen. There are those in our country today, too, who speak of the protection of the country. Of survival. The answer to that is: survival as what? A country isn't a rock. And it isn't an extension of one's self. It's what it stands for, when standing for something is the most difficult. Before the people of the world—let it now be noted in our decision here that this is what we stand for: justice, truth ... and the value of a single human being.

Also of Note

Night and Fog (Alain Resnais, 1955)

One of the most wrenching scenes in *Judgment at Nuremberg* takes place during the prosecution's case in chief when a brief newsreel from one of the Nazi concentration camps is shown and introduced into evidence. However, the first real public showings of these horrors came a few years before this in 1955 (still a decade after the end of the war) with the release of the documentary *Night and Fog*. Certainly, still pictures of these atrocities were available before this. However, none of this seemed to have the power and the impact that the moving picture did. Even after all these years, the film footage from *Night and Fog* remains overwhelming. Although the film itself moves from the past to the present, the only thing the viewer will ever remember—and will never forget—are the black-and-white images of heaped humanity taken from the Auschwitz and Majdanek concentration camps.

48
The Road to Guantanamo
(Michael Winterbottom and Mat Whitecross, 2006)

The distinction between documentaries and feature films can be blurred at times, and the next film is an excellent example of this. In many respects, The Road to Guantanamo *could be considered a documentary. However, the reason I place it here is that there are more elements of a feature film—even if these scenes look frighteningly "real"—than there are of a documentary.*

✳ ✳ ✳

The Road to Guantanamo presents the saga of the "Tipton Three"—Ruhal Ahmed, Asif Iqbal, and Shafiq Rasul—British citizens who went to Pakistan for a wedding and then decided to travel to Afghanistan for fun and excitement, and who ended up at Guantanamo Bay, Cuba, in the custody of American authorities before their eventual release. Much of the film is told through reenactments, but these are not the cheap-looking reenactments that we are so accustomed to seeing. Instead, the viewer gets the strong sense of watching a documentary unfold: from the mayhem in Afghanistan leading up to their arrest as Al-Qaeda supporters, to the desperation of their lives while in custody at Guantanamo. In that way, what is especially jarring are the "real" scenes involving actual interviews with the Tipton Three after their eventual release. These seem less real than the reenactments.

Although some will be bothered by the blurring of the distinction between reality and fantasy, since there is no publicly available footage of what life is like for the Guantanamo Bay detainees (aside from the interrogations shown in *You Don't Like the Truth*), the present film provides the most accurate, and certainly the most compelling, portrayal that is available.

49
City of Life and Death
(Lu Chuan, 2009)

Rape has always been a part of war, which, in part, helps explain the longstanding cavalier attitude towards the practice and those who have carried it out. However, more recently there has been a growing recognition of the heinousness of the act and the manner in which wartime rape is simply not a private offense but the result of deliberate state policy—and a crime against humanity. One of the things that helped bring this issue to the fore was the practice of forced impregnation that was used by Serbian and Bosnian Serbian soldiers on Bosnian Muslim women. However, the following film depicts these horrors in an earlier time and a different setting.

✳ ✳ ✳

This black-and-white feature film is dedicated to the 300,000 victims of the rape of Nanking, following Japan's invasion of China in 1937. Obviously, the story it tells is a gruesome one, and the film wastes no time in telling it. The film opens with Japanese troops massed outside the city gates of Nanking. Inside there is mass hysteria, especially after the Chinese military commander has fled. One of the more affecting scenes involves the internal battle between troops that want to remain to fight against the invaders and those who are looking to flee. What ensues is a massive mosh pit of sorts, but finally the lines are broken. Still, many of the Chinese troops remain and fight bravely, and these battle scenes are startling in their realism. But this is nothing compared to the wholesale slaughter of Chinese POWs that subsequently takes place.

There are two main characters. Kadokawa (Hideo Nakaizumi) is the "good" Japanese soldier who throughout the film attempts to do the right thing, whether it is protecting POWs, bringing candy and food to a "comfort woman" he has fallen in love with, and even shooting and killing a Chinese woman before she could be subjected to gang rape. At the close of the film, Kadokawa marches a former Chinese soldier and a young boy out into the fields, but rather than executing them he sets both free. He then proceeds to shoot himself, moments after observing to another Japanese soldier that "life is more difficult than death." Kadokawa has seen and lived through a lot and his effort to resist the barbarity all around him finally takes its toll.

The "bad" Japanese soldier is represented by Ida (Ryu Kohata), who really does not do anything worse than the rest of the soldiers around him, but this is not saying an awful lot. Murder and rape are everyday events, even in the area of the city that is purportedly a safety zone. Another character is Mr. Rabe (John Paisley), a German official who is in charge of the safety zone and, in one of the more poignant moments in the film, has to announce to a roomful of young Chinese women that the Japanese soldiers will agree to stop raping—but only if they are provided with 100 volunteers to "service" them. Ever so slowly, one hand and then another is raised. Rabe's assistant is Mr. Tang (Fan Wei), and although he believes his position gives him some protection he later finds out that it offers him very little, as his young daughter and his daughter-in-law are both raped and killed. However, Tang displays his true courage when he declines safe passage with his wife and allows another official to depart instead. He maintains that he is needed to protect the refugees, but he no doubt knows that he will be quickly executed, which is exactly what takes place.

This film does a stunning job of conveying the horrors of the brutal invasion of Nanking. However, there are a few moments of cinematic melodrama. For example, Tang's decision not to flee with his wife is played out over several minutes where, apparently, no other character speaks a word. This causes the film to lose some of its realism, but given the carnage on display here perhaps the audience needs a break as well as a personal connection to the story.

Also of Note

The Greatest Silence: Rape in the Congo (Lisa Jackson, 2007)
Lumo (Bent-Jorgen Perlmutt and Nelson Walker III, 2007)

These two documentaries focus on rape in the current conflict in the Democratic Republic of the Congo. Needless to say, both films are disturbing. In addition to hearing from so many of the victims, one of the most important achievements of *The Greatest Silence* is its willingness to hear from members of the militia who have repeatedly committed acts of rape. The filmmaker (Lisa Jackson) is a former gang rape victim herself. This is made note of more at the beginning and then at the end of the film, but it is generally not overplayed. Rather, it seems to provide the filmmaker with a means of making a special connection with those who have been abandoned by their own families and Congolese society alike. In many ways, the filmmaker's small acts of kindness in the form of soap and nail polish provide vastly more comfort and solace to these women than do the slight efforts of the international community.

Lumo focuses on fistula—a debilitating medical condition brought on by these repeated acts of rape. The film shows us the remarkable community of women and the doctors who make a valiant effort to treat the sufferers. This film has much to say about war and those who survive it, but perhaps it has even more to say about human resilience and courage.

50

Rabbit-Proof Fence
(Phillip Noyce, 2002)

Genocide has often been carried out against indigenous peoples. This was certainly the case in Australia, where the state sought to eliminate the country's aboriginals.

✱ ✱ ✱

On February 13, 2008, Australian Prime Minister Kevin Rudd gave one of the most resounding political apologies ever uttered by a head of state when in a nationally televised address he apologized for the forced removal of aboriginal children from their parents in what came to be termed the "Stolen Generation." *Rabbit-Proof Fence* is a feature film that brings these decades-long racist policies to life, telling the true story of three young "half castes" (their father was white), Molly (fourteen years old), Gracie (ten), and Daisy (eight), who were abducted from their mother in the northern town of Jigalong and sent to a concentration camp (there is no other way to describe this) at Moore River some 1,500 miles away. The girls eventually escape from the camp and make the long and grueling journey back home, guided by the country's rabbit-proof fence, which was erected to prevent rabbits from having access to certain farmland and which passed through their home town. Only Molly and Daisy are successful. Gracie is tricked by a poacher and never heard from again. In the film's epilogue, the viewer is introduced to the real Molly and Daisy, now in advanced age. Molly relates the story of how two of her own daughters were also stolen from her and, incredibly enough, how she was able to escape with one of them, much in the manner shown in this film.

One of the great strengths of the film is that the evil behind the government's policy is never overdone. Kenneth Branagh plays the part of A. O. Neville, the protector of Western Australian Aborigines, and what we see is a government policy intended to wipe out the indigenous strain from the country—but with the goal of improving the quality of life for these children. It was only later (much later) that this policy was recognized for what it was: as a form of genocide against aboriginal people. *Rabbit-Proof Fence* provides a sample of the human manifestations of this genocide.

Images from Selected Films
(and Their Human Rights Dimensions)

City of Life and Death (Security of the Person). The Rape of Nanking (Literally).
CREDIT: CHINA FILM GROUP/MEDIA ASIA / THE KOBAL COLLECTION/ART RESOURCE

Rabbit-Proof Fence (The Rights of Indigenous People). Daisy, Gracie, and
Molly: the abducted aboriginal sisters, part of the "Stolen Generation." CREDIT:
MIRAMAX/DIMENSION FILMS / THE KOBAL COLLECTION/TWEEDIE, PENNY/ART RESOURCE

Days of Glory (Indigènes) (Freedom from Discrimination). First class soldiers, but second class citizens. CREDIT: TESSALIT/IFC / THE KOBAL COLLECTION/ART RESOURCE

Norma Rae (The Right to Form and Join Trade Unions). Norma Rae (Sally Field) fighting for the right to form a union. CREDIT: 20TH CENTURY FOX / THE KOBAL COLLECTION/ART RESOURCE

Precious: Based on the Novel "Push" by Sapphire (The Right to Social Security). Precious (Gabourey Sidibe) with her brain damaged child and abusive mother, Mary (Mo'Nique). CREDIT: LEE DANIELS ENT/THE KOBAL COLLECTION/ART RESOURCE

Hunger (Freedom from Political Oppression). Bobby Sands (Michael Fassbender) about to embark on a hunger strike for the rights of political prisoners in Northern Ireland. CREDIT: FILM4BLAST FILMS / THE KOBAL COLLECTION /ART RESOURCE

The Lives of Others (The Right to Privacy). Gerd Wiesler (Ulrich Mühe) as a Stasi spy who eventually finds his own humanity. CREDIT: CREADO FILM/ THE KOBAL COLLECTION/ART RESOURCE

The Killing Fields (Genocide). Dith Pran (Haing S. Ngor) in the maelstrom of the Cambodian genocide. CREDIT: ENIGMA/GOLDCREST / THE KOBAL COLLECTION/ ART RESOURCE

Darwin's Nightmare (The Right to Food). How "others" attempt to live. CREDIT:
SAGA FILMS/COOP 99 / THE KOBAL COLLECTION/ART RESOURCE

4 Little Girls (Children's Rights). The Four. CREDIT: 40 ACRES & A MULE/HBO /
THE KOBAL COLLECTION/ART RESOURCE

Hoop Dreams (The Right to Education). Basketball: perhaps the one means of escape for those denied their human rights. CREDIT: FINE LINE/KARTEMQUIN / THE KOBAL COLLECTION

Enemies of the People (The Right to an Effective Remedy). Journalist Thet Sambath with the chilling Nuon Chea, Brother #2. CREDIT: OLD STREET FILMS / THE KOBAL COLLECTION/ART RESOURCE

Crude (The Right to a Clean and Healthy Environment). The indomitable Ecuadoran human rights lawyer, Pablo Fajardo. CREDIT: RED ENVELOPE ENTERTAINMENT / THE KOBAL COLLECTION/ART RESOURCE

Burma VJ (Religious Freedom). Buddhist monks beaten by Burmese security officials. CREDIT: MAGIC HOUR FILMS / THE KOBAL COLLECTION/ART RESOURCE

The Interrupters (The Right to Human Dignity). Interrupter Ameena Matthews with Caprysha Anderson. CREDIT: KARTEMQUIN FILMS/RISE FILMS / THE KOBAL COLLECTION/ART RESOURCE

Taxi to the Dark Side (Freedom from Torture). The "War on Terror": making the world safe—for whom? CREDIT: JIGSAW PRODUCTIONS / THE KOBAL COLLECTION/ ART RESOURCE

Part II

Documentaries

1

Darwin's Nightmare
(Hubert Sauper, 2004)

A good documentary is neither emotionally manipulative nor didactic. Nor should the director tell the viewers what to think or feel or be overly explicit in connecting all the dots. Life is much more complicated than that, and films should be as well. Darwin's Nightmare, the top-rated documentary, meets all these criteria. There are no talking heads, no swelling music, and really no attempt to package a particular political message for the viewer. Instead, we are introduced to a destitute village in Tanzania that seems a universe removed from us. Those who watch this film will find out that the truth is something much different from this.

* * *

A. O. Scott of the *New York Times* has called *Darwin's Nightmare* a "masterpiece," and I will go even further and describe this documentary as nothing less than one of the best movies ever made. The film takes place in a small fishing village on Lake Victoria in Tanzania. The only visible means of subsistence involves the Nile perch, an enormous predator fish not indigenous to the lake into which it was mistakenly introduced a number of years back. The Nile perch is now killing all of the other species of fish, which is effectively killing the lake itself. Thus, as dire as the story that unfolds in the film is, one can be certain that things will eventually get much worse.

The town's dilapidated airport plays a central role in this story. Large planes depart frequently, stuffed with Nile perch that have been caught, cleaned, packaged, frozen, and then flown off to various European restaurants and markets. What remains unclear, at least for some period of time, is what (if anything) these planes are carrying when they fly into Tanzania. The party line echoed throughout the beginning of the film is that these planes are empty. However, as the film advances, the viewer begins to learn that this is anything but the truth. Instead, their cargo consists of military weapons, which are then unloaded and transferred to many of the civil wars on the African continent. Arms traded for fish. In addition, at the time the film was being shot, Tanzania was in the midst of a severe famine that threatened to take the lives of upwards of two million people. In one scene, as fish are being loaded for transit to Europe, one of the filmmakers asks one of the workers loading the plane whether he realizes that there is a famine in that country. The answer comes in the form of a puzzled look, as if to say: so?

There are a number of reasons why *Darwin's Nightmare* is such an effective and thought-provoking film. For one thing, the movie does not employ any "talking heads," commentators whose explanations of events interrupt the main narrative. Instead, the film leaves it to the viewer to see and interpret what is going on—even if nearly all of the people in the film cannot seem to see it themselves. Certainly one of the most searing images is that of the skeletal fish remains that are sold to the local townspeople who cannot otherwise afford to buy fish from the lake they live on. One of the most basic human rights is the right to food, but as one sees these revolting maggot-filled cauldrons of fish entrails, it becomes impossible to think that this right is being met here. No narrator needs to tell the viewer this, and no swelling music is necessary to convince anyone that this is not how human beings should live. Children are shown throughout the film. The Convention on the Rights of the Child is the single most widely adopted international human rights treaty, and it guarantees all children human rights protection. Unfortunately, there is not an ounce of human rights protection for children to be found anywhere in *Darwin's Nightmare*. In one of the most gruesome scenes, two children living on the streets, neither of whom could be more than eight years old, sniff glue late in the evening in an attempt to ward off hunger and to render themselves unconscious so that they will not be aware of the horrible things that they know will be done to them. And in an earlier scene at the lakeshore, a group of children turn into something resembling a pack of wild animals as they fight furiously over a small portion of food. But perhaps the most telling scene comes late in the movie during the course of trade negotiations that will provide European concerns with continued access to the Nile perch—at least until the lake dies out and fish will no longer be found there. As dignitaries sitting on an outside veranda talk on and on about how trade has been a boon to all countries and all people involved, the eye is drawn to the reality in the background of Tanzanian street children, who will continue to live (and die) in abject squalor. The title "Darwin's Nightmare" might simply be referring to the ascendancy of the Nile perch over all other fish in Lake Victoria. But the survival of the fittest is mirrored on land as well. Despite all the promises of international human rights law, most of the people in this small Tanzanian village live a Hobbesian existence where life remains solitary, poor, nasty, brutish, and, perhaps mercifully, short.

2

Nero's Guests: The Age of Inequality
(Deepa Bhatia, 2009)

For some viewers, Nero's Guests *will be nothing more than a quirky documentary about suicides among farmers in rural India. The film is certainly about this, but it also provides one of the most insightful and devastating critiques of the perpetuation of the inequities in the global order that I have ever watched, and the revelation of the meaning of the title at the end of the documentary is enough to knock you back in your seat and, more importantly, make you think about your own role in the protection of human rights.*

✳ ✳ ✳

Nero's Guests builds slowly. At the outset, the film focuses on the massive number of suicides among Indian farmers, as the viewer follows the incredible P. Sainath, a passionate journalist who wonders why the mainstream media is more interested in such things as Fashion Week than in the deaths of more than 200,000 farmers in the previous decade. As the film points out, notwithstanding all the modernization and advances made in India, it remains a poor agrarian society, with approximately half the country's population attempting to live on less than 50 cents per day. In response to this societal and personal distress, desperate farmers began to take their own lives. In 1998 there was an average of one suicide per week, but a decade later this had turned into a daily event.

Sainath is virtually a one-person press corps trying to bring this story to the public at large. He visits the family of the dead men—in India, women are not farmers themselves, but only the wives of farmers—and he talks to the survivors and takes their pictures for journalist purposes but also for posterity. In a particularly moving scene, the daughter of a farmer-poet who has just killed himself reads his suicide note aloud, which can only be described as both beautiful and haunting.

After giving the viewer a glimpse of the magnitude of the country's forced displacements and its societal consequences, Sainath and the filmmaker broaden their scope and consider the structural reasons for the worsening plight of India's poor. Sainath makes note of the enormous differences between rich and poor, not only within India itself but beyond. For example, he explains that while the rich get "incentives" from the government, the poor get "subsidies"—if they get anything at all. Going beyond this, Sainath also points out how Western subsidies are killing people the world over. He uses the American cotton industry as an example, where the annual government subsidy ($3.9 billion) is more expensive than the entire output of the American cotton industry ($3 billion). This might only seem to be a case of bad economics, but it's more than that.

These practices are having a terrible effect on millions of cotton growers in some of the poorest countries in the world, who can no longer compete with the cheaper (because of the government subsidy) Western cotton.

But, as Sainath points out, it is not only cotton. There are also massive subsidies for coffee, paper, grain for European cattle, and so forth. Farmers in the Third World have been looted and plundered by the policies and practices of the rich, domestically as well as internationally. In Sainath's words: Western subsidies are "inhumane, unjust—and obnoxious." The film begins with Sainath speaking to an enraptured university audience, and he talks about the guests at Nero's palace in Rome. The film ends by returning to this talk, and now the viewer is equipped with more knowledge and context and hopefully more conscience. Sainath tells the story of a party that Nero threw, which was reportedly the biggest bash in the entire ancient world. The party was held in the evening and in order for the guests to be able to see, criminals were burned at the stake as a means of providing illumination. Nero was certifiably crazy. But Sainath says what has always intrigued him is how the most intelligent and successful citizens of Rome could be at this party and allow this inhumanity to occur right in front of them—without saying a single word. Sainath does not accuse his audience of being like these guests, but it is clear that this is exactly what he is implying. And with the release of this incredible film, we are now all Nero's guests.

Also of Note

Black Gold (Nick Francis and Marc Francis, 2006)

If the World Bank and the International Monetary Fund come in for rough treatment in such films as *Bamako, The End of Poverty?* and *Life and Debt,* the World Trade Organization (WTO) gets its share of blame in this documentary about the world's coffee trade, a commodity that a number of poor countries have been banking on to lift themselves out of poverty. Although heralded as promoting free trade and leveling the international playing field for everyone's trading interests, the WTO is really run for and by Western states. As is shown in the film, Third World countries are lucky to even get a seat at the negotiating table, not that their concerns, most notably widespread violations of ESCR due to falling commodity prices, ever get much of a hearing even when they do.

3

Hoop Dreams
(Steve James, 1994)

As a general rule, I find that documentaries are better able to capture violations of economic, social, and cultural rights better than feature films do. The previous two films certainly prove this as does the following documentary, set in inner-city Chicago. People of a certain age should be familiar with Hoop Dreams *because it received a fair amount of publicity when it was released, and people would make references to William and Arthur as if they were speaking of old friends, which in a sense they were.*

✳ ✳ ✳

The flattops and razor slash haircuts are no longer in style, but the story told in this film is every bit as relevant today as when it was released in the mid-1990s. William Gates and Arthur Agee are two young men attempting to escape from ghetto life. Both have been recruited to play basketball at St. Joseph's High School in Chicago's lily-white suburbs. Gates is an immediate star, and his future seems to be paved with gold, until he wrecks his knee and never fulfills the promise he showed when he was young. Still, he not only earns a degree from St. Joseph's but a basketball scholarship to Marquette University.

While Gates enjoys at least some initial success on the court and in the classroom, things in his personal life remain unsettled. For one thing, William is never able to develop any kind of relationship with his father, who had abandoned him and the rest of the family when William was young. The scenes where he meets up with his dad are quite awkward, although one gets the sense that it is not because of the presence of the accompanying film crew. In addition, William has to contend with his brother Curtis, who seems intent on doing everything in his power to prevent William from making all the mistakes that he himself has made. And to complicate matters even further, William and his girlfriend have brought a young daughter into their lives. But William's story shows that if you are willing to put up with a three-hour commute to school each day, are blessed with and develop superior basketball skills, and are willing to outwork all of your classmates both on and off the court, there is some chance you just might escape from the ghetto.

Arthur is not the immediate basketball success that William is, and his scholarship to St. Joseph's is revoked after only one year, forcing him to go to a public high school in Chicago. The contrast could not be starker. One school produces graduates who will all go on to college; the other does not produce many high school graduates at all. But in many respects Arthur's is the more interesting story. In terms of basketball, Arthur's team goes from being terrible to contending for the state title and all the excitement that accompanies this exciting run. Because of his own improved and spirited play, Arthur receives a college basketball scholarship, although to a school with only six black students—all basketball players.

But it is Arthur's personal and family life that makes this such a compelling story. Two scenes in particular stand out. One takes place at an outside basketball court where Arthur and others have long honed their skills. Arthur is involved in a game, but his attention is really on a group of men in the distance. These are known drug dealers, and Arthur's father is with them. Although his father maintains that he has now gone clean, Arthur knows his father better than this. And as he nervously gazes at this worthless crowd it is evident that he wants to stop what he knows is going on but is powerless to do so.

The second scene involves Arthur's parents traveling out to St. Joseph's in order to pay money owed on tuition so the school will release Arthur's freshman year transcript. St. Joseph's is a school that essentially has done nothing for Arthur except to renege on a scholarship offer when it appeared that he was not going to turn into a superior ballplayer, and yet his parents are forced to grovel before the school treasurer and promise to make payments to the school each month—money the family simply does not have—just for the "privilege" of receiving Arthur's grades.

One important reason why *Hoop Dreams* is such a beautiful and effective movie is that there is nothing about it that would shout out: HUMAN RIGHTS! Yet, in its exposition of the mixture of class, socioeconomic status, the horrible educational opportunities for inner-city kids, drugs, the insecurity of the person, the lack of meaningful work, and so on, this is exactly what this incredible film is all about.

Also of Note

On the Ropes (Nanette Burstein and Brett Morgen, 1999)

The four protagonists in this powerful documentary are on the ropes, both literally and figuratively. Three are young boxers hoping to escape ghetto life while the fourth is a trainer who had gotten out once and is attempting to do so again. One of the characters is a saucy and talented young female fighter, and her wrongful conviction for possession of crack cocaine found at her uncle's house is a searing indictment of the criminal justice system and painfully difficult to watch. But I assure you of one thing: good things also happen.

4

USA vs. Al-Arian

(Line Halvorsen, 2007)

In addition to giving great insight into ESCR, documentaries can also capture violations of civil and political rights (CPR). The next film offers a devastating portrayal of one of the casualties in the American "war on terror."

✳ ✳ ✳

This disturbing film covers the criminal case brought by the US Attorney's Office in Tampa, Florida, against Sami Al-Arian, a University of South Florida professor accused of providing "material support" to Palestinian terrorists. The crux of the prosecution's case is that as one of the leaders of the Palestinian Islamic Jihad, Al-Arian, a man who previously had been feted by the likes of President George W. Bush, was criminally responsible for acts of terrorism carried out in Israel. Despite widespread publicity and heightened tensions that surrounded this post–September 11, 2001, proceeding, a Florida jury acquitted Al-Arian of all major charges and deadlocked on the others. When a reporter asks one of the jurors after the trial what it would have taken to convict Sami Al-Arian, the juror quickly replies: "Evidence."

Although there are interviews with representatives of the US Attorney's Office, all of which only hurt the government's case, the film is told principally through the eyes of the Al-Arian family, especially Sami's remarkable and tireless wife, Nahla, who has assumed the responsibility of keeping the family together during this ordeal. Many moments are touching and some are even funny, including one scene where the family sits around and listens to a government wiretap from a decade ago as their young son orders a "Bigfoot" pizza from Domino's. Yet as silly as this moment is, it also indicates how long the Al-Arian family has been subject to government surveillance.

Like the jury, the viewer is easily convinced of terrible overreaching and political machinations by the US Attorney's Office. However, if the trial itself is Kafkaesque, what happens afterward almost defies description. Rather than Al-Arian walking out the courtroom door a free man, the US Attorney's Office decides that it will re-try the deadlocked charges and that it will keep him in detention until the completion of the second trial, which will mean several more years in prison. To avoid this, Al-Arian pleads guilty—to charges that he has already been acquitted of. Matters get even more bizarre at the plea bargaining hearing, where the presiding judge refuses to honor the agreement that had been reached between the prosecution and the defense, and instead sentences Al-Arian to additional time in prison.

At the outset of the film there is a video clip of President George W. Bush declaring after the September 11 attacks that international terrorists will come face to face with American justice. What he means by this is that American law and American justice will stop terrorists dead in their tracks. Yet, as *USA vs. Al-Arian* proceeds and as injustices are heaped on Al-Arian in the manner of Job from the Old Testament, the viewer is left to ponder about the true meaning of American justice.

Also of Note

The Prisoner or: How I Planned to Kill Tony Blair (Petra Epperlein and Michael Tucker, 2006)

This is the story of Yunis Khatayer, an Iraqi journalist, who, along with two of his brothers, was accused by American occupation forces of planning to kill British Prime Minister Tony Blair. This might sound preposterous—and it *is* preposterous—but this did not prevent the three of them from being detained for a full nine months while their human rights were repeatedly violated. Yunis is a journalist and after the American invasion in 2003 he did what journalists do: he took pictures, wrote stories, and asked questions, especially about the devastating effect the war had on civilian populations. And for this he was marked as a dangerous man. Despite his travails, he tells his story with almost no emotion, up to the point when he describes how the US military eventually apologized to him. His reply tells it best: "Sorry? I don't need sorry."

5

The Agronomist
(Jonathan Demme, 2003)

In 2010, Haiti was featured on the front page news when an earthquake leveled most of Port-au-Prince, including the presidential palace. Since then, rebuilding has been maddeningly slow, cholera has been an enormous problem, and human rights violations continue apace. Yet the people of the poorest country in the Western Hemisphere have long suffered gross and systematic violations of both CPR and ESCR, particularly under the brutal dictatorships of "Papa Doc" Duvalier and then his son, "Baby Doc."

✳ ✳ ✳

All too often, human rights victims are tenderly thought of as passive and unfortunate souls who need our attention, our protection, our money, and most of all our pity. Jean Dominique, a staunch opponent of the military regime in Haiti, needs none of this. Rather, what makes this documentary so powerful is that "powerful" is perhaps the best way to describe Jean Dominique himself—along with passionate, vibrant, and heroic. Although he often referred to himself as a mere "agronomist" because of his early training in agriculture, Jean Dominique is so much more than this. For years, he operated Radio Haiti-Inter, and in this capacity he served as the voice of Haiti's poor and oppressed.

The most moving scene of all comes at the end of the story after Dominique has been assassinated by government goons. In a brave but chilling act, his wife, Michele Montas, opens the radio broadcast by announcing what has long been eminently clear to the viewer: "Jean Dominique is alive." Indeed, you will never meet a person with as much life.

6

4 Little Girls
(Spike Lee, 1997)

Civil rights are human rights, and the horrible struggle that African Americans went through to achieve both has been wonderfully told in this Spike Lee masterpiece.

* * *

Although Denise McNair, Cynthia Wesley, Carole Robertson, and Addie Mae Collins are not household names, one could make a strong case that these four little girls—the victims of the bombing of the 16th Street Baptist Church in Birmingham, Alabama—were key figures in the American civil rights movement. By 1963, the year of this terrorist attack, Birmingham was already well known for its violence. From the late 1940s on, there had been a series of bombings directed at black populations, especially on what came to be known as "Dynamite Hill," an upper-scale part of the city that black families were attempting to move up into. And in May 1963 the American public was introduced to the unforgettable (for all the wrong reasons) Eugene "Bull" Connor, the police commissioner of Birmingham, who was the living embodiment of the bigoted southern sheriff. It was Bull Connor who drove around his city in a shiny white tank, and it was Bull Connor who gave the orders to turn water hoses and police dogs on those peacefully marching for their civil rights. These images were shown on American television, and the raw racism was simply too vivid to ignore. But to plant a bomb in the house of God and murder four young children attending Sunday school services? This was something that showed in stunning clarity the depravity of those who would defend racial segregation at all costs.

One of the great strengths of this film is the manner in which the civil rights movement is depicted. One of the bravest people one would ever encounter is Rev. Fred Shuttlesworth, who not only survived a bombing of his own home some time before this but who, in an attempt to integrate the Birmingham city schools, took on a group of white thugs who were armed with chains and other weapons—and from the film footage shown, was more than holding his own against them. What we also learn is the manner in which the Birmingham marches were driven by young people, local college students at first but eventually high school and even grammar school students. And their meeting place was 16th Street Baptist Church.

The heart of the film is the personal portrayal of these four little girls. Interviews with family members and friends are interwoven into the film, and viewers feel the profound effect that the lives—and deaths—of these girls have had on others, even years after the tragedy. As one would imagine, many of those who are interviewed are quite emotional in describing the bombings and the joint funeral (for three of the girls) held a few days later, which attracted worldwide attention. As one relative states: while you forget some of the details, you never forget how you felt at that time.

Two scenes in this great movie stand out. The first involves an interview with Maxine and Chris McNair, the parents of Denise, as they describe the first time Denise realized that there was racism in the world. The family was shopping at a department store during the Christmas holiday season when Denise asked her parents if they could get something to eat at the lunch counter there. Her father's description of the alluring smell of the food is so vivid that you almost have a sense that you are in the Kress department store basement with them. What Denise had not been told before is that blacks were not allowed to eat with whites, and what she also had never been told, or apparently had ever realized in her happy world, was that many people hated her because of the color of her skin. Chris said he decided to tell her that evening about racism, and he tells the interviewer (Lee) that this was as painful as the day he saw the horror of his dead daughter. And years have not lessened any of this pain.

The second scene involves George Wallace, the former governor of Alabama who was even better known that Bull Connor, both adopting a take-no-prisoners approach to maintaining the racial superiority of whites. It was Wallace who at his inauguration uttered the infamous line "segregation now, segregation forever" and who later stood in the schoolhouse doorway to block the efforts of federal officials attempting to enforce integration. By now Wallace is a tired old man, himself the victim of an assassination attempt when he ran for president. He gives the standard line that he was brought up to believe that segregation was something that blacks and whites both wanted. But what makes Wallace such a pathetic figure is his need to convince the interviewer and presumably the viewing audience that he is not a racist man and that his "best friend," who he repeatedly orders to come over for the camera, is his black manservant. Who knows, this might be his only friend. But one can tell from Ed's wary look that Wallace has not changed.

One final point involves the film's wonderful musical score. The film opens with the haunting "Birmingham Sunday" sung by Joan Baez about these murders and the tune is replayed in various formats throughout. One of the great surprises is when Bill Baxley, the former Attorney General who successfully brought criminal charges for the killings many years later against Bob Chambliss, recounts how he played this song each morning before trial. After watching this film, one certainly understands why.

Also of Note

The Murder of Emmett Till (Stanley Nelson, 2003)

Emmett Till was a fourteen-year-old boy from Chicago when he and cousin took a trip to Money, Mississippi, where his family had migrated from before relocating in the North. As he was leaving, his mother sternly warned him about how blacks were expected to act in the Mississippi Delta. She gave him his father's signet ring and instructed her only child to give her a kiss, just in case she never saw him again. She eventually did see him again—or at least his mangled body after he had been lynched by a group of whites—but the only way she could identify her own son was because of this ring. What was Emmett Till's crime? Quite simply, he playfully whistled at a white woman in Mississippi. Mrs. Till took her son back home to Chicago and ordered that there be an open casket, where pictures from his funeral were carried by the international press corps, allowing the rest of the world to understand the barbarity of segregation in the American South.

7

Arna's Children
(Juliano Mer-Khamis and Danniel Danniel, 2004)

Documentary filmmakers are attracted to the Israeli–Palestinian conflict the way that moths are drawn to a flame. In my view, Arna's Children *is the most challenging and the most thought provoking of all these. Since the 1967 war against a group of Arab states, Israel has been an occupying power in the West Bank (and the Gaza Strip as well, until quite recently). As shown in this stunning film, this occupation has played a central role in creating a dispossessed and disillusioned Palestinian population.*

✳ ✳ ✳

The Arna in the title is Arna Mer Khamis, an audacious Jew who married a Palestinian Arab and who spent most of her life working with children in Palestinian refugee camps and engaging in never-ending battles with Israeli authorities. One of the directors of the film is her son Juliano, who worked with his mother in establishing a theater troupe for Palestinian children. Much in the nature of the *7 Up* series, one of the most interesting aspects of this film is to see these young people when they were adolescents and then to view them several years later at the beginning of adulthood—or at least those who have survived to adulthood. The young people have hardly changed at all in terms of their looks, temperament, and mannerisms—but in other ways all have changed enormously. When they were young and playing various theatrical roles, they all dreamed of having their pictures and names plastered on billboards announcing a starring role in some new stage production. Many of Arna's children have indeed achieved fame and have had their pictures plastered all around the refugee camp where they live—not as stage actors, but as martyrs to the Palestinian cause.

What *Arna's Children* does better than anything else is to show the humanity in those who would commonly be hated as "terrorists." The viewer enjoys the company of these children when they were young and joyful, and yet something has changed dramatically since then. Despite Arna's entreaty to turn away from violence, several of her "children" have not been able or willing to do so—and the viewer gets a strong sense of why this has happened. *Arna's Children* is an extraordinarily powerful and thought-provoking film with no ready answers. The simple truth is that those who are victims of political violence will almost naturally turn to violence themselves.

Also of Note

To See If I'm Smiling (Tamar Yarom, 2007)

The film is a somber and effective documentary that is based on a series of interviews with several female Israeli soldiers as they recount their actions while patrolling the Occupied Territories. To be clear, the movie makes no pretense that these individuals speak for all women (or all soldiers) who served in the Israeli Defense Force. For all the viewer knows, the deep discomfort and shame expressed by these former soldiers might be atypical.

Still, it is fascinating to watch these women recount their wartime experiences. One gets a strong sense that until these interviews were conducted, not one of these former soldiers had ever reflected on such matters before. The most intense encounter involves a woman whose comments provide the title of the film. She relates a story of the death of a Palestinian and comments that it was her experience that in such circumstances there was often a swelling of the man's penis, giving him an erection in death. She then goes on to say that there was a picture taken of this "event," and what she begins to wonder—in growing horror and agitation—is whether she happened to be smiling for the camera when her picture was taken with the dead Palestinian. And it is at that moment that this former IDF soldier realizes what an unfeeling monster she has become. It is something that apparently sends chills down her spine, but it has the same effect on the viewer as well.

Hot House (Shimon Dotan, 2006)

In October 2011 Israeli Staff Sgt. Gilad Shalit, who was captured in June 2006 at the age of nineteen and held by Hamas, was released in a prisoner swap for more than a thousand Palestinian prisoners. Shalit's name and face are widely known, not only in Israel but throughout the world. But what do we know of the Palestinians who were released? Or the tens of thousands who remain in detention? Almost nothing.

More than any other film, *Hot House* comes closest to providing some insight into who these prisoners are. Perhaps the most surprising thing of all is that Israeli authorities would allow the film to be made in the first place; while the Israeli government considers these people to be dangerous terrorists, these men come across as articulate, committed, and disciplined. Indeed, these are people you would want to share a drink with or discuss politics.

8

We Were Here
(David Weissman, 2011)

The 1980s AIDS crisis in San Francisco show us how fragile and fleeting the human right to health care oftentimes is. It also shows the kinds of punitive measures that politicians seriously considered at that time as a way of dealing with the crisis. Only through political action were such measures defeated. This is a scary film but a deeply moving one as well.

* * *

We Were Here tells the personal stories of five individuals who survived the AIDS epidemic that decimated San Francisco's gay population throughout the 1980s. This was a period where gay men were dropping like flies from some mysterious disease that was called the "gay cancer." Sufferers endured a gruesome death, as their bodies became plastered with horrible lesions and quickly wasted away to almost nothing. They resembled concentration camp survivors, only there were no survivors from this disease, at least at that time.

Guy is a flamboyant black man who came to the city in the late 1970s thinking he was really something (he is) and who has run a flower shop for decades. Eileen is a nurse who helped develop some of the first AIDS testing studies. Paul is a policy expert, often seen in old film footage leading various political demonstrations. Daniel is an artist who has lost two partners to the disease and attributes his still being alive to being a "wuss" because of his unwillingness to stay in an AIDS testing regimen that turned out to be disastrous. Finally, Ed is a gay man who was out of his element during the heyday of free and open love. He says he was terrible at anonymous sex, but he has a wonderful talent of connecting with other people, and he was able to put these skills to great use counseling scared young gay men facing death.

These personal stories are balanced very nicely with the political atmosphere at various times. In the 1970s, the gay community in San Francisco was quite hopeful. The Castro was transformed into a gay mecca, and Harvey Milk had just been elected to the city's board of supervisors. Then two terrible things occurred almost at the same time. The first was Milk's assassination in 1978 and the virtual exoneration of Dan White. The second was AIDS, although no one knew this at the time. Medical authorities now estimate that by 1979, 10 percent of the city's gay population was already infected, and by two years later this was up to 20 percent. Ed tells a horrifying story of going to a drug store to buy some rolling papers and seeing a poster with pictures of an AIDS victim (although it was not yet known as such) with purple lesions all over his body and the enormous impact this had on him. And yet this was just the beginning of the war, and each commentator tells about close personal friends dying all around them.

No one knew what was causing these deaths, and here the film provides a nice reminder of the great public fear of this "gay cancer." Eileen recounts how the hospital she worked at sought to exclude those with this disease, lest it be thought of as an "AIDS hospital." Public opinion polls at that time indicated that half of the population was in favor of quarantining AIDS patients, and another 15 percent advocated placing a tattoo on those infected so that they could be identified by the public at large. There was much discussion of mandatory testing along with proposals that those with AIDS be fired from certain jobs (most notably as school teachers). But what this did was to bring the gay community closer and closer together. Not only did they have to fight against public opinion, which they were able to do, but also to tend to their own.

One of the interesting changes was in the public perception of gays. Before the epidemic, gays were thought of as being entirely hedonistic, and the truth is many fit this stereotype or at least tried to do so. However, the AIDS crisis transformed the image of gays into something very different, mainly as caregivers. Yet, at the same time, the epidemic radicalized many gays, who were convinced that the government had little interest in protecting them, which resulted in the creation of organizations such as ACT-UP.

Medicines were eventually developed to combat AIDS, first AZT and then the kinds of cocktails that have now done so much to keep those infected with the disease alive—including people like Daniel who recalls how suicidal he was after losing his second partner. Daniel has the last word in the film and I will give it to him here, although I cannot match the emotional quiver that filled his voice. Speaking not only of his lovers but of his friends, he says: I miss a lot of them, a lot.

9

Long Night's Journey into Day
(Frances Reid and Deborah Hoffmann, 2000)

South Africa is widely hailed for its political and social transformation. In the space of less than two decades, South Africa has gone from being a pariah nation that was ruled under the banner of apartheid to a society founded on the principle of equality and justice. The vehicle for achieving this was the country's Truth and Reconciliation Commission (TRC), which operated under the principle that the best way of moving the society forward was to first establish the truth about the horrors that had taken place under apartheid rule. In that way, the TRC was set up so that amnesty would be granted to those who had committed a political crime and were willing to come forward and tell the truth about this.

* * *

Long Night's Journey into Day uses four separate stories to tell the story of the TRC. It begins with that of Amy Biehl, an exchange student from the United States who had been killed by a young black man (Mongezi Manqina) while she was working in one of the black townships. Biehl's story is best told by her parents. This American couple attended the amnesty proceedings for their daughter's killer, and they speak eloquently and passionately in favor of a grant of amnesty for Manqina. As they explain, their ultimate wish is to honor their daughter's life the best way that they could—and they are certain that Amy would have been a staunch supporter of the TRC process. The Biehls also used the trip to meet Manqina's family, something that totally overwhelms his mother, who expresses her own grief over Amy's death.

A second story involves the amnesty application of Eric Taylor, a white security officer who comes forward to admit his wrongdoing in the killing of four black activists known as the Cradock 4. Taylor maintains that his great revelation came from reading Nelson Mandela's autobiography and from watching the film of the US civil rights movement *Mississippi Burning*. However, Taylor's amnesty is opposed by the widow of Fort Calata, who is not at all convinced of Taylor's transformation. Another story involves Robert McBride, an African National Congress "freedom fighter" who set off a bomb at a Durban nightclub, killing three women and injuring a host of other people. What is most interesting about the McBride case is that he had previously been pardoned by the new South African government, but he still chose to go forward with his amnesty application. Aggressively opposing it is Sharon Welgemoed, the sister of one of the deceased. It would be too much to say that Ms. Welgemoed represents the face (and fury) of white South Africans, but she simply seem incapable of reconciliation.

The last story involves the slaughter of the Guguletu 7—and if slaughter seems too strong a word, the best proof of this comes from a breathless television newscast that covered this story at the time it occurred. In this report, the black activists are described as "terrorists," and the killings by the security forces are justified as a measure of self-defense. Yet what is eminently clear from the film footage itself, especially the amateurish placement of weapons on the dead black men, is that the event had been entirely staged and used as a pretext to eliminate these irritants to the apartheid regime.

Some twenty-five officers were involved in these killings, but only two—one black and one white—have come forward and applied for amnesty. Consistent with what appears to be white denial more generally (as the film points out, more than 80 percent of the amnesty applicants were black), the white officer attempts to have it both ways. On the one hand, he maintains that he did not commit a criminal act. But, on the other hand, if he had done so, he is asking the TRC for amnesty.

The black security officer is Thapelo Mbelo. It is evident to the viewers—as it is becomes evident to the widows, who he meets with privately and to whom he profusely apologizes—that this man has been racked with guilt, not only for his participation in these murders but the undercover role that he had assumed under the apartheid regime. The title of the film might seem to be a cute play on words of Eugene O'Neill's classic, but what is shown here truly is a long, winding, and uncertain journey into the future. The film does not judge, but it is evident from the setup of the film, particularly the many scenes of white opulence, that the filmmakers are convinced that the white minority has gotten off quite easily—while at the same time, so many remain disinterested in seeking out the truth or in bringing about a larger societal reconciliation.

10

Waiting for "Superman"
(Davis Guggenheim, 2010)

The right to education is one of the most important ESCR. Article 26 (1) of the Universal Declaration of Human Rights states: "Everyone has the right to education. Education shall be free, at least in the elementary and fundamental stages. Elementary education shall be compulsory. Technical and professional education shall be made generally available and higher education shall be equally accessible to all on the basis of merit."

The second paragraph of Article 26 goes on to specify the kind of education that human rights mandates and it goes well beyond the 3Rs: "Education shall be directed to the full development of the human personality and to the strengthening of respect for human rights and fundamental freedoms. It shall promote understanding, tolerance and friendship among all nations, racial or religious groups, and shall further the activities of the United Nations for the maintenance of peace."

In terms of the United States, which is the setting for the next film, one of the problems in enacting meaningful reform in this area is that education is simply not thought of as a human right. The US Constitution does not offer much protection in this area. In San Antonio v. Texas *(1973), the Supreme Court ruled that education is not a "fundamental right," and it thereby upheld a state funding scheme that has led to enormous inequalities in per-pupil expenditures. The end result of all this is that some American children get a wonderful education, while others are shunted aside to inferior schools.*

* * *

This thought-provoking documentary on the dysfunctions of the American educational system presents some of the most gut-wrenching scenes you would ever wish to see in a film. The film documents the lotteries that are used to determine which children will receive a coveted spot at one of the "good" schools they have applied to or whether they will be consigned to the underachieving one they are currently enrolled in. At this point, the viewers know exactly what is at stake and the enormous difference that a good teacher—let alone a good school—will have on a young child's life prospects. So we watch and anguish as numbers and names are being pulled out of a computer system, or balls rolled out just like in a real lottery, and we see some joy but much more consternation. In a clever move, the drama is heightened even more by keeping a running tally of the dwindling number of places for that particular school still available—until there are none left. Despair is simply too weak a word to describe the feeling of those who have lost.

Quality education is one of those things that everyone is certainly in favor of, but the educational system in the United States is woefully lacking, and there are a lot of villains who share the blame for this, although in this film teachers' unions come in for particular condemnation. The biggest problem, it seems, is the tenure system, which is granted almost automatically to teachers as soon as they start to teach and protects them the rest of their career. If they turn out to be good or even great teachers, there is no problem. However, many turn out to be "lemons" (the actual term used for horrible teachers in Wisconsin), and getting rid of a lemon is virtually impossible. We know this because most of the talking heads in the film are school administrators (or former administrators), who have tried to take on the entrenched school bureaucracy—and have been burned, badly.

But there are some real heroes in this film as well. These include the students themselves, who seem to know at an unnaturally young age the enormous importance that their educational opportunities (or lack thereof) will have on them. Many parents (and in one case a grandparent who is raising her son's child) are also heroes, as they try to arrange meetings with teachers (often to no avail), work odd jobs to make tuition payments at private schools, and generally do everything in their power to provide their child with a fighting chance in life. Finally, several of the administrators profiled in the film are heroes, especially Michelle Rhee, the former superintendent in Washington, DC, and Geoffrey Canada, who has started a charter school in Harlem that, amazingly, guarantees that each child will graduate from college. Unfortunately, these stories are too few and far between and what we have instead is a steady supply of either "dropout factories" in inner cities or else suburban schools that engage in tracking that serves as the death knell for students who do not test well.

One of the most fascinating scenes in the film are the thousands of teachers in New York City who have been removed from the classroom for incompetence but who still get full pay and benefits. These people are required to report to school authorities each day, although most spend their time playing cards, reading the newspaper, or looking like bored fifth-graders and sleeping with their heads on the desk. It would have been interesting to hear from this group in an attempt to find out how and why these teachers are so horrible. Related to that, the film might have explored how teachers become teachers in the first place. Is it because teaching provides one of the few secure occupations in the United States?

The last point concerns human rights practices. The viewer can certainly feel for these students, and the film provides plenty of information at the end of the film on websites to visit in order to "do something." Yet what is missing is the sense that the plight of these kids is an actual violation of human rights. These children are victims as much as they would be if they had been tortured or kidnapped. Unless and until we are able to recognize the dysfunctions of the educational system as such, we will be showing this film (or something just like it) for generations to come.

11

Roger & Me
(Michael Moore, 1989)

For those who do not think that human rights and comedy can go together, I offer Roger & Me. *But perhaps laughter is the only thing that keeps the viewer from crying at the economic devastation and lost lives depicted in this film.*

✳ ✳ ✳

In my view, *Roger & Me* remains Michael Moore's best film, combining wit, humor, and social insight with the likes of Pat Boone, Anita Bryant, and Bob Eubanks of "The Newlywed Game." The premise of the film is that Moore is intent on saving his hometown of Flint, Michigan, and he thinks this can only be accomplished by bringing General Motors CEO Roger Smith to the city so that he can get a firsthand look at the economic devastation brought on by the GM plant closings in that area. Of course, Moore never gets to meet Smith, and their closest encounter comes at a shareholders meeting where Moore asks Smith a question and promptly has his microphone shut off.

Still, most of the fun and insight comes from the chase itself. Because this was Moore's first film, his schlep character was at this time unknown to viewers, and watching the response that he gets for his audacity in trying to enter GM headquarters to make an appointment with Smith is hilarious on one level but also telling; the staunchest defenders of social stratification are quite often those at the bottom of the heap.

Likewise, the constant foibles of the Flint city government are incredible to witness, with the city's "economic development" plans going from one failed policy to another, including a new prison, a new convention center, prayer meetings with nationally recognized televangelists, and a museum dedicated to the automobile that closes within six months after its opening. Yet behind this black humor is a system of governance that is at the mercy of Darwinian forces—both public and private—that lead directly to violations of economic rights, particularly the lack of food and shelter.

Roger & Me has any number of truly memorable scenes. One that deserves special mention takes place at the exclusive Flint Country Club, where a group of female golfers are offering their own "insights" into the laziness of today's workers, just as they are about to tee off for what certainly looks like a leisurely round of mid-day, mid-week golf. While the film is populated by all sorts of clueless people—including the GM mouthpiece who tries to convince Moore (and himself) that auto workers will actually be better off from being laid off—what remains real throughout are the people who have lost their jobs, their homes, their livelihoods, their health care, and perhaps worst of all at least some part of their humanity.

12

White Light/Black Rain: The Destruction of Hiroshima and Nagasaki
(Steven Okazaki, 2007)

With the exception of the two atomic bombs the United States dropped on Japan that quickly brought World War II to an end, the world has been spared a nuclear attack, although the "nuclear club" continues to grow larger and larger and the world more dangerous. It's easy to lose sight of the fact that the detonation of a single nuclear bomb would make all the other human rights violations under consideration pale in comparison.

White Light/Black Rain is the one film that I truly believe everyone needs to see. It contains actual film footage of the survivors of the nuclear attack on Japan, and it is an overwhelming experience. At the outset of the documentary it is mentioned, almost in passing, that for a quarter century the US government suppressed film footage of the devastation, but there is no mention of why or how this was done or why it took so long to bring the footage to light. Of course, one reason is that there is a kind of collective amnesia, or perhaps some strange need to forget. At the outset of the film it is pointed out that 75 percent of the Japanese population was born after 1945, and not a single teenager who is interviewed on the street is able to provide the correct answer regarding the importance of August 6 and 9, 1945, the days that atomic bombs were dropped, first on Hiroshima and then on Nagasaki.

What makes this film so fascinating and so important are the survivors, as they recount the horrors they somehow lived through. They describe in painful detail, almost as if they are experiencing it for the very first time, the flesh falling off of bodies, people losing arms and legs, intestines and brains falling out, and bodies that were burned beyond all recognition—as one survivor describes it, like fish cooking on a grill. One survivor describes his face looking like a black ball and another describes pain so intense that he would frequently pass out, and maggots that would eat away at his exposed flesh. Even acts of compassion could turn out to be anything but, as one of the survivors remains haunted by the two people he insists he killed—by giving them water to drink, not realizing the effect this would have on severely dehydrated bodies.

Given the fact that these individuals are still alive, one might naturally conclude that these constitute the "lucky" ones, but that is by no means certain. One survivor describes how those receiving treatment in the hospital begged constantly to be killed, while several of the others continue to suffer a kind of survivor's guilt. The loss of loved ones is particularly poignant. Another survivor relates how her sister initially survived but then threw herself in front of a speeding train when the pain—both physical and psychological—became too overwhelming. She goes on to relate that she went to the same exact spot, intent on ending her own life in the same way, but jumped away at the last moment. She said that she realized then that there are two kinds of courage: the courage to die, which her sister had, and the courage to live, which she herself had. Both of these entail great courage. Notwithstanding the societal discrimination that each one of the survivors experienced, many have gone on to lead happy and productive lives. One created a cartoon titled "Barefoot Gen" that displays the horrors of nuclear weapons through this medium. Another describes her role in life as being there to tell people about what happened to her—so that others will be spared the same fate that she has lived through.

The response of the Americans is both callous and bizarre. Those who took part in the actual bombing seem undisturbed by what they did. One even goes so far as to say that not only did he not have any nightmares about his own involvement in the killings of hundreds of thousands of people but that he has never had a nightmare in his life. After the immediate surrender of Japan, US medical teams rushed to provide help, although it is not clear whether there were also political and scientific ends that were being pursued in addition to humanitarian ones. In terms of the bizarre, in the mid-1950s a group of young female bomb victims was brought to the United States for plastic surgeries that oftentimes went on for years, and this group was called the Hiroshima Maidens. But in a strange way one of the most moving scenes involves the appearance by Reverend Tanimoto, who began the Maidens program, on the popular television show *This Is Your Life,* where one of the guests is Lt. Lewis, who flew the Enola Gay, which dropped the first bomb. The enormity of what he was a part of seems to hit Lewis at that moment. The Hiroshima Maidens are also there, but as explained on air, they are being kept offstage so as not to offend the viewing audience.

Perhaps it is time that the viewing audience is offended. Various countries in the world now possess the equivalent of 400,000 Hiroshima bombs. Like the Hiroshima Maidens and the other brave survivors in this film, not to mention those who are long dead, we certainly need to know of the loss and destruction caused by just two of these weapons.

13

Where Soldiers Come From
(Heather Courtney, 2011)

Some may question whether Where Soldiers Come From *can be called a human rights film. In its own subtle and quiet way, the film shows us how those at the lower rungs of the socioeconomic ladder, with few (if any) real prospects in life, are forced to fight the wars the rest of the population is simply not willing to fight.*

✳ ✳ ✳

The National Guard soldiers who are sent off to fight in Afghanistan in this film are from Michigan's Upper Peninsula. The two main characters, Dom and Cole, are boyhood friends. Cole is a bit of a goofball, while Dom wants to be an artist and spray paints murals in abandoned buildings (and on a wall at Finlandia University after his deployment when he has resumed his studies). A third friend, Bodi, plays a more prominent role later in the film, especially when he is grounded in Afghanistan due to the multiple concussions he has suffered. The seemingly offhand manner in which these young men join the National Guard is, on one level, disturbing because they seem to give little deliberation to the decision or their possible deployment to Afghanistan or Iraq. Yet, on another level, the decision to sign up makes perfect sense. Their parents work in dead-end jobs that pay a pittance, and there is no indication that Dom and Cole would be able to do any better. Moreover, both young men want to better themselves. Dom is already enrolled in classes, while Cole has plans for college and attends Northern Michigan University when he returns from Afghanistan. College is expensive, and both sets of parents are in no position to offer assistance. At this juncture, the signing bonus from the National Guard looks mighty good. It is only later that the implications and the full consequences of this decision become more fully known.

At one point Cole's mother says that the whole scene of this contingent of UP friends going off to war reminds her of the movie *The Deer Hunter,* and she is exactly right. We see the small-town rituals and the tight bonding between people who have known each other—and virtually no one else—their entire lives. After the unit gets deployed, our attention is divided between their lives in Afghanistan and the lives of those left behind. The Michigan National Guard is assigned the task of locating and neutralizing IEDs and the unit's day consists of driving around in enormous vehicles looking for such bombs. Their vehicles are occasionally hit, and it is Bodi's great misfortune to be involved in several of these, causing him to suffer severe concussions, which not only prevents him from going out into the field but transforms his personality. While sitting between his two friends, Bodi describes what the war has done to him. He states that he has come to hate all Afghan people and the entire country of Afghanistan and he goes on to describe himself as a "racist American." Finally, he states, whether truthfully or not, that he never hated anyone before joining the Army. Now, he hates virtually everyone, but most of all he hates himself.

The good news is that no one from the Michigan National Guard is killed. But all suffer severe physical and mental problems. At one point, Cole seems addicted to Nyquil, which at least allows him some opportunity to get some sleep amidst the war raging all around him. After he returns home, Dom displays an irritability that his girlfriend says she has never seen before. As for Bodi, he is shown receiving help for his brain injuries. His greatest fear is that he will end up as a nutcase back home, and there is serious reason to believe that he represents a part of a war-tested generation that will become just that. There are also moments of pride and triumph, especially when the people from their hometown line the streets to welcome "their boys" back home. Life goes on—there simply is no other option. Under the guidance of his art teacher, Dom completes a large mural at his university that seems to help bring meaning to his experiences. Cole's future seems a bit fuzzier, but the viewer is pleased to see that, his Afghan experiences notwithstanding, he still has not lost his endearing goofball manner.

14

In the Land of the Free
(Vadim Jean, 2010)

There are a number of outstanding documentaries that show the failures and the corruptness of the American criminal justice system. Although it is quite difficult to single out any one of these, the following film certainly is deserving of special recognition.

✳ ✳ ✳

The Angola 3 are three inmates who were held in solitary confinement—or, to use the vernacular of prison authorities, closed cell restrictions (CCR)—for decades at the infamous Angola state penitentiary in Louisiana. Herman Wallace and Albert Woodfox were convicted of murdering a prison guard (Brent Miller) in Angola in 1972, and they were placed in CCR from that time until their release into the general prison population at Angola in 2008, after US Congressman John Conyers, the chairman of the House Judiciary Committee, took an interest in their case. The third member is Robert King, who was convicted of another murder and held in CCR for twenty-nine years. King was eventually acquitted of the murder charges that had been brought against him, and he has now dedicated his life to freeing his two comrades.

It is difficult to know where to begin to list the horrible things that have happened to these three men. In terms of the killing of Officer Miller, the filmmaker presents an overwhelming case that Wallace and Woodfox had nothing to do with the slaying, a sentiment that is also shared by the guard's widow. Instead, they were convicted based on the testimony of a single jailhouse snitch (Hezekiah Brown), for whom the prison warden sought special favors. The irregularities in the review of their continued confinement were numerous: The grand jury proceeding was headed by Ann Butler, who was the wife of the warden at Angola and who had already written a book on the first trial in support of its verdict. There was a bloody fingerprint on Miller's body that forensic tests proved was not from either Wallace or Woodfox, but it was never compared with the fingerprints of the other Angola inmates who were at the facility when the murder occurred. By these "standards," King's conviction for a murder that another inmate had confessed to almost seems like the embodiment of justice.

What explains these results? The real crime of the Angola 3 was that they were members of the Black Panthers. And for this they were not only wrongfully convicted of murder but spent between twenty-nine (King) and thirty-six years (Wallace and Woodfox) in solitary confinement. At Angola there are two different levels of solitary confinement. In one, the better one, the prisoner is simply deserted. In the other, the prisoner is strapped to a bed with a football helmet placed over his head—and then deserted. Over the decades, King, Wallace, and Woodfox have experienced both.

As Conyers eloquently points out, solitary confinement violates the prohibition against "cruel and unusual" punishment in the 8th Amendment. And what the filmmaker also shows is that there has come to be increased reliance on the use of solitary confinement in the past decade or so. But the heart of the film is not so much the legal abrogations as the extraordinary ability of these men to endure these barbarous practices and to become more human in the face of all the inhumanity directed against them.

Also of Note
The Trials of Darryl Hunt (Ricki Stern and Anne Sundberg, 2006)

In 1984, Darryl Hunt, a nineteen-year-old black man with no previous criminal record, was charged with raping and murdering Deborah Sykes, a young and attractive white woman. An all-white jury in Winston-Salem, North Carolina, convicted Hunt, although there was no physical evidence linking him to the crime and one of the prosecution's main witnesses was a member of the Ku Klux Klan. Hunt's legal team, most notably Mark Rabil who literally worked on this case for decades, fought for a new trial, but in 1989 Hunt was once again convicted.

However, in 1994, the sperm found on Sykes' body was tested by DNA evidence and it was found not to be Hunt's. One might think that this would lead to Hunt's freedom, but the prosecution stonewalled, taking a two-prong approach. The first was to posit that while Hunt might not have raped Sykes, he could have been the person who murdered her—although eyewitness accounts only placed one man at the scene of the crime. The second was to argue that DNA testing is simply one piece of evidence and that the negative test on Hunt really does not prove a thing. To be fair, at this time the use of DNA evidence was still relatively new. Still, to hear the prosecution and judge discuss the matter as if they are talking about alchemy is quite disconcerting.

Darryl Hunt would go on to spend another decade in prison. As might be imagined, his eventual release was a deeply emotional moment. For Hunt, it represented the exoneration he has been claiming—for anyone who would listen, as he puts it. Unfortunately, Sykes's mother refuses to accept the fact that Hunt is not her daughter's killer. To see Darryl Hunt, without an ounce of rancor, reach out to Mrs. Sykes the way that he does is to show what a remarkable human being this man is.

Murder on a Sunday Morning (Jean-Xavier de Lestrade, 2001)

In 2000 a white tourist staying at a hotel in Jacksonville, Florida, was shot and killed at point-blank range by a young black male who also made away with her handbag. A short while later, a gangly fifteen-year-old black kid is brought to the scene of the crime, where the deceased's husband, who was walking with his wife at the time of the murder, gives a positive identification that this was his wife's murderer. After being arrested and questioned by the Jacksonville police, the young man, Brenton Butler, signs a confession.

Most of the story is told through the narration of Pat McGuinness, the public defender representing Brenton, who should rank with some of the greatest trial lawyers to ever appear on screen. The best scenes involve McGuinness's cross examination of the police. The testimony of the burly black police officer, a former college football player, was that he took Brenton out into the woods in order to look for the murder weapon. Yet, photographs taken immediately after this "walk" establish quite convincingly that this skinny young kid, in shackles no less, had been smacked about the head and the chest area. In addition, through cross-examination we find out that Brenton's "confession" was not written by him at all but by a white police officer who apparently had developed a practice of putting his own words in other peoples' mouth. I will not give away the dramatic ending, but what happened to Brenton Butler should never have happened.

Paradise Lost: The Child Murders at Robin Hood Hills (Joe Berlinger and Bruce Sinofsky, 1996) and *Paradise Lost 2: Revelations* (Joe Berlinger and Bruce Sinofsky, 2000)

On August 19, 2011, Damien Echols, Jessie Misskelley, and Jason Baldwin—better known as the West Memphis Three—were finally released from prison. In 1994, the three were convicted of murdering three young boys: Stevie Branch, Christopher Byers, and Michael Moore. Misskelley was tried separately, and his conviction was largely based on a taped confession. Misskelley has an IQ of 72, and although he had been interrogated by the police for more than twelve hours, only a small portion of these proceedings were recorded. In these statements, Misskelley implicated Echols and Baldwin, who were later tried and convicted. Much of the hysteria surrounding the second trial revolved around whether Echols and Baldwin were part of a Satanic cult, and one of the chief prosecution witnesses was Dr. Dale Griffis, who obtained both a M.A. and Ph.D. without ever having to attend a single class.

Damien Echols took the stand while Jason Baldwin did not. Echols's Goth hair and dress certainly did not help win over this West Memphis jury. Much of the film contains interviews with the parents of the deceased boys, but the main attraction is John Mark Byers, the stepfather of Chris Byers. Byers is not able to shut up when a camera is present, and he is questioned when a knife he gives to the filmmakers (why would he give a knife to the filmmakers?) is found to have blood on it that matches both his and his stepson's. Another one of the key government witnesses is a jailhouse snitch, who maintains that immediately after meeting Baldwin, the latter told him the entire story of how he and the other two had murdered these three young boys. Sound fishy?

This case would have remained in complete obscurity if not for the release of *Paradise Lost,* which eventually drew international attention to the case. After an outpouring of support, particularly from members of the entertainment industry, the defense then had the resources to have expert witnesses re-examine the evidence, pointing to a lot of things that the prosecution had missed such as teeth marks on Chris Byers. After the release of the first film, the families of the other two children refused to speak to the filmmakers, but John Mark Byers filled the void for the follow-up film, *Paradise Lost 2.* His incessant talking was more difficult because he had lost his front teeth—teeth that might well have bitten his stepson at the time he was killed. The level of prosecutorial misconduct and police ineptitude and corruption shown in these two films is nothing short of astounding.

The Thin Blue Line (Errol Morris, 1988)

The "thin blue line" used in the title comes from a line used by the prosecution in the murder trial of Randall Adams and refers to the police as the only thing preventing complete societal anarchy. What this film makes eminently clear is that in an attempt to create the illusion of security, the police can also bring about their own societal anarchy. On the positive side, I suppose, the film caused such a stir after it was released that it eventually resulted in Adams's conviction being overturned. On the negative side, one wonders why it would take the making of a documentary before an obviously innocent man could finally find some measure of justice.

15

You Don't Like the Truth: 4 Days Inside Guantanamo
(Luc Côté and Patricio Henriquez, 2010)

You Don't Like the Truth *is a riveting documentary. To my knowledge, the film footage of the interrogation of sixteen-year-old Omar Khadr, a Canadian-born "enemy combatant" being held at Guantanamo Bay, Cuba, by a Canadian security officer (posing as a diplomat) is the only visual recording of an interrogation at that military facility that is available to the public. It should also be noted that this was not something that the Canadian Security Intelligence Service (CSIS) or the Central Intelligence Agency (CIA) did of its own accord. Rather, in July 2008 the Canadian Supreme Court ordered the release of the tape. We should all be eternally grateful that they did. And it is imperative that other judicial bodies should order the same.*

✳ ✳ ✳

Omar Khadr was captured by coalition forces in Afghanistan and accused of killing a US Army medic, Chris Speer. At the time of his arrest, Khadr was fifteen years old and had suffered horrible wounds to his chest and to his face. Khadr was first taken to

Bagram prison where, by all accounts (including that of Damien Corsetti, an American interrogator at the facility), the young boy was repeatedly tortured. It should be noted that Omar's father, Ahmed, was thought to be in league with Osama bin Laden, and it remains unclear whether this was true or not (Ahmed was killed eight months after Omar's interrogations at Guantanamo Bay).

The interrogation occurs over a four-day period. Day 1 is entitled "Hope," and we see a teenage boy who initially is thrilled to see what he believes are diplomatic officials from his home country who have traveled to Cuba to help him. Jim Gould, who conducts the interrogation, is indeed a Canadian diplomat, but he works in the security wing that is affiliated with the CSIS. After some initial discussion in which Gould goes out of his way to put Omar at ease with offers of food and soda, it is evident that the only reason why Gould is there is to obtain a confession from him and garner whatever information he can get concerning Omar's father, mother, and sisters.

In addition to the visual images of the interrogation itself, one of the things that makes this film so powerful is that we also see the reactions of a host of people, often as they are watching the same segment of the interrogation as the viewer is. Some commentators are current or past members of the Canadian government, who are of one mind that they were wrong to rely on the diplomatic assurances of the US government. Another key individual is Michelle Shephard, a reporter for the *Toronto Star,* who did a story that showed through the use of satellite photographs that a wounded Omar, whose unconscious body is shown lying face down under a pile of rubble from the home leveled by US military forces, could never have killed the American medic. In addition, Shephard also points out that the medic was a member of the elite Delta Force and was serving in this capacity when coalition forces fired on this house where Al Qaeda forces—and Omar Khadr—were staying.

Day 2 is entitled "Fallout." Omar tells his interrogator that he has a dark secret to share with him and what he wants is assurances that he will be protected. The secret is that he lied to American interrogators at Bagram, and he explains that the reason why he did so is that he had to find some way to stop the horrible torture. Surprisingly enough, one of people who comes out looking the best in all this is Damien Corsetti, the large and intimidating interrogator who also plays a central role in *Taxi to the Dark Side,* who talks quite frankly of the manner in which he and his fellow interrogators turned into monsters and regularly tortured this fifteen-year-old kid, among others.

Day 3 is "Blackmail," and much of the conversation between Gould and Omar relates to the attempt to get information about Omar's family and the people they associate with. As before, Gould pretends to be worried about the well-being of his fellow Canadian citizens. He is not terribly convincing, and Omar tells him very little about their goings-on and whereabouts, further frustrating the interrogator. This day's session ends with Omar alone in the interrogation room praying.

Finally, Day 4 is titled "Failure." As the head of the Canada Centre for Victims of Torture notes, at this point Gould is getting increasingly more desperate, repeatedly accusing Omar of withholding information and the truth from him. Omar responds by simply saying what has been used as the title of this documentary: "you don't like the truth." The "truth" according to Canadian and American officials is that because Omar was in a house with Al Qaeda operatives, he was guilty by association, and these same authorities have also continued to accuse him of killing Speer. Omar maintains that his father placed him in the house but that he was not involved in any fighting.

What is more certain is that after Omar was arrested he was systematically tortured, and this is corroborated by Corsetti as well as some of his former cellmates. What others might disagree on is whether the interrogation conducted at Guantanamo is itself a form of psychological torture. In October 2010 Omar pleaded guilty to killing Speer and also signed a statement saying that he had extensive knowledge of his father's political activities. The Military Commission handed down an eight-year term, but he avoided the forty-year sentence sought by the US government. The film closes by noting that not once did Canadian officials ever press for his repatriation. Earlier in the film Corsetti, an unlikely one-man Greek chorus, drily notes that he seems to have more compassion for Omar than the Canadian government and the Canadian people. Few who watch this film will doubt this for a moment.

16

An Inconvenient Truth
(Davis Guggenheim, 2006)

Global warming will have an enormous impact on human rights, especially when people resort to violence over diminishing resources. Yet environmentalists and human rights practitioners and scholars are in the bad habit of talking right past one another—if they even speak to each other at all.

✳ ✳ ✳

An Inconvenient Truth is certainly the best known and most widely watched of all the documentaries included here. In essence, this film is in the nature of a slideshow presentation on global warming given by former vice president Al Gore. In his inimitable way, Gore is able to poke fun of his personal and political persona, but he is decidedly serious and extraordinarily effective when he presents an avalanche of empirical evidence of the greatly increased levels of CO_2 that have been pumped into the atmosphere—and the enormous problems that will ensue from this. Gore delivers a command performance, not only in delivering the frightening news of where our collective actions are leading us toward but also in detailing how, with personal and political will, this catastrophe could be avoided altogether.

What the film could have done better is to tie environmental issues and human rights issues together. Instead, there is a tendency in this film, and elsewhere, to treat global warming as merely an environmental problem when in fact it is a human rights problem of the highest order.

Also of Note

Manufactured Landscapes (Jennifer Baichwal, 2006)

The opening scene of this documentary is unlike anything else I have ever witnessed. For what seems an eternity, the camera is rolled at floor-level through a Chinese manufacturing plant, and through this the viewer begins to get some sense of the enormity of this operation. Much of *Manufactured Landscapes* is focused on the extraction industries and the effect this has on our own lives. As artist Edward Burtynsky rightly points out, all of the things that we use come from someplace, and all will eventually end up someplace after we have thrown these things away. Burtynsky's role is to introduce the viewers, for what is probably the first time, to where the material of their lives comes from: cell phones, computers, cars, and so on. He also spends a great deal of time in China simply because so much of what we use in our lives is produced there, and also because so much of what we throw away will be housed there in the form of mountains of trash.

Burning the Future: Coal in America (David Novack, 2008)

Perhaps the most startling scene in this fine, but extended, documentary concerning the ravages of mountaintop coal removal in West Virginia is when a group opposing such practices travels to New York City, where they have a rather unsuccessful meeting with officials on sustainable development at the United Nations. Given the fact that this is their first trip to New York, one would certainly understand if these mountain folks were rendered speechless by the overwhelming sights and sounds of Times Square. Instead, Maria Gunnoe, one of the community organizers on the trip, speaks for her group and many of those in her home community in West Virginia when she suddenly turns to the camera and angrily asks whether people realize the connection between the environmental devastation that she and her neighbors have been suffering from and the teeming lights all around them.

The Last Mountain (Bill Haney, 2011)

The Last Mountain tells much the same story (with some of the same activists in fact) as *Burning the Future*. Some 2,500 tons of explosives are used every day in mountaintop removal operations in Appalachia—the equivalent of the atomic bomb that was dropped on Hiroshima *every single week*. At the time this film was made, more than 500 mountains had already been destroyed, one million acres of forest had disappeared, and 2,000 miles of stream had been buried.

Although the local activists are truly inspiring, the star of this documentary is Bobby Kennedy Jr., who wears his celebrity status quite well. Kennedy is an environmental lawyer, and he makes repeated trips to the Coal River Mountain area to advocate for its residents. Although he is from a political family, he speaks quite candidly about the dysfunctions of American politics and the manner in which the interests of millionaires are repeatedly placed ahead of the well-being of young children, whether it is the unfortunate children in this West Virginia hollow, who go to school right next to a filthy coal silo, or his own asthmatic children, who cannot escape from the emissions of coal-burning plants.

17

Last Train Home
(Lixin Fan, 2009)

Much of the attention given to Chinese cinema has focused on feature films such as Raise the Red Lantern *or* To Live. *As outstanding as these films are, one should not overlook many of the documentaries that are coming out of China that expose such things as the exploitation of the country's workers, the frightening levels of environmental degradation, and the epidemic political corruption at all levels of government.*

✳ ✳ ✳

This documentary works on two different, but related, levels. The first involves a husband and wife who work in a sweatshop in a dirty, industrial city in China, who, along with 130 million laborers, return to their home town to celebrate the New Year. Home includes a teenage daughter (Qin) and adolescent son (Yang), who have been raised by their grandparents for the past thirteen years, and the first (and seemingly only) thing that the parents can ask their children—even after a full year's absence—concerns the children's grades in school, which are never deemed to be good enough.

Thus, much of the film chronicles the enormous tension between two parents who think they are sacrificing their own well-being in order to give their children a chance at a university education and advancement, on the one hand, and two children who are almost complete strangers to their parents, having only spent a few weeks each year with them. While what ensues is predictable enough, it is not easy to watch. Qin quits school and moves to another city to work as a seamstress and then in a disco bar. It is not clear whether she is doing this because she is not a great student, because of the financial independence that it gives to her, or because it is her only means of establishing that she is her own person. In one of the most bizarre scenes near the end of the film, Qin travels back home with her parents and intentionally drops an F-bomb, which sends her father into a rage. But it is clear that his anger, and hers as well, did not arise from this one utterance. Instead, it comes from years and years of separation and estrangement.

The larger issue of migration from rural areas to industrial sites serves as a backdrop for this family drama. What the viewer sees is a China that is terribly inefficient, desperately poor, and seemingly ready to burst apart at the seams—just like Qin and her parents.

18

Jung (War) in the Land of the Mujaheddin
(Fabrizio Lazzaretti and Alberto Vendemmiati, 2001)

Absent the events of September 11, 2001, and the subsequent US-led invasion of Afghanistan, it is unlikely that the next documentary, released a year before the September 11 attacks, would have attracted even the slightest bit of attention in the West, or anywhere else for that matter.

✳ ✳ ✳

Jung tells us a part of the story of the decades-long suffering of the Afghan people. What we see is the systematic oppression of women by the Taliban (not that their enemy, the Northern Alliance, are all that much better); young children who have lost limbs due to land mine explosions; and soldiers who have fought for years and years. What the viewer now knows is that there will be more, much more, of this to come for at least another decade.

Despite all this, *Jung* is a hopeful story, or at least somewhat hopeful. The protagonist is Gino Strada, an Italian doctor who is attempting to build a hospital. This would be difficult enough in an impoverished country like Afghanistan, but his plan is to place it where it would do the most good and alleviate the greatest amount of suffering, namely, a war zone. In this venture he is joined by Kate Rowlands, a British nurse, and Ettore Mo, an Italian journalist. The fact that Strada et al. succeed in establishing and staffing a well-functioning hospital is remarkable enough. But he is by no means content with this miracle and the film closes with Strada about to embark on a seemingly even more quixotic project: establishing another hospital in a Taliban-controlled area of the country.

Also of Note

Triage: Dr. James Orbinski's Humanitarian
Dilemma (Patrick Reed, 2008)

It is not clear what Dr. James Orbinski's humanitarian dilemma happens to be. Orbinski is the former director of Doctors Without Borders, and he currently is the head of Dignitas, which focuses on AIDS prevention and treatment in the Third World. Orbinski certainly has seen more than his fair share of human suffering and this documentary recounts some of what he has experienced. The viewer goes with Orbinski as he visits sites in Somalia and Rwanda where he had worked previously, during the time the former suffered from a terrible famine and the latter genocide. During the course of these travels, Orbinski recounts events and meets up with old friends, in some instances people whose lives he had saved.

Orbinski is a remarkable and courageous man. He is also a reflective person who simply refuses to live in a world where there is so much human suffering. So he does his part—actually, vastly more than his part—by leaving his family in Canada and putting himself in the line of fire in some of the worst hellholes imaginable. He is also writing his memoirs, in part to explain these horrors to those who have not witnessed them but seemingly also as a way to make sense of them to himself.

Living in Emergency: Stories of Doctors Without Borders (Mark Hopkins, 2008)

In many ways this documentary comes across as an infomercial for Médecins Sans Frontières (Doctors Without Borders). The viewer tags along with several physicians working under hellish conditions in Liberia and the Democratic Republic of the Congo. All are young, determined, and smart. Some are on their first (but maybe their last) mission, while others might best be described as "lifers" who have been with the organization for quite some period of time and who, in all likelihood, will continue to fight the good fight. MSF operates in some seventy countries, so the film makes no pretense of covering the entirety of its work. But one has a strong sense that it would not matter much where the filming took place. We would see the same thing: doctors operating in a war zone attempting to save the lives of at least some of those caught up in the deadly crossfire, all the while never having much to work with, sometimes not even something as rudimentary as clean surgical gloves.

The film closes by pointing out that MSF treats some 10 million patients a day—in a world where some 2 billion have no access to any form of medical treatment. The problem, then, is not only the existence of war. Rather, it is a world where the promise of a right to health care is denied to many.

19

Pushing the Elephant
(Beth Davenport and Elizabeth Mandel, 2010)

Here is a pop quiz. What country has experienced the highest levels of political violence? Is it the Sudan? Afghanistan? Iran? Columbia? Iraq? The correct answer is the Democratic Republic of the Congo, where in the past decade and a half between 4 and 5 million people have been killed in a civil war that now also involves several neighboring states. The following documentary is about a remarkable woman who was one of the few lucky ones able to escape this hellhole.

* * *

Pushing the Elephant is a documentary that tells the remarkable story of Rose Mapendo and her ten children, Congolese Tutsis who went through hell before they eventually were granted refugee status in the United States. Rose forgives but she does not forget, and she has now dedicated her life to assisting displaced and unfortunate people. This is not easy to do when you have ten children and two grandchildren to raise, but what keeps her going is her overwhelming passion.

One of the central stories in this film is Rose's reunification with her daughter Nangabire after thirteen years. Nangabire had been living with her grandparents in another part of the Democratic Republic of the Congo when Rose and the other children fled the country (her husband had already been killed in the fighting). Much of the film follows this young woman as she is introduced into a completely foreign culture—and at this juncture an equally foreign family, with their skateboards, bikes, basketball hoops, and those funny things they use to put food in their mouths.

One of Rose's goals is to return to the DRC, despite the enormous danger that she would face upon her return. That she is able to do this is no surprise to the viewer, who would readily believe that this woman is capable of doing anything. As Rose says at one point in the film, everyone suffers in war, but especially women. It is only as the story in the film unfolds that the viewer gets a true sense of the depth of her suffering, as Rose describes something that happened to her in prison that is akin to that decision made by the protagonist in *Sophie's Choice*.

20

Pray the Devil Back to Hell
(Gini Reticker, 2008)

Liberia and Sierra Leone are two neighboring West African states that suffered through years of conflict through the 1990s and into the early years of the new century. Fortunately, since then, both countries have now achieved peace and a certain level of security, and the following documentary tells the unique and inspiring story of the vital role that a group of women in Liberia played in bringing the fighting to an end.

* * *

The story told in the film is quite simple. A group called the Women of Liberia Mass Action for Peace starts a campaign to end the conflict in their homeland. They all dress in white t-shirts to symbolize peace, and the group is somehow able to convince government and rebel officials to begin talks in Ghana for a ceasefire. A contingent of these women travel to Ghana as well, and after the peace talks stall and appear doomed, they take it upon themselves to prevent the men from being able to leave the room where the negotiations are taking place. Soon thereafter, a peace agreement is reached and the horrible fighting in Liberia ends.

Although perhaps not as dramatic as the women in Aristophanes' play *Lysistrata* who go about ending a war by withholding sex, or as visible as the Mothers of the Plaza de Mayo in Argentina who wear diapers on their heads as symbols of their lost children, what the Women of Liberia Mass Action for Peace is able to achieve is nothing short of miraculous. Equally impressive is the manner in which Muslim and Christian women bonded together in this effort. In addition to playing a central role in ending the Liberian conflict, the movement also helped lead to the election of Ellen Johnson Sirleaf as president of the country, the first female head of state on the African continent and a 2011 Nobel Peace Prize winner. In the end, *Pray the Devil Back to Hell* provides enormous inspiration that there can be another way.

21

Enemies of the People
(Rob Lemkin and Thet Sambath, 2009)

The horrible genocide in Cambodia from 1975 to 1979 was portrayed in the feature film The Killing Fields *(FF-5). The documentary* Enemies of the People *moves the story ahead several decades and shows one journalist's attempt to preserve and document this tragic period of Cambodian and world history. What also plays a central role in the film is the special UN tribunal for Cambodia that has brought some of the worst human rights offenders to trial.*

✳ ✳ ✳

Few films will send a chill down your spine in the manner of *Enemies of the People*. Thet Sambath is a Cambodian journalist who leaves his lovely family each weekend in search of those responsible for directing and carrying out that country's genocide from 1975 to1979. Sambath's goal is to uncover and document this part of Cambodia's history before it disappears into oblivion. All that he brings with him is a small video camera with which he records interviews, mainly with low-level operatives and oftentimes at locales where the killings had taken place. *Can you show me where you killed people?* And Mr. Suon and Mr. Khoun, two former members of the Khmer Rouge, dutifully point to the ditches where they systematically carried out their tasks, usually at dusk, with thirty or forty bodies stuffed into each ditch. In one incredible scene, they even demonstrate how they went about their business. Although troubled enough by what they have done that they would even speak to Sambath, still, of all these deaths there is only one that seems to stand out for them, and this involves the murder of a beautiful young woman.

What makes Sambath's project even more incredible is his decision to befriend Nuon Chea, known as Brother 2, who along with Pol Pot led the Khmer Rouge. As the film progresses, Sambath describes his own personal history. His father and brother were both killed by the Khmer Rouge and his mother was forced to marry a Khmer Rouge official. He does not tell Nuon Chea any of this. Instead, he slowly and painstakingly builds his relationship with this pathetic old man and in many ways serves as a surrogate son. Sambath states that over the years there were many instances when Nuon Chea would not be able to recall anything from his past. Yet the viewer has a strong sense that Nuon Chea remembers everything but is incapable of coming to terms with the genocidal nightmare that he was a key figure in creating. Still, towards the end of the film, as Nuon Chea is about to be placed under arrest by the UN Special Court for Cambodia, and after Sambath describes his own victimization, Nuon Chea tells him how deeply sorry he is for Sambath's suffering. With respect to the Cambodian people themselves, Nuon Chea never wavers in his belief in the rightness of the Khmer cause and the imperative of eliminating the "enemies of the people."

At the outset of the film Sambath states that his project is for all Cambodian people. This is the only palpable error in this film because his brave efforts are in fact for *all* people.

Also of Note

Brother Number One (Annie Goldson, 2011)

This documentary takes up where *Enemies of the People* leaves off. The film is organized around the first trial of the Extraordinary Chambers in the Courts of Cambodia. The defendant, Duch, is the former warden of the most notorious prison camp, S-21. Duch now professes to be a Christian, and he tries to deflect his own responsibility by taking a cue from Eichmann and claiming that he was merely a cog in the larger Khmer Rouge killing project. The tribunal has what is known as a civil process, which allows victims, broadly defined, to testify. The victim the viewer comes to know and deeply admire is Rob Hamill, whose older brother Kerry had been tortured and killed by Khmer Rouge operatives after his sailboat had mistakenly gone into Cambodian waters. It was years before this information was released, and it led to the decimation of the Hamill family.

Given the incredible suffering by the Cambodian people, one could be critical of all this attention to one of the few Westerners who were victimized by Khmer Rouge. Rob Hamill oftentimes seems to feel this same way, and he is forever both grateful and apologetic for the many efforts of others to assist him. But there is a wonderful line in the film about the "cry of all humanity," and the point is that the Hamill family's suffering is no greater—but also no less—than that of the Cambodian people.

22

Presumed Guilty
(Roberto Hernández and Geoffrey Smith, 2008)

Rather than preventing crime and defending freedoms, all too often the criminal justice system is where violations of civil and political rights take place. What we see in the following film is the nightmare of Mexican "justice."

✳ ✳ ✳

In the United States and other countries, criminal defendants enjoy a presumption of innocence—at least in theory. However, in Mexico there is a presumption of guilt for those who have been arrested by the police. This harrowing film follows the fortunes (and misfortunes) of Antonio Zuniga, better known as Tono, who at the outset of the film is attempting to overturn a prior conviction for homicide. It is quite fair to say that if Tono had never met the filmmakers/lawyers who became involved in this case, he would still be rotting away in a Mexican prison.

As the movie points out, approximately 95 percent of the verdicts in Mexico are convictions, and in 92 percent of the cases there is no physical evidence. In Tono's case, he was convicted by an eyewitness who, in two previous interviews with the police, had never even mentioned Tono. It was only in his third interview with the police that Tono is referred to for the first time. This is all the police needed to place him under arrest and all a judge needed to convict him and hand down a sentence of twenty years. This is where the film begins and the viewer is hopeful that the hiring of a trial attorney for Tono and the presence of a film crew will make some kind of difference, particularly when the police commander is obviously lying; the eyewitness subsequently recants having seen Tono at the shooting; the presiding judge (the same judge as in the first trial) is more of a stenographer than an officer of the court; and the prosecutor in the case states that she will deliver her closing argument to the judge on a floppy disc.

Yet, even with all this, Tono is convicted a second time. It would be tempting to say that his trial had a number of irregularities, but these things are not irregular in Mexican courts. One of the most surprising revelations is that the defendant's attorney cannot conduct a cross-examination of the prosecution's witnesses. Instead, this is something that the defendant himself has to do, as the viewer watches as Tono struggles mightily to represent himself, with his lawyer beside him, neutered in the proceedings. The cross-exam probably wouldn't matter anyway because what seems to matter is what the police have already placed in the defendant's file.

Tono seems like an earnest young man, with a lovely wife and child, and the prospect of him serving two decades in prison for a crime that a host of people (who can verify his whereabouts at the time of the killing) claim he did not commit is quite difficult to swallow. However, his conviction is finally overturned on appeal when the filmmakers are able to offer their video of the trial as proof of the mendacity of the investigating officers and the purported eyewitness. Yet while the viewer most certainly breathes a sigh of relief that Tono can go home and return to the life he had been living, one also wonders about the levels of gross injustice in the Mexican judicial system.

Also of Note

Reportero (Bernardo Ruiz, 2012)

Reportero is another outstanding documentary about human rights violations in Mexico, in this case regarding the government's deep involvement in the country's brutal drug trade. What the viewer sees is the inner workings of *Zeta Weekly*, a newspaper that since 1980 has shined a light on government corruption. During this time, editors and reporters for the newspaper have been targeted for assassination and several have been murdered. Yet, like our narrator, Sergio Haro, these brave men and women work to expose the truth because of their abiding commitment to the protection of human rights.

23

Taxi to the Dark Side

(Alex Gibney, 2007)

The war on terrorism serves as the backdrop for the next two films. In both cases what the viewer sees is that under the banner of fighting terror the US government readily engages in terror itself. Taxi, which won an Academy Award for Best Documentary, does this by focusing on the death of a single Afghan citizen, while Ghosts uses the atrocities at Abu Ghraib as a means of excoriating American policies and practices.

✻ ✻ ✻

Dilawar is a young Afghan taxi driver who was taken into custody by US officials on December 1, 2002, and who was dead five days later, the consequence of the repeated torture he had been subjected to while in detention. Dilawar was the second Afghan to be murdered in this manner within a week, and although the death certificate listed the cause of death as homicide, the initial Army "investigation" had concluded that he had died of natural causes. A short time later, Carolyn Wood, the chief investigator in this matter, was awarded the Bronze Star. However, after *New York Times* reporters Carlotta Gall and Tim Golden looked into Dilawar's death, a second investigation was carried out, resulting in several American servicemen being court-martialed and sent to prison.

Not a single military commander or political leader has been touched by any of this. Rather, like the subsequent abuses at Abu Ghraib, the government claimed that Dilawar's murder at the Bagram Prison was the result of a few bad apples. This excuse ignores both the grossly insufficient training of these interrogators and the fact that the brutal interrogation methods were tacitly ordered by higher-ups in the chain of command, going all the way up to the office of the vice president.

The interrogators make a convincing case that they were simply doing their job. One of them, Damien Corsetti (who also plays a prominent role in the documentary *You Don't Like the Truth*) calmly explains that he received all of five or six hours of training before he and other American teenagers were thrust in a position of having to obtain useful intelligence from the thousands of Afghanis who were brought to Bagram. Corsetti explains that there were many instances when he was absolutely certain that the person he was interrogating was innocent of having any links with the Taliban, but this did not matter. Rather, like the others, he was expected to put this person through the wringer—which invariably consisted of very loud music, sleep deprivation, and getting in the face of the prisoner, even if it was all just gibberish. At one point, Corsetti relates how his interrogations oftentimes consisted of nothing more than shouting out the ingredients in a box of Kellogg's Frosted Flakes cereal that happened to be available. However, what was most useful, at least to the interrogators, was having all prisoners shackled with their hands over their heads and forced to stand for days on end. And while in this position, the American interrogators would beat them mercilessly. In fact, Dilawar was so badly beaten that his legs were later described as being "pulperized," and medical officials say that if he had lived both of his legs would have required amputation.

One of the great strengths of the film is that it provides both the political and legal backdrop that led to this criminal lunacy. A good deal of time is spent on the "torture memos" written by John Yoo and Alberto Gonzalez, which re-defined the meaning of torture so that it was limited to death or pain that would lead to severe organ failure. Anything short of this was not torture—or so the US government would now claim. Taking this Alice-in-Wonderland approach a step further, the memos took the position that when exercising his commander-in-chief powers, the president is not bound by either domestic or international law that prohibits torture. And as perhaps the last straw, the US Congress subsequently passed legislation that provides an amnesty to top political and military leaders for any war crimes committed in the war on terror. This amnesty does not cover those fighting on the front line, the soldiers we get to meet in this film. *Taxi to the Dark Side* covers a lot of ground. Not only are we informed of the brutal treatment afforded detainees at Bagram in Afghanistan and

Abu Ghraib in Iraq but also the US military base at Guantanamo Bay, Cuba, where the government's cheery attitude goes well beyond the surreal. The public relations people who provide guided tours to reporters talk about such things as the excellent dental treatment the detainees receive, and how prison cells come equipped with board games such as checkers—although it is not clear who the detainee would play against since he is in solitary confinement.

One of the great moral voices in the film is that of the British national Moazzam Begg, who like the overwhelming majority of detainees at Guantanamo was not arrested on the battlefield. His perfect English notwithstanding, Begg was held for years, and he talks quite candidly about assuming that he would never be released and that he would die while in detention. Begg's offense seems to be that he witnessed the treatment afforded Dilawar and, in the eyes of the US government, this made him a very dangerous man. On the positive side, I suppose, at the time the film was released "only" thirty-seven Afghan and Iraq prisoners had been murdered while in American custody. But there is still plenty of opportunity. As of 2007, more than 83,000 prisoners remained in detention. Like Dilawar, would they also be beaten and killed?

24

Ghosts of Abu Ghraib
(Rory Kennedy, 2007)

Ghosts of Abu Ghraib *can be seen as a fitting companion to* Taxi to the Dark Side.

✳ ✳ ✳

Ghosts of Abu Ghraib opens with a short black-and-white film from the Milgram experiment. For those not familiar with this study, subjects in New Haven, Connecticut, were instructed to ask a person in another room certain questions. Each time a wrong answer was given the person was supposed to press a lever that would administer an electric shock to this person, and with each wrong answer the voltage would increase. (The voice at the other end who played the person being punished was a part of the experiment, and no one was actually being harmed.) The Milgram experiment was deeply disturbing because so many people were willing to administer the highest levels of "punishment" (450 volts) even when they could hear this person's desperate cries for help.

The conclusion to be drawn from this is that people will not question orders so long as the person issuing commands says he will take full responsibility. As Milgram comments in the film, if people are willing to follow the commands of complete strangers, imagine what they will be willing to do when they are ordered to act by their political leaders. But Milgram and others do not really need to wonder what will happen in a real-world situation because we have more than enough evidence that otherwise ordinary law-abiding citizens are capable of being ordered to carry out all kinds of atrocities. Didn't the Holocaust already prove this?

Add Abu Ghraib as another sad chapter. Although the Bush administration did everything in its power to separate itself from these atrocities after the images were shown on *Sixty Minutes II* and immediately displayed the world over, like *Taxi*, the present film makes a compelling case that the military interrogators at this former Iraqi prison were simply following the wishes and implicit orders of their superiors. Rory Kennedy, who directs this film, examines not only the "torture memos" that the president's legal advisors had drawn up, but the manner in which General Geoffrey Miller was transferred from the US military base at Guantanamo Bay, Cuba, to Abu Ghraib, with the intention of introducing harsher interrogation techniques—torture— against Iraqi detainees. Soon thereafter, General Sanchez, at that time the top US military commander in Iraq, issued an order approving the use of these techniques, although he rescinded this order a month later. What all seem to agree on is that complete confusion reigned.

The film also points out that Charles Graner, the ringleader of these abuses, was issued a commendation for his outstanding work well *after* his superiors knew of his role in stripping detainees, putting woman's panties on their head, stacking prisoners in a pyramid on top of one another, forcing naked Iraqi men to masturbate, and so on—but I suppose you have also seen these pictures. And what also has to be said is that the very worst abuses were not photographed.

One of the more important features of this film is learning how these photos saw the light of day. Serviceman Joseph Darby describes how he knew that Graner was fond of shooting pictures, and one day he asked to see some of his photographs. The first CD he looked at consisted of shots Graner had taken of various places in Iraq, much in the nature of photos that any tourist might take. But the second CD Darby looked at contained many of the terrible images that all of us are now familiar with. In a singular act of bravery, Darby went to inform his superiors. He met with top military brass, only to find out that sitting in the waiting room were Graner and many of the others involved in the Abu Ghraib scandal. Giving his superiors the benefit of the doubt, Darby speculates that this was simply a foul-up. More sinister, perhaps, is when Donald Rumsfeld mentions Darby by name while testifying before Congress. Ostensibly, this was done to praise the young man, but anyone who has served in the military knows full well the danger that "snitches" face, even (perhaps especially) snitches who are reporting war crimes.

The military has carried out all sorts of studies and investigations of the Abu Ghraib incident. However, as one commentator in the film points out, not one of them looked up the chain of command. Rather, all looked down, and most carried the party-line espoused by the Schlesinger Commission (named after former Secretary of

Defense James Schlesinger) that this was nothing more than "Animal House on the night shift." Kennedy shows here that the true Animal House was in the White House.

Also of Note

Standard Operating Procedure (Errol Morris, 2008)

Errol Morris has a special knack for blending the real with the unreal. The goal of his film *Standard Operating Procedure* is to challenge the notion that the well-known images from Abu Ghraib tell all that actually happened there. Thus, this is a film about other media images. Morris is certainly correct in positing that images can lie. However, what he never grapples with is why the viewer should believe the images and explanations he provides here any more than those they already have seen from Abu Ghraib.

Certainly, Morris has scored a coup in publicly airing the voices of those we think we know from the images themselves—especially the infamous Lynndie England, perhaps better known as the woman holding the dog collar. Yet, so much of the film involves these actors (and this term is used purposely) trying to explain that their actions were not nearly as cruel and sadistic as the images would suggest. Much like his earlier film *The Fog of War*, which is an extended interview with Robert McNamara, secretary of defense during the Vietnam War, one would wish that Morris would not be content to let his subject ramble on in self-justification. One last point involves the artistic quality to Morris's work in *Standard Operating Procedure*. Although he uses this same technique in his other movies, in the present film one gets a sense that this is being used to distract the viewer more than anything else, as if Morris' dazzling display will somehow push aside the images of Abu Ghraib already seared in our collective minds.

25

Crude

(Joe Berlinger, 2009)

It is no great secret that many multinational corporations (MNCs) wield an enormous amount of economic and political power. However, one of the great concerns of human rights practitioners and scholars is the degree to which MNCs are oftentimes left unregulated in their operations in developing countries. This is due to the fact that the host state is either unable or unwilling to regulate corporate practices and that home states have shown little willingness to protect against the extraterritorial abuses committed by their own corporations. As a result of all this, as the next film shows, citizens in developing states have suffered greatly due to the unregulated practices of Western MNCs.

*** *** ***

There are not many documentaries that engage the viewer in the nature of a political thriller, but *Crude* certainly does. The story line is fairly straightforward. Texaco (which merged with Chevron in 2001) is an American-based corporation that had drilled and operated in the Amazon region of Ecuador for many years, before selling its interest to a state-run operation. As a result of environmental malfeasance, an area the size of the state of Rhode Island has been turned into what has been called the "Amazon Chernobyl." The issue the film explores is who is responsible for this environmental nightmare—Texaco/Chevron or the Ecuadoran government—and some of the most intriguing aspects of the film involve judicial hearings that are literally carried out in the jungle.

Crude is also in the nature of a "buddy flick." The odd couple here consists of Steven Donziger, a loud, relentless, overbearing, and almost stereotypical American lawyer, and Pablo Fajardo, a quiet but equally dogged young Ecuadoran lawyer from very modest means whose brother was assassinated at the outset of the litigation in what appears to be an attempt to silence Pablo.

Despite the overwhelming odds against them, the dynamic duo hit upon some good fortune. One is that Fajardo was part of a feature story in *Vanity Fair* magazine (with Leonardo DiCaprio adorning the cover) dealing with environmental themes. Pablo was also awarded the prestigious Goldman Award for environmentalism. And finally, more fame enters into both of their lives when they are able to convince Trudie Styler, the wife of musician Sting and an ardent environmentalist in her own right, to visit the site and take up this cause.

Notwithstanding the feel-good quality of the film, what remains unclear is whether liability against Texaco/Chevron will ever be established, and if it is, whether victims will ever be compensated. In early 2011, the Ecuadoran judge who heard the case ruled against Texaco/Chevron and awarded monetary damages of $8 billion. However, the corporation has already appealed this decision, and in all likelihood the litigation will remain in limbo for years and years to come. Meanwhile, tens of thousands of indigenous people in this region continue to be poisoned by land and water that are saturated with environmental poisons.

26

Better This World
(Katie Galloway and Kelly Duane de la Vega, 2011)

One of the reasons for using the documentary Better This World *in a college class is that students can relate to the two idealist protagonists in the film. What they see on film is what many already feel. They think the world is too corrupt, too unequal, too callous, too money-driven, and too violent—but they are at a complete loss in terms of how to go about changing things.*

✳ ✳ ✳

This absorbing documentary tells the story of David McKay and Bradley Crowder, two likeable young men from Midland, Texas, who are prosecuted by the US government for planning terrorist activities at the 2008 Republic National Convention in Minneapolis. How could two idealistic boys like this become terrorists—or, more accurately, be considered by their own government to be terrorists? Two words: Brandon Darby.

Darby is a government snitch who posed as a self-styled radical and approached the younger McKay and Crowder and then egged the two on, repeatedly telling them that violence was a necessary component to fighting injustices. Initially, McKay and Crowder were both dubious about this. However, after arriving in Minneapolis with Darby and a few others and being subjected to all kinds of police harassment, including the stripping of their rental van, the two made the grave mistake of buying materials to make Molotov cocktails. In the early part of the film the viewer gets a strong sense of the political passion of David and Bradley. The latter recalls watching the "shock and awe" military campaign at the outset of the war in Iraq and feeling helpless to stop the human slaughter. He responded by wearing an antiwar tee-shirt to school— remember, this is Midland, Texas—and he soon found common cause with David McKay. Two liberals in a sea of red.

This is when Brandon Darby comes into the picture. Darby certainly had liberal credentials, particularly his work founding Common Ground in New Orleans to assist the victims of Katrina, and he also worked on the case of the Angola 3 (documented in *In the Land of the Free*). It is not clear when Darby decided to become a government snitch or what prompted this. His ex-girlfriend explains that Darby always had to be "the man," and spying on others seems to fill this psychic need. But Darby did much more than spy. As a former FBI agent explains, in the old days government informants simply watched and listened, but they were not allowed to talk, meaning they were not allowed to coax others into committing crimes. This has changed since September 11 and Darby is a perfect example of this.

In one particularly illuminating sequence, the viewer sees a series of text messages sent from Darby to McKay in the early morning hours, constantly prompting the latter to take some kind of action. Beyond buying the bomb material, the two boys (and at the time they were boys) never do take action, but government agents soon swoop in and arrest both of them on a myriad of domestic terrorism charges. The prosecutor tells them that if they make use of their constitutionally protected right to go to trial and are found guilty, they will receive at least ten years in prison. Unfortunately, the government's use of informants will not be placed on trial, only their own acts of "terrorism." Bradley takes a two-year plea, but David is only offered a seven-year deal and he decides to go to trial.

The case results in a hung jury, but the government decides to go for a new trial. In the period before the second trial, the viewer sees David back in Midland with his girlfriend and his family. They have wrenching conversations about whether he should simply take the government's new plea agreement, which he eventually does: four years for obstruction of justice. One of the more interesting aspects of the case is that David had made the claim that it had been Brandon Darby's idea to make Molotov cocktails, but this is not completely accurate, and the government was prepared to call Bradley at the second trial as a witness for the prosecution. One of the reasons why David took the new offer was to spare his friend from having to testify against him.

Yet, while Molotov cocktails might not have been Brandon's ideas, what is clear from the film is the manner in which Darby controlled and manipulated these two young boys. The FBI agents interviewed in the film make the claim that none of this constitutes entrapment. However, if this isn't entrapment it is difficult to understand what would be.

Also of Note

If a Tree Falls: A Story of the Earth Liberation Front (Marshall Curry and Sam Cullman, 2011)

This film tells the story of Daniel McGowan, who grew up in a middle-class neighborhood on Long Island with nary a political thought in his head. By a series of seemingly chance encounters and luck—both good and bad, I suppose—he eventually moved to Eugene, Oregon, and while there became a member of the Earth Liberation Front. As such he participated in a number of ELF torchings, which resulted in such things as the burning of an SUV lot. Like *Better This World,* the film raises the question of how far one should go when acting on behalf of one's deeply held political beliefs. Or as one ELF member comments, if 95 percent of the country's forests have already been cut down, is it really such a radical idea to take direct action in an attempt to save the remaining 5 percent?

Bidder 70 (Beth Gage and George Gage, 2012)

The reader might remember an event from a few years back when a young man "bought" various parcels of federal land in Utah that were being auctioned off by the Department of the Interior in the waning weeks of the George W. Bush administration. This would not be unusual except for the fact that the bidder—bidder 70, to be exact—had no money to pay for it. Instead, in a glorious

moment of moral clarity, Tim DeChristopher decided, apparently on the spot after he had errone-
ously been given access to the auction, that the thing he must do was to throw a monkey wrench into
the proceedings to stop the sale of some of the most pristine land in the continent that was about
to be sold to private concerns for gas and oil drilling. And this is exactly what DeChristopher did.

What the film shows is the manner in which the government pursued the case against him,
even after the Obama administration acknowledged that the auction itself violated federal law. After
more than a dozen postponements, DeChristopher was brought to trial, but the presiding judge ruled
that he could not offer the defense that he had acted for the greater public good. Thoreau spent a
night in jail for his civil disobedience. DeChristopher was given a two-year sentence

27
The Pinochet Case
(Patricio Guzmán, 2001)

*General Pinochet, the former Chilean dictator (1973–1990) was been mentioned previously in
our discussion of* Missing *(FF-3). His name is now synonymous with the "Pinochet principle,"
under which any state can bring to trial those who directed or carried out gross and systematic
human rights violations or violations of peremptory norms (such as torture). The following
film provides an insightful account of this case and its aftermath. Unfortunately, a short time
after these legal proceedings in the United Kingdom, the International Court of Justice ruled
that while former heads of state (such as Pinochet) can be tried in this manner, present heads of
states (and other government ministers) cannot legally be held to account in the domestic courts
of another country; such measures could only be conducted through international institutions,
such as the newly created International Criminal Court (ICC).*

✷ ✷ ✷

Patricio Guzmán has produced several important films on the 1973 military coup in
Chile and its aftermath, most notably his three part series *The Battle of Chile*. The present documentary is his finest work, and it begins in the desert in northern Chile where
family members of those "disappeared" by the Pinochet dictatorship are attempting
to locate the remains of their loved ones. This work goes slowly and unsteadily, but
each new body provides some measure of closure, while at the same time adding yet
another piece of evidence of the brutality of this regime. Pointing to a picture of her
son, who was only eighteen when he was disappeared, one mother announces to the
camera: "this is Pinochet's government." Only the most hardened or most ideologi-
cal would doubt this. The film presents the legal case against General Pinochet. The
proceedings against Pinochet began a few years after he was removed from office via
a referendum; it does not commence in Chile but in Spain, where Spanish magistrate
Baltasar Garzón lays the groundwork for his extradition based on the legal principle

of "universal jurisdiction." The spark that would create an international furor occurs a few years after this when Pinochet went on a shopping trip to Great Britain, where he was placed under arrest per Garzón's extradition request. At first, Garzón sought the extradition on behalf of Spanish citizens who had been Pinochet's victims, but this was later extended to include all victims—Chilean and non-Chilean alike.

Guzmán does a splendid job of not only distilling the arguments in the case but constructing the narrative like a legal thriller. There are interviews with Pinochet supporters, as well as those working toward his extradition and trial. Certainly the most insightful interviews are those who were victimized by the military dictatorship. In one amazing sequence, a mother talks about the torture she endured while in captivity, while her daughter, who is about her age at the time she was abducted, looks on with a mixture of curiosity and horror. This is the first time that her mother had spoken of these events. Her daughter admits that she knew that some terrible things had happened, but that she did not want to delve too deeply and know too much, for fear of offending her mother but also fearing her own reaction. Perhaps much the same can be said of Chilean society. There is a desire to know about the horrors of the Pinochet years—but not know too much. On the other hand, there are still some, such as former British Prime Minister Margaret Thatcher, who think of Pinochet as a hero for his fight against communism and his support in the Falkland Islands war.

In the end, the British High Court ruled that Pinochet could be extradited to Spain. However, the Home Secretary (Jack Straw) decided that the General was too weak, mentally and physically, to withstand the rigors of a trial. He was allowed to fly home, where he was greeted as a hero, at least by the military and political leaders who met him at the airport, and where, miraculously enough, he bounds out of the wheelchair he had confined himself to in England.

But Pinochet is no longer able to get off scot-free. In one of the most noteworthy developments, Chilean Judge Juan Guzmán not only interrogates Pinochet and subjects him to house arrest but visits the locations where torture had been carried out, including the infamous Grimaldi camp. At the end, things come full circle. A new statue of Salvador Allende is erected outside the Ministry of Justice at the same time that Pinochet, the man who headed the military coup that ousted him, is spending the last years of his life defending himself and desperately trying to stay out of prison.

Also of Note

Carla's List (Marcel Schüpbach, 2006)
Milosevic on Trial (Michael Christoffersen, 2007)
War Don Don (Rebecca Richman Cohen, 2010)
The Reckoning (Pamela Yates, 2009)
My Neighbor, My Killer (Anne Aghion, 2009)

There has been a spate of documentaries about the work of the regional human rights tribunals and the ICC itself. *Carla's List* provides an intimate and somewhat flattering view of the work of Carla Del Ponte, who at the time the film was made served as the chief prosecutor for the International Criminal Tribunal for the former Yugoslavia (ICTY). Former Serbian President Slobodan Milošević remains the only sitting head of state ever to be brought to trial for international war crimes, and the documentary *Milosevic on Trial,* which is drawn from over 2,000 hours of the court proceedings against him before the ICTY, provides the best video account of this. The War is Over—*War Don Don.* The reference in the title is to the bloody civil conflict in Sierra Leone from 1991 to2002. With this as a backdrop, the film's focus is the Special Court that was created by the United Nations and the government of Sierra Leone and its prosecution of Issa Sesay, one of the leaders of the rebel group Revolutionary United Front (RUF), which sought to overthrow the government. *The Reckoning: The Battle for the International Criminal Court* is a documentary that almost comes across as a primer, if not something almost resembling an infomercial, on the ICC. Finally, focusing on one small hamlet in the Rwandan countryside, *My Neighbor, My Killer* tells the story of the victims and perpetrators of the 1994 genocide and the role played by the gacaca courts—almost in the nature of neighborhood gatherings—in attempting to bring justice and closure to this country.

28

Budrus

(Julia Bacha, 2009)

In order to protect its own national security, Israel has built a security wall around much of the Occupied Territories. For many Palestinians this has had severe consequences, separating families and preventing people from living and farming on ancestral lands. This action not only constitutes a violation of the laws of war in the sense that it has had a detrimental effect on civilian populations, but it represents a violation of international human rights standards as well.

✳ ✳ ✳

In its own quiet way, *Budrus* is an awe-inspiring documentary that tells the saga of how a nonviolent protest movement in this small Palestinian town (population 1,500) in the Occupied Territories was ultimately able to force Israeli officials to re-direct the construction of the Israeli security wall. The protagonist of the film and the conscience behind the movement is Ayed Morrar, a father of a brood of children, who, like many Palestinian men, has spent his fair share of time over the years in Israeli prisons. For reasons that are probably not even clear to him, Ayed rejects violence and he displays a calm demeanor and adopts a commonsense approach to matters, traits that seem to elude so many in this part of the world.

Yet, notwithstanding his physical and spiritual grace, Ayed has a steely resolve that is not to be underestimated. The filmmaker's use of maps helps to make matters clear. What the viewer sees is the manner in which the Israeli security wall veers inside the Green Line—the 1967 armistice line—and as a result takes away land owned by

Palestinians. In the case of Budrus, the wall would result in the removal of hundreds of olive trees that are the lifeblood of the community. In an early organizational meeting, Ayed tells his fellow townspeople that they can either accept the security wall as the will of God or they can organize to try to stop it from happening. Adopting the second approach, what ensues is a tense and at times bloody ten-month standoff. The Israelis are able to remove some trees, but the resolve of the Palestinians is not diminished. And one of the central stories is the vital role played by women. Although the original protests were male only, women soon took the lead. In a scene reminiscent of the person in China who bravely stood in front of a moving tank, at one point Ayed's daughter jumps into the hole being dug by a steam shovel, daring the operator to kill her. Fortunately, he does not.

All this would be remarkable enough, but what truly transforms the movement as well as the film is the involvement of Israeli activists as well as those from other parts of the globe, including some who served in the anti-apartheid movement in South Africa. For their part, the Palestinians seem utterly astonished that Israelis would stand with them against the IDF. But the converse of this is also true. When Israeli soldiers attempt to arrest Israeli demonstrators, the Palestinian protesters—their newfound brothers and sisters—prevent this from occurring.

Much of the middle part of the film chronicles the months of standoff. Notwithstanding Ayed's entreaties, some of the Palestinian youth take to throwing stones, which in turn sets off a reaction by the Israeli soldiers so that at times events on the ground look like Fallujah, as Ayed puts it. For their part, the Israeli soldiers come across as both frightened and clueless. Although the film is mainly told from the Palestinian perspective, the filmmakers intersperse this with interviews of two of the Israeli commanders. One (Spielman) has an American accent and although at times he seems both patient and reasonable, his view that the security of Israeli citizens is more important than the livelihood of all Palestinians sends a cold chill down one's spine. The other officer (Yasmine) comes across much better than this, and certainly more human, although her own role is somewhat complicated by her gender and the manner in which the Palestinian demonstrators (particularly the women) respond to this.

At the end of the day the Palestinians and their allies win this battle and the security wall is not placed where it was originally planned, although Spielman cannot concede that the protests had anything to do with this. In addition, the cause has spread to other Palestinian towns, which have attempted to adopt the nonviolent methods of Budrus. Of course, the war will be won when the security wall, like other infamous walls before it, is torn down and Israelis and Palestinians live in peace, side-by-side with one another—just as some have in Budrus.

Also of Note

Encounter Point (Ronit Avni and Julia Bacha, 2006)

This rather uplifting documentary is about the Bereaved Families Forum, which at the time of filming had brought together some 500 Israeli and Palestinian families who had all lost loved ones in the conflict. The organization is premised on the simple but powerful idea that it is better to recognize and understand the pain in others, especially those who you have been taught to think of as your enemy, than it is to blindly lash out, and thereby create even more suffering.

29

When the Levees Broke: A Requiem in Four Acts (Spike Lee, 2006)

Violations of ESCR are oftentimes hidden, at least for those who do not want to be confronted by such reality. Places with failing schools, high unemployment, dilapidated housing, and so on, are almost always in areas people purposely avoid. However, every so often we are confronted with the reality of the denial of basic human rights protection, and in 2005 Hurricane Katrina showed the world the utter despair of the "other America."

✳ ✳ ✳

Spike Lee is the single best chronicler of racism in American today, and he has made an outstanding four-part film on the Hurricane Katrina disaster. Act I provides us with the immediate backdrop of the approaching storm. Quite belatedly, New Orleans Mayor Ray Nagin orders a complete evacuation of the city; but as a study conducted a few years earlier had shown, tens of thousands of people had no access to cars, and there was no city, state, or federal government plan to help those who were without transportation. The storm hit, enormous flooding ensued, and disaster struck for many, especially those who could not get out of the city.

We have all seen the images from the aftermath, but they are equally stunning to watch even now. Perhaps the hurricane and the flooding could be attributed to an act of God, to use terminology from the insurance industry (more on them later), but it was the near-complete inaction of the federal government in the ensuing days that borders on the criminal. We see some of this at the end of Act I and more in Act II, with George W. Bush's infamous "Brownie, you're doing a heck of a job" repeated three times for effect. And when the feds finally do respond, it is as much by pointing weapons at people as it is giving a helping hand.

Act III focuses on the diaspora. Several commentators likened this scattering of black folks to all parts of the United States as something resembling slavery in that, as in those days, there was little apparent thought given to keeping loved ones together. Instead, parents were often separated from children, husbands from wives, and the sick and the elderly were often left to fend for themselves—without their medicines, without adequate food and water, and without their loved ones to help take care of them. More than that, those lucky enough to get out of New Orleans were only given one-way tickets, which seems to be sending quite a strong political message—does it not?

Act IV begins joyously with the Mardi Gras celebration the following year. Given the continuing dire circumstances in the city, some had suggested that these events should be cancelled. However, the viewer can see how and why this would have been an enormous mistake. Lord knows, the good people of New Orleans needed something to celebrate, and at least for some brief period of time their lives assume some degree of normalcy—if it is possible to describe Mardi Gras as anything even remotely approaching "normal." One of the more interesting things referenced in Act IV is how little insurance companies actually paid out. There are no "good hands" stories here. Instead, after being neglected by their government, many people were then shafted by their insurance companies, on the basis that the damage they sustained was the result of a hurricane and not a flood—although the hurricane caused the flood.

The musician Wynton Marsalis sums it up best when he says that Katrina showed us all what is wrong with these United States. But the citizens of New Orleans are determined to get their city back on its feet. The first order of business is to bring its people back home. Appropriately enough, this four-part series closes with Fats Domino's classic "Walking to New Orleans."

Also of Note

Trouble the Water (Tia Lessin and Carl Deal, 2008)

Most home movies cover the mundane—things like birthdays and weddings. *Trouble the Water* is a home movie, of sorts, of Hurricane Katrina. Kimberly Roberts lives in New Orleans with her husband, Scott. With the hurricane approaching, but with no means of evacuating, Roberts decides the best thing she can do is to prepare for the worst—and to start filming. This results in a frightening firsthand account of the young couple's ordeal, including scenes where the family has taken refuge (of sorts) in their attic to escape the angry sea of water that has enveloped nearly the entirety of their home.

One of the most revealing aspects of the film is not so much how useless the government was, but how it actively battled citizens attempting to survive. When they finally were forced to flee their home, the Roberts and others sought refuge at an abandoned US Naval base—only to be turned away at gunpoint. They were finally able to locate safety at the Frederick Douglass High School, where the couple had to sleep on school desks drawn together. But the most telling aspect of this whole story is the smugness of the white National Guardsmen, one of whom makes a disparaging remark that "these people have no concept how to survive." But it is not easy to "survive" when your own government knowingly and purposely thwarts such efforts.

30

Well-Founded Fear
(Shari Robertson and Michael Camerini, 2000)

There are few, if any, ways in which a country can more directly influence the human rights protections of foreign nationals than through the asylum process. Article 14 of the UDHR provides: "Everyone has the right to seek and to enjoy in other countries asylum from persecution." However, no country is obligated to provide protection to refugees. Instead, states are only obligated not to send a person back to a country where his life or well-being might be threatened.

✳ ✳ ✳

This documentary provides an insightful look into the asylum determination process in the United States. Throughout the course of the film, the viewer is introduced to asylum seekers from various countries, including Russia, Romania, Bulgaria, El Salvador, China, and Algeria. Some parts of the movie involve the actual asylum hearing itself, which is a rather informal affair invariably consisting of the applicant, along with a translator and any legal representation the applicant can afford to bring, and the asylum hearing officer. The other part of the film consists of interviews with the various parties involved.

This might not sound like high drama, but it is. And the reason for this is that viewers get the very real sense that they are watching peoples' lives and fates determined right in front of them. It is not only the applicants who the viewer gets to know. One of the great strengths of *Well-Founded Fear* is that it introduces the hearing officers as well. Some are likable and garner the viewers' respect, while others display a cynicism or even an intellectual arrogance that is quite unsettling. One of the most maddening aspects of the film relates to the communication gap that so often takes place between the hearing officer and the applicant. In several instances, the oral translation that is being given at the hearing itself is nowhere close to what is actually being said—which the viewer knows because of the use of subtitles. One of the most egregious examples of this occurs late in the film, and it relates to a female applicant from Algeria, who brings both an Arab translator and a French translator to her hearing; yet neither one is able to accurately convey that the applicant's family is highly political and that the violence and threats directed at her are on account of her (and her family's) political opinions. Rather, all that the well-intentioned asylum officer hears is that there is violence in Algeria, which in his view does not differentiate her claim from that of any other Algerian applicants. As a result he rejects her claim.

The title comes from the refugee definition under international and domestic law. A refugee is an individual who is outside of his or her country of origin and able to establish that he or she has a "well-founded fear" of persecution on account of one of five enumerated grounds: race, religion, political opinion, nationality, or membership of a particular social group. What is shown so effectively in this film is not only the humanity of the asylum seeker, but also the human element involved in making the refugee determination. In that vein, perhaps the most eye-opening scene occurs during the end credits. Much earlier in the movie a woman's claim for asylum based on grounds of religious persecution has been rejected because when the hearing examiner asked her who the head of the Anglican Church is (of which she claims to be a member), she answered incorrectly—or so it is thought. However, as the credits roll the viewer is provided information that the head of the Anglican Church is the Bishop of Gibraltar, just as she said. At that moment, the viewer has a deep sense of dread that this human error, and perhaps others like it as well, will lead to even further cruelties.

Also of Note

Sierra Leone's Refugee All-Stars (Zach Niles and Banker White, 2005)

There are at least two reasons to watch the *Sierra Leone's Refugee All-Stars*. The first and arguably most important is that the film provides an insightful account of what the refugee experience is like for literally millions of people. The central players in this film are those who escaped from the brutal civil war in Sierra Leone and who have been "warehoused" (the terminology used in refugee protection) in various West African refugee camps for years. As the film shows so well, the life of a refugee is anything but a glamorous one. Rather, it is alternately made up of enormous fear and anxiety, but also boredom and aimlessness of purpose. To help fill the void, a group of refugee-musicians forms a band, and it is the sweet music of the Sierra Leone Refugee All-Stars that is the second reason for watching the film.

In many ways, this is an uplifting movie. As part of a repatriation project, UNHCR officials fly all but one of the band members back to Sierra Leone after the civil war has abated, where they are able to return home and be reunited with their family and friends who survived the terrible onslaught. The movie certainly inspires hope, and the band itself has now gone on to a certain amount of international fame. But amidst all the good cheer and wonderful music, the most devastating scene occurs when the one musician who does not return to Sierra Leone explains to the filmmaker why: during the country's civil war he was forced at gunpoint to crush the skull of his infant. It is at this moment that the music and repatriation are placed in proper perspective and the viewer comes to understand the horrors that these individuals have lived through.

Sentenced Home (David Grabias and Nicole Newnham, 2006)

Sentenced Home is a documentary that presents two different sides of the refugee experience in the United States. The first involves those who fled from Cambodia during the reign of terror of the Khmer Rouge. The families of the three young men featured in this film—Many Uch, Kim Ho Ma, and Loeun Lun—all arrived in the 1970s when they were children. This first immigration story, then, involves refugee flight and resettlement in the United States.

The second story describes the young people's subsequent fortunes in the United States and does not have anywhere near the same happy ending. During their teen years, all three committed petty crimes that under US law were categorized as "aggravated felonies." An aggravated felony is a deportable crime, and the film tracks their deportation to Cambodia, their country of origin, but a country that they have had only the most fleeting connection with (if that) since their arrival in the United States.

31

Children Underground

(Edet Belzberg, 2001)

The most important human rights treaty for young people is the Convention on the Rights of the Child. Recognizing the unique vulnerability of children, the treaty provides a litany of rights and human rights protection. There are only two countries—Somalia and the United States—that have not signed and ratified the CRC. Thus, one might naturally conclude from all this that children's human rights are well protected. Unfortunately, the truth is just the opposite of this.

✳ ✳ ✳

Children Underground is not for the faint hearted. One of the policies of the old communist regime in Romania was to proscribe abortion and birth control, and as a consequence there was a surge in unwanted children, many of whom came to live on the streets. At the time the film was released, there were approximately 20,000 street children in Romania. *Children Underground* presents us with five who live at a subway stop in the heart of Bucharest. The leader of the gang is Cristina, a fifteen-year-old girl who disguises herself as a boy in order to avoid being raped. Cristina is alternately cruel and kind as she disciplines her unruly underlings but also caresses and tends to them. Macarena's gender is also indeterminate, but the viewer eventually learns she is a girl. Macarena, along with the others, spends much of her day sniffing paint, oftentimes in public, and when she is not doing this she is continually screaming and crying and fighting with the other children. There are three younger children. Ana (ten) and Marian (eight) are sister and brother, and one of the most chilling scenes in the film is when they return to their parents' house in the countryside after an absence of two years. The mother seems to have some sense of guilt at what has happened to her children, but the stepfather encourages the children to return to Bucharest—while at the same time pretending to be concerned about their welfare and saying that he wants them to return and stay at home. The children go away again, and it seems certain they will return to the grubby subway stop and a life (albeit a short one) of begging and sniffing and prostitution. Yet a year later the filmmaker returns, and Ana has been reunited with her mother and stepfather, while her brother seems quite content at an orphanage.

The last child is Mihai, who is twelve at the time of filming. Mihai claims that what caused him to leave home were the beatings administered by his father, and yet when a social worker pays a visit to the family it is not certain that this has been the case. Everyone in the household seems quite distraught at Mihai's departure, and even the father, a person who the viewer expects to hate, shows signs of love and affection for his son.

Children Underground is an intense viewing experience. There are only a handful of scenes where there is any kind of peace and quiet, and really only one—where the younger children go to a park and go swimming in a wading pool—where there is anything even resembling childhood. The paint sniffing is constant and in many scenes Marcarena's face is smeared with the stuff. There are a few responsible adults, but not many. Some of the social workers shown in the film actually attempt to do some good, but others seem to have the attitude that these kids are actually better off living in an underground subway stop. And the saddest thing of all is that, given the lack of alternatives, they might well be right.

Also of Note

We'll Never Meet Childhood Again (Sam Lawlor and Lindsay Pollock, 2007)

Nearly all human rights films are sad and disturbing affairs, and there is good reason for this: nearly all focus on situations where human rights have been violated. *We'll Never Meet Childhood Again* is completely different from this because it is about a group of young adults who really should not be alive. The political background for this film involves the policy of the old communist regime in Romania to allow infants infected with HIV/AIDS to die. However, in stepped the nongovernmental organization Health Aid Romania, which undertook to place as many of these neglected children as it could with various health care workers who raised them as their own.

At the time of filming, most were teenagers, although old film footage of birthday parties and the like shows some of the children from the time they were toddlers on. In many ways, these teens are no different than any others. They are worried about looks, boyfriends and girlfriends, careers, school, parents, jeans, and so forth. But in addition to these things, these young adults are also burdened with the knowledge of their HIV/AIDS status, worries about how this will affect their relations with other people, and of course anxiety about how long they might live. Yet the most remarkable thing about these youngsters is just how unremarkable they are, and much the same could be said of their heroic caretakers.

32

Invisible Children

(Jason Russell, Bobby Bailey, and Laren Poole, 2006)

In the spring of 2012, one of the most talked-about videos on the Internet was "Kony 2012." The Kony in the title is Joseph Kony, the leader of the Lord's Resistance Army in Uganda, and this half-hour video, which went viral nearly the moment it was released, was produced by Jason Russell, who had put out Invisible Children *six years earlier. Certainly, many more people have viewed "Kony 2012" than have ever watched the earlier film, although the popularity of "Kony" might well spark additional interest. The plea in "Kony 2012" is that by the end of the calendar year Joseph Kony will be arrested and turned over to the International Criminal Court and be brought to trial for crimes against humanity and war crimes. Those interested can even order a "Kony kit" with information on the warlord's activities and two bracelets to show off support for the initiative.*

✳ ✳ ✳

Invisible Children starts off as if it will be something on the order of *Bill and Ted's Excellent Adventure,* only set in Africa. The viewer is introduced to three seemingly goofy American college students who are about to take off for a trip to the Sudan because they have developed some kind of interest in the genocide in that country. When they finally arrive, there is not much to see and so they take their "innocents abroad" act to Kenya.

At this point they come face to face with the conflict in Northern Uganda. There are several scenes in the film that almost defy description, especially the nightly migration where teeming numbers of young people flee into the town of Gulu, seeking shelter anywhere they might find it in order to avoid being abducted by the Lord's Resistance Army. These shelters are reminiscent of slave ships, as hundreds of young children are squeezed together, whether in a hospital basement or on a wet floor in what is referred to as the "crib." Early on, one of the filmmakers comments that these children do not cry. This seems to be true, but near the end of the film one of the boys (Jacob) does break down when he is describing the killing of his brother. His howls of repressed grief seem to be for all members of his "family"—the term used for the brotherhood and sisterhood of Ugandan youth.

A film that at the outset appeared so trite and trivial turns into a profound testament of the human condition, with an expressed commitment to help make these human wrongs right. As someone in the film comments, "we are human beings just like you." The filmmakers certainly believe this and part of their mission in making this movie is to convince the viewer of this as well.

Also of Note

Soldier Child (Neil Abramson, 1998)

Soldier Child is an extraordinarily difficult film to watch. For fifty-five minutes (although seemingly much longer) what the viewer sees children who had previously been abducted by the Lord's Resistance Army in northern Uganda but were able to escape. The bulk of the film deals with the efforts to rehabilitate these devastated and crippled children. This, of course, is no easy task. They have not only seen things that would be unimaginable for most of us but have been forced to do things such as kill their parents and other members of their families. Given the horrors these young children have lived through, it is no wonder they are often in a near-catatonic state, and accompanying social workers end up not only translating but seemingly telling the child's story.

These are extraordinarily brave and resilient children, and the film depicts the manner in which some are reconnected to their families and to their communities. First, they are encouraged to draw pictures of what had happened to them, and they are repeatedly assured that they were forced to commit these horrors and that under normal circumstances they would not have done so. In addition, they are never referred to as traumatized rebels, but simply as "our children." Through such things as school, play, and music, some of these children are able to assume their proper role—as children.

War/Dance (Sean Fine and Andrea Nix Fine, 2007)

War/Dance tells the story of a group of children from the Patongo refugee camp in Northern Uganda who compete in the country's national music competition, which is the first time that a school from the conflict zone has competed. The story is primarily told through the eyes of three children, all of whom have experienced incredible trauma.

The film does not dwell on the suffering of these children or the other refugees in the camp, nor does it provide an extended political background. What we do know is that there is a tragic civil conflict in Uganda, which has had a terrible effect on the Ocholi people, particularly the children of this tribe. The musical competition, and perhaps even the making of the film itself, serves as a respite from the suffering and deprivation all around them.

ABC Africa (Abbas Kiarostami, 2001)

ABC Africa also deals with Ugandan children, in this case on how AIDS has helped create some 1.6 million orphans. The film offers a snapshot of Ugandan youth and the desperate lives so many lead. A number of scenes are filmed inside a hospital, where the viewer is exposed to the routine of daily suffering and death. In one of the most uncomfortable scenes, a small dead body is wrapped up and placed in a cardboard box, as it is transported from the hospital to a burial ground on the back of a bicycle. But the documentary tells more than just the suffering of Ugandan children. In a number of scenes cute and curious children mug shamelessly for the camera crew—just like children anywhere else in the world.

33

The Inheritors
(Eugenio Polgovsky, 2008)

We move from children who fear being abducted by the Lord's Resistance Army to the plight of rural children in Latin America who work tirelessly from dawn to dusk in order to help their families survive. Child labor is a tricky issue; while most agree that children should be in school rather than in the fields and in the factories, the reality is that without the contributions of their children, many families would not be able to survive.

✳ ✳ ✳

Until the closing credits it is not clear where the rushing display of wonderful images the viewer has just seen were filmed—or what the meaning of it all is. There cannot be more than ten lines of dialogue in the entire film, and even this consists of little more than stray background comments. Rather, what we witness are children working from dawn to dark and working as if their lives depended on it—which it very well might. We see children running into forests trying to find firewood; children dragging buckets of water back to their homes; children who seem no older than four or five years old picking tomatoes, cucumbers, peas, and peppers; children carrying corn great distances to be ground up for tortillas; children making rugs; children starting fires for cooking and washing the family's dishes; children wading up to their knees in cement in order to produce cinderblocks; and children planting seeds in the fields.

There is no apparent schooling and almost no evidence of play, although there is something joyous about these children. In this regard, two scenes in particular stand out. In one, three boys who are out tending to some goats spontaneously break into somersaults and then take their shirts off and begin to twirl them over their heads. The other is the film's final scene, where the children don masks and break into a spirited version of "Dance of the Devils." And when they are done, they do it all over again.

Also of Note

The Devil's Miner (Kief Davidson and Richard Ladkani, 2005)

One of the first questions about *The Devil's Miner* is how the filmmakers came up with the concept of making a documentary about a fourteen-year-old boy (Basilio) who along with his twelve-year-old brother (Bernadino) works in the dusty and dangerous Cerro Gordo silver mine in the remote town of Potosi, Bolivia, while also attending school and making every effort to lead an otherwise normal adolescent life.

The filmmakers are able to bring the scary lives of these young boys into view, especially by filming mining conditions that are essentially no different from when the Spanish introduced such practices in the sixteenth century. The lives of indigenous people were certainly not valued then, and little has changed over the past 500 years. Most miners die in their thirties and forties, mainly from silicosis. Whether the two boys will make it to that age remains to be seen, but they are determined to provide for their family and equally determined to escape the mines. And what keeps the two going are a combination of dreams, determination, and the coca leaves that all miners chew almost incessantly.

The title of the film comes from the miners' belief that while the outside world is under God's domain, the mountains are ruled by the Devil. Thus, the miners have created a subterranean sanctuary of sorts. But rather than worshipping God, which they do at Sunday mass, they have created a large figure of the Devil and adorned it. Of course, whether worshipping the Devil really does serve to protect miners is a matter of some conjecture. However, what certainly would help would be some form of health and safety regulations, although there is simply no evidence of any of this. These two young boys are left to their own devices with no human rights protection.

34

Out in the Silence

(Joe Wilson and Dean Hamer, 2009)

It is a violation of international human rights standards to discriminate against a person on the basis of his or her sexual preferences. But these standards apply only to the state. Private individuals, even groups, are generally exempt.

✳ ✳ ✳

Perhaps there should be a colon after the title with this added on: how small-town America hates gays. The town in this instance is Oil City, Pennsylvania, and perhaps the only thing that sets this town apart from countless others like it is that it produced one of the filmmakers (Wilson), who went to college and seemingly left Oil City behind forever. Wilson moved to the nation's capitol and while there he met his partner Hamer. The two began dating and eventually married. But rather than cutting himself off from a past where he pretended to be something other than what he is, Wilson sent a wedding announcement and photograph to the town newspaper, which, surprisingly enough, published both.

This brought about an avalanche of hate mail. However, there was one other letter, and it came from Kathy Bills, who wrote about the terrible treatment that her gay son C. J. was subjected to at school. This prompted Wilson and Hamer to take the unusual step of making an extended road trip to Oil City. The couple not only stayed a while but became central players in helping to bring about at least some amount of civic change. Rather than ignoring those who had written the hate mail to him, Wilson decided to try to reach out to these individuals. Only one couple (Reverend Miklos and his wife) responded, but after a jittery first meeting, where Mrs. Miklos tries to explain her opposition to gays on the basis of the need to make use of both male and female plumbing parts, what eventually develops is a warm and meaningful relationship.

We learn that their letter of protest to the local paper was fueled by Diane Gramley of the American Family Association, a conservative organization that seeks to prevent what they term the "homosexual agenda" from gaining ascendancy in Oil City and elsewhere. Wilson's response is right on point: what straights oftentimes describe as the "gay agenda" is what gays simply call their lives. But this story is really not Wilson's but C. J.'s. Here is a young man who looks and acts like any other teenage boy. He plays sports, loves awful music, tinkers with old cars that will never run—and he is attracted to boys. And for this, he is subjected to all kinds of cruelties at school, including repeated death threats. Wilson and Hamer form an immediate bond with both C. J. and his wonderful mother, and they, along with Roxanne and Linda, a lesbian couple, are able to make headway in opening minds and hearts in Oil City in ways that did not seem possible. This was aided by the ACLU, which brought a successful suit against the school system on C. J.'s behalf, resulting in desperately needed diversity training in the city's schools. Presumably, at the end of the day Wilson and Hamer will go back to their lives in Washington. But they do so by leaving a good part of themselves in Oil City and the residents will be enriched by this.

Also of Note

Paragraph 175 (Rob Epstein and Jeffrey Friedman, 2000)

Paragraph 175 was the provision of the German criminal code, first enacted in 1871, that made sexual relations between two men illegal. Yet, until the Nazis assumed power, Paragraph 175 was mainly ignored, and in the period immediately following World War I, Berlin was arguably the gay capital of the world. All this was to eventually change after Hitler was elected into office in 1933, although it is interesting to find out that Ernst Roehm, initially one of Hitler's closest advisors and the head of the SA (Storm Battalion), was himself openly gay.

Under the Nazi regime, some 100,000 gay men were arrested for their sexual preferences and somewhere between 10,000 and 15,000 were sent off to concentration camps. (Interestingly, gay women do not appear to have been targeted.) In this film, the viewer meets the handful of survivors who tell their story, some for the first time.

35
Public Housing
(Frederick Wiseman, 1997)

Housing is a basic human right. Article 25 (1) of the Universal Declaration of Human Rights provides:

> *Everyone has the right to a standard of living adequate for the health and well-being of himself and of his family, including food, clothing, housing, and medical care and necessary social services, and the right to security in the event of unemployment, sickness, disability, widowhood, old age, or other lack of livelihood in circumstances beyond his control.*

Individuals are expected to find and maintain their own housing. If, however, they are not able to do so, the government must provide it for them. In the United States, one means of government support involves public housing. Yet, as can be seen in the following film, such housing often fails to meet human rights standards.

***

Frederick Wiseman makes films—very long, but very good films—about institutions. These documentaries are not easy to watch—which is exactly Wiseman's point. They show us exactly what we do not want to see: the outcasts of American society and the institutions that have been designed to keep them in their place.

Public Housing takes viewers to the Ida B. Wells homes in Chicago. At the outset of the film these homes look like something resembling slave quarters, with black folks crammed into a small and dingy space. Yet, there are other times when shots of these same homes and this same neighborhood are nothing short of beautiful, with excited children running around on the blacktop playground and lush gardens being attended to. This same ambivalence is shown in those who appear in the film.

A case in point is Helen Finner, the tenants' advocate and the only person the viewer gets to know by name (and only because she has a name plate on her desk). The first time we see Finner she is in an outlandish outfit, and when she opens her mouth the viewer can see that nearly all of her teeth are missing. In short, Finner is almost a caricature of a welfare mom. Who could ever take this woman seriously? But we eventually see that Helen Finner is not only tireless in her efforts on behalf of others but canny as well. And before opponents can set forth their own harsh criticism of public housing, Helen Finner does it for them: acknowledging that it is poor, dirty, and unfair and that it brings together in one place the very worst aspects of American society. No one knows this better than Helen Finner does.

There are many scenes in *Public Housing* that will confirm the viewer's worst stereotypes. There are a lot of drugs floating around and a lot of violence. Residents are repeatedly told that there are jobs out there—is starting a company that does nothing but shuts off lights really a business?—but in the depressed areas surrounding the projects there is very little evidence of much opportunity. Downtown Chicago, occasionally seen in the background, seems to be another galaxy away. And in one of the most memorable scenes, residents do their food shopping from the outside of a convenience store, directing as best they can the storekeepers who are on the other side of a bullet-proof window. There are other scenes that almost defy description. One is a grandmothers' sewing circle that, except for the black faces and hands, might have been filmed in a rural farming community in Iowa. Another involves a talk on safe sex that is given to a group of girls who look much too young to have had any experience in such matters, but whose crying babies suggest that this talk came several years too late. Wiseman's films often focus on what used to be referred to as "the other America." But this was when the other America might actually have meant something to the rest of American society.

Also of Note

Welfare (Frederick Wiseman, 1975)

This earlier Wiseman film takes the viewer into the bowels of a public welfare office, and what we (and the recipients) suffer through are endless waiting lines, calloused caseworkers, and mountains of paperwork, all of which seem to drain the life out of all those who enter into this system—welfare recipients as well as employees of the DDS. The lesson of the film is this: in exchange for any kind of government support, the recipient should expect to be treated like a piece of meat.

36

Harlan County, USA
(Barbara Kopple, 1976)

American Dream
(Barbara Kopple, 1990)

Although the right to establish and join a labor union is a basic human right (UDHR Art. 23), this battle continues to be fought in countries all over the world. In the United States, where the following two documentaries by Barbara Kopple were filmed, union membership in the private sector has now been reduced to less than 10 percent of the working population.

✳ ✳ ✳

The old labor song "Which Side Are You On?" is heard repeatedly in *Harlan County, USA*, but there is little question that producer and director Barbara Kopple is on the side of the striking coal miners at the Eastover Mine in Harlan County, Kentucky. One certainly cannot blame her for this. We see the claustrophobic work the miners do every day and also witness the wheezing and coughing of those who have contracted black lung, a disease that the company's doctors claim does not exist. Much of the film occurs on the picket line, where violence always seems imminent as the striking miners attempt to prevent "scabs" from passing.

The problem is that the scabs and the owners of the mines have guns and the miners do not. Another problem is that the coal operators also have law enforcement on their side, if not in their deep pocket. And finally, it is not even clear that those who profess to be on the miners' side—the United Mine Workers Union, which the miners at Eastover are attempting to join—truly have the miners' best interest in mind. One of the most riveting subplots involves the battle for the leadership of the UMW, which ends up with the reform candidate (Jock Yabloski) being murdered at the behest of sitting president, Tony Boyle.

The strike lasts for almost a year and much of the film concerns itself with the hardships faced by people who have known almost nothing but hardship their whole lives. Their teeth are rotting away; their lungs no longer deliver much oxygen; there is no heat in the house; and you can simply forget about indoor plumbing. Mining is a dangerous hell, but it is the only option in a place like Harlan Country.

Special mention has to be made of the women in the film who essentially are the ones who take the fight to the coal operatives. There is both purpose and passion behind them, and it seems clear to the viewer that without their brave efforts this strike would have been lost a long time ago and the miners would have been forced to crawl back to work.

What also deserves special praise is the music that is played throughout the film. There is not a false note here, so to speak, as Kopple is so effectively able to tell her story through the music and also to show the manner in which this music plays a central role in their lives. In the end, the miners win, although it takes the killing of one of the strikers to finally bring about this result. Yet the viewer will be excused for being somewhat cynical about how much of a victory this really is. While some conditions will change for the better, it is clear that the owners of the coal mines will do everything in their power to fight real reform and obstruct safety measures.

A number of years after *Harlan County*, Barbara Kopple released *American Dream*, a documentary about the labor strike at the Hormel meatpacking plant in Austin, Minnesota. While the conflict in Harlan County centered around the workers' attempt to unionize, the meatpackers at Hormel already are unionized. However, there are two conflicts. The most immediate conflict is with the management at Hormel, which is seeking to reduce hourly wages from $10.69 to $8.25, notwithstanding a $30 million profit the year before. The second conflict is intramural, and it pits the local union (P-9) against the international union (United Food and Commercial Workers), which refuses to support the strike.

The conflicts and the arguments on both sides are depressingly the same as in the earlier film, although the outcome, at least from the workers' perspectives, is not nearly as hopeful. What we see are family members on opposing sides of this issue and acts of solidarity that are eventually ripped apart at the seams. What Kopple also sees—and which economic conditions over the past two decades have borne out—is the unraveling of the American Dream, at least for those who had made their living in something like meatpacking or manufacturing. The lesson here is that no matter how much money a corporation makes, it always has to make more. Kopple offers us a thoughtful analysis of the human consequences that ensue from this.

37

Shipbreakers
(Michael Kot, 2004)

Article 23 of the UDHR demands that working conditions be "just and favorable." In addition, Article 24 provides: "Everyone has the right to rest and leisure, including reasonable limitation of working hours and periodic holidays with pay." In the following film there is absolutely no evidence that either of these two rights is even remotely being met.

✳ ✳ ✳

Perhaps there are dirtier and more dangerous jobs in the world than breaking up enormous tankers on the shores of Alang, India, but I would be hard pressed to name one. Approximately half of the dismantled ships in the world are handled by a workforce of 40,000, but there is no specialized training for this, no safety nets to catch those working in ships that are ten stories high, no goggles for welders, and no protection from the fumes that workers ingest (equivalent to ten to fifteen packs of cigarettes a day). This does not even address the asbestos and the PCBs that these ships are loaded with. The common expression is "a ship a day, a death a day," and it is estimated (because no formal recordkeeping is done) that there are 300 deaths a year, not to mention that upwards of eight in ten workers will be injured at some point in their (short) careers.

But as this film explains, this is better than living in destitution at home, and because of this, old and young alike descend on Alang to provide for themselves. Mittu is a young man who came to work as a shipbreaker against the wishes of his parents, who had already lost one son there. Mittu takes care of his uncle who is now nearly blind because of sparks that repeatedly flew into his eyes. Except for a tiny room where he lives, Mittu's uncle has almost nothing to show for his years of toil. On the other hand, he is still alive, and in this treacherous job this is no small feat.

As *Shipbreakers* notes, the Basel Convention on the Control of Transboundary Movements of Hazardous Wastes and Their Disposal prohibits the transnational shipment of toxic wastes, but this does not include ships, which nearly all originate in the West and are loaded with toxic wastes. The viewer is also shown how regulations are easily avoided, as "The Tulip" is being dragged to shore, waiting to be dismantled. However, this is not the real name of the ship. Rather, it is quite common for a ship about to be dismantled to frequently change its name—as well as the flag it is flying under—any number of times, all with the intent of evading legal responsibility. In this case, "The Tulip" was a Norwegian ship that had originally been called "The Gird." But that was a long time ago, at least in terms of assigning any responsibility to the Norwegian government.

At the end of the film Mittu talks about his desire to sail the world someday. This young man is not looking for anyone's pity. Rather, as he points out, ships die so people like him can live. But there has to be a better way for ships to die than they presently do in Alang, and certainly a much better way for people to live than these shipbreakers do.

38

Mardi Gras: Made in China
(David Redmon, 2005)

Last Train Home *(D-17) focused on Chinese laborers who returned home each year to celebrate the New Year with family and old friends, who were more like complete strangers due to their yearlong absence. The following documentary spends more time on the factory floor and shows the cruelty of company practices and the inhumanity of employees' work lives. Nearly all criticisms of China's human rights policies have zeroed in on such things as the imprisonment of political dissidents. What also has to be kept in mind are the massive human rights violations that are carried out every single day at the workplace.*

✳ ✳ ✳

This is a story of different worlds colliding. One involves the revelry and drunkenness of Mardi Gras, where shiny colorful beads are tossed to women who flash the crowd in exchange. The other world is the Chinese factory where these beads are made. While the excesses in New Orleans will not be new to anyone, at least not to anyone from the West, those who make these cheap beads were absolutely astonished when, later in the movie, the filmmaker shows these workers how and where the beads they had made were being put to use.

There are two central themes to this film. The first involves Chinese labor practices. Not only do the laborers work incredibly long hours and at a constantly frenetic pace, but the manner in which the workers are controlled almost defies belief. For example, for merely speaking to another employee, a person is charged an entire day's pay, while any consorting among and between the sexes in the bleak dormitories where the workers live results in the loss of a month's pay—and in all likelihood dismissal as well.

The other theme is our own involvement in human rights abuse. It is much too easy to watch this film and merely express disgust at the conditions these Chinese laborers are working under, but the film highlights our own connection with these practices. By showing the sordid origins of our throwaway products, Redmon helps viewers see the world much differently than before.

39

The Interrupters
(Steve James and Alex Kotlowitz, 2011)

Although human rights are oftentimes divided into two main categories—ESCR and CPR— the truth is that all rights are interdependent and indivisible and there are times when these neat divisions get in the way of understanding this. The following film underscores this point by showing how deprivations of ESCR so often lead directly to instances of political violence.

All of us have grievances, but seldom do these wrongs (or perceived wrongs) escalate into anything but a heated argument. However, in inner-city Chicago hundreds of young people have been gunned down and killed over grievances that lead to violence, which lead to acts of revenge, which in turn lead to even more acts of violence, and the only thing that breaks the cycle is either death or incarceration—certainly not the best of options. How and why do young poor people kill each other like this? As one person comments in this film, those who have been ostracized by mainstream American society have a special need of dominating the surroundings around them. What also adds to this is the belief that many young people have—and in many instances, not a mistaken one—that their own life is going to be quite short. Or as this same person says: "fuck tomorrow, I am going to survive today." But there is also a good chance that they will not survive today. Some of the most haunting scenes in this film are small street memorials for the fallen that seem to be everywhere. And on a brick wall with the names of teens who had been killed before their lives really even began, there is a space with these words written on it: I am next.

This is where "violence interrupters" come in. These are people who put their lives on the line and attempt to prevent violence from escalating further. Each of the interrupters we meet in this film was once a street hood, and all would readily admit that it is no small miracle they are still alive today to do their vital work. Tio Hardiman is now a professor at the University of Illinois–Chicago, and he certainly looks the part, with his glasses and easy demeanor in front of the classroom. Yet, these are not traditional students in class but gang members who have vowed to kill one another. Tio is trying to convince them not to.

Certainly the most riveting violence interrupter is Ameena Matthews. Ameena is the daughter of one of the most notorious gang leaders in the history of Chicago, Jeff Fort, and she was well on her way to getting killed herself. The turning point came after she was wounded and her father called her to find out who he had to go kill for vengeance. She simply said to him: Why, Daddy? After this, she converted to the Muslim faith and decided to devote her enormous passion to halting violence rather than spreading it. Watching this petite women get in the face of menacing gang members is certainly captivating, but perhaps her best work is with a young high school dropout (Caprysha Anderson) who is well on her way to going nowhere. There is no magic wand to do this work, and the two of them struggle mightily in the process.

Eddie Bocanegra is a former member of a Hispanic gang, and he talks as dispassionately about shooting a guy who had shot a friend of his as if he is talking about going shopping. Eddie has been an interrupter since getting out of prison, and although he has forsaken the baseball cap and the gang colors and now dresses in Ralph Lauren, he still has "the street" in him. So does Cobe Williams, although he has moved his family to a suburb where the only violence seems to be in the form of the Friday night football game. In one of the more remarkable stories, Cobe finds out the police have busted into the house of Flamo, a hardened criminal, and in the process have disrespected Flamo's mother, an egregious insult. Flamo is about to go out and kill someone—preferably a police officer, but in his state of mind anyone would do. Here we see how Cobe and the other interrupters work. As Cobe explains, what you try to reach is the soft side, the person's humanity: "Are you hungry? Would you like to get something to eat? Sure you're pissed off, but the police know you are pissed off and they are just waiting for you to go out and do something dumb—and then what?" And at the end of the film the viewer sees Cobe dropping off Flamo at his job working security in the Chicago Transit Authority. I am not sure if there has ever been such a complete metamorphosis shown on film.

The film does not deal much with issues of poverty and class, and this is both a strength and a weakness. It is a strength in the sense that the interrupters have a job to do, and discussions about youth unemployment rates or vastly inferior education opportunities are simply not going to get young people the intervention they need immediately. However, as brave and as remarkable as the interrupters are, one has a sense that they are fighting a losing battle. One certainly hopes that these efforts, and the film itself, will spawn much greater attention to how young people deal with violence. People like Tio, Cobe, Eddie, and Ameena are not miracle workers, even if they seem like it. Their incredible efforts will take the young people of Chicago only so far.

40

The Age of Stupid
(Franny Armstrong, 2009)

Although the connection between environmental degradation and violations of human rights standards is not made as strongly in the following film as it could have been, the film is clever and informative in using the horrors of the future to remove viewers from their present worldview.

✳ ✳ ✳

The age of stupid is the present day, and the reason for this moniker is our collective unwillingness to address global warming, although we are well aware of the enormous harms that our current practices will bring about. *The Age of Stupid* transports us to the future (2055), when the Earth is in utter ruins: Las Vegas is a desert, Sydney is burning, London is completely flooded, and so on. Our narrator (Pete Postlethwaite) lives in a lonely building in the Arctic, where his job is to safeguard mankind's artifacts now that the human race is at the edge of extinction—due to our own stupidity.

This fictional narrator introduces six real-life people from our own time to explain how humankind did itself in. One of the more interesting involves Al DuVernay, a resident of the Gulf Coast who stayed behind after Hurricane Katrina and helped a lot of distressed people. DuVernay is an engineer for Shell, and he staunchly defends the policies of the oil companies, while at the same time he is willing to acknowledge the great harm that the industry and its policies are bringing to us all, manifested clearly by Katrina itself.

A second story revolves around Indian entrepreneur Jehangir Wadia, who wants to bring low-cost airline travel to his country while also reaping in the appropriate personal rewards. One of the great secrets revealed in the film—is it really such a secret?—is the amount of environmental damage caused by air travel. Yet, as Wadia asks, why shouldn't Indians have the same travel opportunities as those in the West?

Arguably the least effective vignette concerns two young Iraqi children whose family had to flee the country after their father was killed in the war. The connection to the film's larger theme seems to be that the Iraq war was fought for the country's oil reserves, although this is never made particularly clear. Another story introduces us to Fernand Pareau, the oldest mountain guide in the Alps. Fernand is able to draw upon decades of hiking experience and rather incontrovertible evidence in terms of rapidly shrinking glaciers to show the effects of global warming. But Pareau is not one to passively complain, and the film shows his efforts to halt a further widening of the roads in the Alps that are needlessly shipping goods back and forth throughout Europe.

Western audiences should readily identify with Piers Guy, a wind turbine expert whose family makes a strenuous effort to reduce its carbon footprint, including cancelling a ski trip to France because this would necessitate flying. However, what makes this story so frustrating is the manner in which Guy is continually stymied in his efforts to place wind turbines in the English countryside—and the threats directed towards him all come from those who would staunchly consider themselves "environmentalists." What the film also shows is the manner in which such intransigence is not the exception but the order of the day. Finally, there is Layefa Malemi, a young woman who is studying to become a doctor and who is living amid the environmental ruins left by Al DuVernay's company in the Nigerian Delta.

Will *The Age of Stupid* help make us any less stupid? Well it certainly couldn't make us any stupider than we already are, that's for sure.

41

Amandla! A Revolution in Four Part Harmony
(Lee Hirsch, 2002)

As the next film shows, visual images are not the only thing that can bring about political and social change. What we see—and hear—is how the fight against apartheid was carried out by means of music, and beautiful music at that.

✳ ✳ ✳

Although this documentary depicts the cruelties of apartheid rule in South Africa, it is next to impossible to watch the film without a certain sense of joy at the manner in which music played such a central role in the anti-apartheid movement. The name Vuyisile Mini is not familiar to most Westerners, but South Africans (or at least black South Africans) consider him to be the greatest composer of freedom songs in the country's history. Because of this, and because he was considered by the ruling white government to be a subversive, Mini was executed, reportedly singing as he was led to the gallows. The country lost a singer, composer, politician, and poet. Or as one commentator puts it: Mini was physically hung and we were politically hung. Yet his work helped fuel the opposition, and after the new black government came to power, his remains were unearthed from the pauper's cemetery, and he was given a much more proper and appropriate burial.

There are different songs for different occasions and for different generations. A song like "Nkosi Sikelel'I" was written in the late 1800s, and its prayer-like quality has long served as an alternative national anthem for blacks. In contrast to this, there are revolutionary and even threatening songs, such as "Watch Out Verwoerd" (Verwoerd is a former prime minister). Then there are songs that serve both purposes—where the word "Bible" could be used in certain circumstances, but the term "AK-47" in other situations.

Every phase of the struggle had its own song, and to watch old comrades sitting around jumping from one song to another, almost in a juke-box fashion, is to understand the power and influence of the music, but also the connection between different generations. But things changed in the 1980s. The government instituted a state of emergency, and the African National Congress responded by opening up a military wing that was situated outside of South Africa. The music also changed, and one new element was the Toyi-Toyi, commonly used at funerals of slain anti-apartheid leaders, which is almost in the nature of running. One of the more remarkable sights is watching thousands of South Africans, black and white alike, running down the street chanting and breaking into the Toyi-Toyi. The object was to "scare the shit" out of the apartheid regime, which is exactly what happened. On February 11, 1990, opposition leader Nelson Mandela was released from decades of imprisonment, and within a short period of time, he became president of South Africa—the new South Africa. And you might recall Mandela dancing at his inauguration, dancing to the rhythms of the songs that helped bring this transformation about.

42

The Devil Came on Horseback
(Anne Sundberg and Ricki Stern, 2007)

According to the Genocide Convention (1948), genocide consists of an act committed with the intent to destroy, in whole or in part, a national, ethnic, racial, or religious group by: killing members of the group; causing serious bodily or mental harm to members of the group; deliberately inflicting on the group conditions of life calculated to bring about its physical destruction in whole or in part; imposing measures intended to prevent births within the group; and forcibly transferring children of the group to another group.

However, in popular parlance, the term refers to any gross and systematic violation, even if these atrocities would not technically constitute "genocide." Such has been the case with Sudan. A special UN commission reached the conclusion that events in the Darfur region in Sudan did not constitute genocide. In large part, the international reaction was to ignore this finding and to demand that the massive levels of killings be stopped. The following film explains how worldwide attention came about in the first place.

✳ ✳ ✳

The film is told through the eyes of Marine Captain Brian Steidle, a former American military officer who served on a peacekeeping mission in the Sudan. Certainly, the film itself is important in its own right. The title comes from the translation of the word "janjaweed"—man on horse holding gun—the paramilitary force in league with the Sudanese government. What the viewer sees is incontrovertible proof of the savagery of these two forces combined.However, the film underscores a larger point, which is that until Steidle's pictures were published and then became known internationally, there had been almost no attention given to the conflict in the Darfur region of the Sudan. The film shows quite convincingly that without accompanying images, it is not likely that human rights abuses, no matter how widespread or how atrocious, will gain international attention without the ability of others to "see."

Also of Note

Darfur Now (Ted Braun, 2007)

This documentary on Darfur focuses on six people—four Westerners and two Sudanese citizens—who either are directly affected by the conflict or make themselves become involved. Perhaps the only household name in the group is the actor Don Cheadle, who says that he became interested in Darfur during the course of making the film *Hotel Rwanda*. Cheadle is honest with himself and the viewer when he acknowledges that others will become interested in Darfur if he and other celebrities, including his good buddy George Clooney, speak out on this issue, and this is exactly what Cheadle does.

To its credit, by focusing on disparate people united in one cause the film avoids being impersonal. However, it may have been stronger if it stayed longer with each person rather than constantly cross-cutting between stories. Also, the music can be heavy-handed; perhaps documentary filmmakers should take some kind of pledge akin to the Dogma Commandments, which prohibits the use of music altogether.

43

When the Mountains Tremble
(Pamela Yates and Newton Thomas Sigel, 1983)

Granito: How to Nail a Dictator
(Pamela Yates, 2011)

The brutal civil war in Guatemala certainly did constitute genocide, as upwards of 200,000 people, the large majority of whom were indigenous people, were killed. Not only did the United States organize and help carry out the coup that overthrew President Arbenz in 1954, which had the effect of throwing the country into a decades-long civil war, but it also armed and equipped the various military dictatorships that directed and carried out the war. In response to the findings of the Guatemalan Truth and Reconciliation Commission, which tied US policy directly to this genocide, in 1999 President Bill Clinton issued a state apology for the country's support for "unjust regimes." The following film focuses on efforts to bring the Guatemalan perpetrators to justice. To my knowledge, there has not been a comparable effort to hold US operatives accountable as well.

✳ ✳ ✳

Because of the unique relationship between these two films I will treat them together. *When the Mountains Tremble* was released in 1983, just as the violence in Guatemala was beginning to reach genocidal proportions. The film provides some of the historical backdrop, particularly the United States' involvement in the overthrow of the Arbenz government in 1954. What followed were decades of civil war, which would result in the death of some 200,000 people, the overwhelming majority of whom were from the country's indigenous population. Without question, the bloodiest time was the decade of the 1980s, a period that coincided with the presidency of Ronald Reagan in the United States. The star of the movie—if this term is appropriate in a documentary about genocide—is Rigoberta Menchú, one of the young leaders of the indigenous movement, who would later be awarded the Nobel Peace Prize in 1992 for her efforts to end the conflict.

After making *When the Mountains Tremble*, Pamela Yates went on to other things, but years later she was approached by a group bringing a genocide case in Spain—which was spearheaded by Rigoberta Menchú. The group wanted Yates to help establish that genocide had taken place in Guatemala and wanted to make use of some of Yates's outtakes from her earlier film, which she had stored in a New York City warehouse.

One of the more interesting aspects of *Granito* is Yates's explanation of how she made her earlier film. Her contact with the rebels came through Naomi Roht-Arriaza, a fellow American who was working with indigenous groups. Through her, Yates was able to gain access to the guerrillas, including one of their leaders (Mueno), who would play an important role later on in the story. But Yates did not simply want to give the rebels' point of view, and her entrée to military leaders is in many ways even more interesting. She was with one of the military commanders when their helicopter was shot down over the jungle. All survived, but Yates was unexpectedly viewed by important military officials as a kind of lucky charm, which gave her access to many military operations and allowed her to document at least portions of the government's indiscriminate killing. At this same time, Yates also interviewed the president of Guatemala (Rios Montt), and the outtakes from these interviews played a key role in helping the Spanish judge conclude that genocide had been carried out and that proceedings should go forth. However, when the Spanish government attempted to extradite six people (including Rios Montt) to face these charges, their extradition was blocked by the Guatemalan Constitutional Court.

Although the Spanish inquiry was stalled, in 2005 tens of thousands of documents were uncovered in the basement of a government building in Guatemala. This prompted the creation of an archival unit to sift through these documents and the person chosen to head this operation was Mueno, the former rebel commander, a most thoughtful and insightful man, but also a man of action and resolve.

In Spanish, "granito de arena" means a grain of sand, and the importance of this expression in the present context is that one person can only do so much, but the combined efforts of all will be able to bring about meaningful change in the world. In the film's epilogue we learn of the conviction of two former police officers who had killed former guerrilla leader Francisco Garcia. Working on this case as an attorney was Garcia's daughter Alejandra, who was just a little girl at the time of his murder. Some of the best parts of this film are scenes where she describes her memories of her father and the work that she does, and now the intersection between the two. Given the fact that more than 200,000 were slaughtered in the genocide in Guatemala, these two convictions really do not amount to much. But they are two grains of sand.

Also of Note

State of Fear (Pamela Yates, 2005)

Yates's film *State of Fear* tells the story of the rise and fall of the revolutionary Shining Path in Peru—what one observer describes as a "rebellion against reality"—and the government's brutal response to this indigenous-based uprising. In total, over the course of approximately two decades some 70,000 civilians were killed, and a dictatorship was created but eventually removed from office. What the film shows quite clearly is the manner in which the rulers were able to use popular fear as a vehicle for exerting their own authoritarian power.

44

Fahrenheit 9/11
(Michael Moore, 2004)

The political use of fear is also the theme of the next film. And for American readers the locale is certainly much closer to home.

✳ ✳ ✳

The heart of this film is the manner in which the Bush administration used the September 11 attacks to purposely keep the American people in a constant state of fear, and the manner in which they used this fear to then invade Iraq, a country that posed no security threat to the United States. In film clips that I had never seen before, immediately after coming into office several members of the Bush administration, most notably Secretary of State Colin Powell, espouse the position that Saddam Hussein was not a security threat to the United States. However, after September 11, Vice President Dick Cheney and Secretary of Defense Donald Rumsfeld began to exert more authority and influence and created the public impression that such a threat existed.

Although Moore works on the macro-level, his films always include individuals, oftentimes from his hometown of Flint, Michigan, and in this film he makes very good use of Lila Lipscomb. Lipscomb is a God-fearing, flag-flying American who was quite proud when her son, Michael Pedersen, joined the military and was sent to Iraq. But this joy and pride turned to horror, shame, and outrage at the lies of the Bush administration when he returned home in a box.

Moore is also good at slyly showing the hypocrisy of the powerful. In one sequence, he goes around trying to get members of Congress to sign up their young sons and daughters to fight a war they supported—only one member of Congress has a son or daughter in Iraq. Of course, Moore has absolutely no success and some members of Congress actually even run away from him. Yet one wonders whether all of this is lost, not only on the powerful and well connected, but on the American people themselves. One also wonders if someone like Lila Lipscomb would be outside the White House waving an American flag in support of the war if her son had not been killed. The film closes with an observation by George Orwell that wars are not meant to be won but sustained in order to maintain a certain fear and social order. In light of the fact that the Iraq and Afghan wars are still going on as this is being written, and there is absolutely no indication that the USA Patriot Act will be removed—either by Congress or by the courts—any time soon, this certainly seems to describe the state of the United States over the past decade.

Also of Note

Why We Fight (Eugene Jarecki, 2005)

Why We Fight purposely takes its title from the Frank Capra films made during World War II to buttress public support for US involvement in the war. Certainly the Second World War is viewed, almost universally, as the good fight, but as this documentary explores, contrary to its self-image, the United States has become a militaristic nation, and this is true of all presidents and both political parties. Consider, for example, the invasion of Grenada (Reagan) or the military intervention in Panama (the first Bush). To its credit, the film explores how and why the United States so readily resorts to war, and its take-off point is President Eisenhower's farewell address in January 1961 where he warned about the rise of the military-industrial complex. Although the farewell address is best known for this term, what is seldom referenced is his depiction of how every bomb that is built, every plane that is added to the American arsenal, and every ship added to an ever-expanding fleet means less education and fewer social services for the average American. What also adds a nice touch is that it is not merely liberal talking heads who make this point in the film, but Eisenhower's son and his granddaughter.

45

Petition (The Court of Complaints) (Zhao Liang, 2009)

While Last Train Home *(D-17) and* Mardi Gras: Made in China *(D-38) are two documentaries that explore the issue of workers' rights in China, the next film focuses on the country's massive political corruption.*

✳ ✳ ✳

This documentary details aggrieved people in China who seek redress by traveling to Beijing where they petition government authorities, in many instances for years on end. It's hard to tell whether their persistence is a hopeful sign of the human spirit fighting against injustices and government oppression or whether these people are simply crazy. Maybe both of these things are true; or perhaps this level of government corruption is so massive that it would drive even the sanest person to complete and utter distraction.

Perhaps the craziest person of all is the director, Zhao Liang, who has been filming these petitioners for the better part of a decade. What we see is squalor all around the petitioners and the homesteads they have created for themselves, the anger and recrimination in the petition office itself (when filming can only be done clandestinely), and finally and perhaps inevitably in this oppressive society, the people who are forcibly removed from the petition office when government authorities reject their claim, as they inevitably seem to do.

The viewer spends a lot of time with Qi, a widow who during the first part of the film is accompanied by her daughter Xiaojuan. Qi's grievance is that her husband was killed in an industrial accident, and she has been pressing her grievance since 1996 when her daughter was twelve. Xiaojuan is now a grown woman, and yet the two of them persist in traveling to Beijing and persist in pressing their claim, again and again, although the prospects of achieving success are seemingly nonexistent, while the prospects of detention are excellent.

No one else will stand up to government abuses and apparently it is left up to this rag-tag group to do so, even if it means leaving home and family and living in squalid conditions, and even if there is a good chance that this will get them into an even more precarious position with government officials. There is a lot of talk about establishing a democracy in China, but people apparently place much more hope in the central government than they do in the regional and local units, which send "retrievers" to Beijing to try to "persuade" people not to file a petition. In the most chilling scene we see a retriever tell a woman that in their city of millions, the disappearance of one citizen (meaning her) would go unnoticed. Yet she does not balk for a moment. Instead, she informs him that a wrong has been committed and that she will be pressing ahead with her claim—although the film itself gives little indication that the petitioners are in any way successful, and the viewer (and, presumably, the petitioners) knows that plenty are beaten for their efforts.

Despite some weaknesses, *Petition* is the single best window for understanding how government works (or does not work) in China. The pursuit of justice might take decades and is often futile, but aggrieved citizens continue to press their claims. And because they are willing to do so, there is at least some hope for a better future for everyone.

46 (tie)

Burma VJ
(Anders Østergaard, 2008)

Burma Soldier
(Nic Dunlop and Ricki Stern, 2010)

Myanmar (Burma) is one of the last remaining military dictatorships in the world, although a political liberalization of sorts seems to be taking place, and the country's leading political dissident, Aung San Suu Kyi, is now free. However, military officers remain firmly entrenched in power, and the cruelties this regime is capable of carrying out are on display in the following two documentaries.

✳ ✳ ✳

Virtually any film footage that comes out of Burma/Myanmar is to be treasured, especially any that presents such riveting and important stories as the footage in these films. *Burma VJ* follows a group of guerilla human rights advocates who risk their lives and well-being in order to film and document human rights abuses by the military junta, which they then send through satellite images to Norway.

Burma VJ can be viewed on a few different levels. One is as a spy thriller where the viewer is taken on a joyride (sometimes literally) in foiling government authority. Of course the acts of daring are in service to an extraordinarily serious purpose. Because of their efforts, the world now has visible proof of the terrible beatings of those who would dare criticize the government; what was then the decades-long house arrest of government dissident Aung San Suu Kyi; and the butchery delivered against Buddhist monks who would dare march in support of human rights.

Burma Soldier is a documentary that tells the story of Myo Myint, who like thousands of other poor and illiterate peasants joined the military as a teenager in a combination of blind patriotism and the desperate need for a steady paycheck. Myo Myint dutifully served his country, and he fought its battles against government insurgents, losing an arm and a leg in the process. However, what this army (like many others) will not countenance is a soldier who thinks on his own—and this is exactly what Myo Myint began to do. It was this act that led him to take the courageous step of joining the opposition.

For these activities, Myo Myint was harshly imprisoned by the military junta for fifteen years. But the person the viewer gets to know is unbowed, and his new patriotic mission is to help spread the very same dissent that he, and others, sought to suppress for so long. In the final act, Myo Myint has moved to Fort Wayne, Indiana, where his brother and his family now reside. However, it is clear that Myo Myint's work has just started and that he and other disillusioned soldiers can play an important role in helping to bring down the country's military dictatorship.

48

One Day in September

(Kevin Macdonald, 1999)

The relationship between human rights and international terrorism is complicated. The entire basis for human rights is to ensure the security of the individual, and what this translates to, among other things, is that people are not to be kidnapped, beaten, or killed. On the other hand, common Article 1 of the International Covenant on Civil and Political Rights and the International Covenant on Economic, Social and Cultural Rights recognizes the principle of self-determination. This article provides: "All peoples have the right of self-determination. By virtue of that right they freely determine their political status and freely pursue their economic, social and cultural development." Perhaps like most other political conflicts, where one stands on the Palestinian-Israeli issue depends on whether one places a premium on self-determination (Palestine) or on security (Israel).

✱ ✱ ✱

For people of my generation and older, the advent of international terrorism took place at the 1972 Summer Olympic Games in Munich where a group from the Black September Movement abducted a number of Israeli athletes. What ensued was an internationally televised drama of cat-and-mouse negotiations that ended in a massacre at the city airport.

The Munich games were the first Olympics to be held in Germany since the infamous 1936 Games in Berlin. In response to its ugly history, every effort was made to demilitarize and even denationalize the Munich games, and viewers were shown repeated images of athletes of different countries intermingling with one another. These truly were the Feelgood Games.

All this changed overnight when members of the Black September Movement, a group affiliated with the Palestinian Liberation Organization (PLO), breached the scant security at the athletes' village and took hostage a small contingent of Israeli athletes. What followed were hours and hours of high drama, manifested for the world by the shadowy figure with a blackened face and a white summer hat who would intermittently appear on the balcony where the Israelis were being held hostage. What added to the bizarre but compelling nature of all this was ABC's coverage of these proceedings, hosted by Jim McKay, who was also the anchor of *The Wide World of Sports*.

The Black September members demanded flight out of the country, and German officials appeared to comply with this. However, they had set a trap at the airport, and things went awry almost immediately. In the end, all of the hostages were killed in a barrage of bullets and explosions. Although there is no video of what occurred at the airport, the documentary shows in gruesome detail pictures of the charred bodies and destroyed vehicles.

Although the drama took on overtones of David and Goliath, at least in the United States and certainly in Israel, the film is not overtly biased. One of the commentators used throughout the film is Jamal Al-Gashey of Black September, who is purportedly the only living survivor. Another constant presence, from the other side, is Ankie Spitzer, the widow of Andre Spitzer, the coach of the Israeli fencing team, who is first shown in her wedding gown the day the two were married.

What did these events achieve? Arguably nothing. But they helped develop a narrative that continues to exist today. On one side there are Palestinians with the blood of Munich on their (collective) hands and Israelis who readily can play the role of innocent underdogs. This film does not explore these politics so much, but what it certainly does show is how and when politics and sports became mixed in blood.

Also of Note

Munich (Steven Spielberg, 2005)

Munich begins where *One Day in September* ends. This feature film is director Steven Spielberg's attempt to tell how the Israeli government plotted to kill all of those associated with the Munich massacre. One thing that is now particularly jarring is the seemingly cavalier attitude toward terrorism that was taken at that time, particularly the quick decision by the West German government to swap the Black September operatives in its custody following a Syrian skyjacking.

The best part of this less-than-thrilling political thriller is that the film explicitly raises the question that is only implied in *One Day in September*: what has all this violence achieved? And another question that is also raised directly in this film is whether, by engaging in acts of terror itself, Israel has lost the moral high ground, if not its national conscience.

49

The Farm: Angola, USA
(Liz Garbus and Wilbert Rideau, 1998)

Article 10 of the International Covenant on Civil and Political Rights provides: "All persons deprived of their liberty shall be treated with humanity and with respect for the inherent dignity of the human person." One would certainly be hard pressed to find much humanity and respect for the inherent dignity of the human person in the next film.

✳ ✳ ✳

Fully 85 percent of the inmates sent to the Angola state penitentiary in Louisiana will die there. Thus, of the 5,000 prisoners who are there at the time this documentary was made, approximately 4,250 will never get out alive. This documentary focuses on six inmates, and their prospects do not look particularly good, no matter what they have (or have not) done before, or what they do while incarcerated. As the film opens, the viewer meets George Crawford, who has been convicted of murder and is being sent to Angola to begin his life sentence. Crawford is twenty-two years old, and he is understandably scared. Although Crawford's mother comes to visit him, the viewer learns that in almost all cases, visits by family and friends virtually cease after the first year. To the outside world, Crawford is already dead.

Eugene "Bishop" Tannehill is in his thirty-eighth year of incarceration. The moniker "Bishop" comes from his activities in the prison spreading the Lord's word. As the Bishop acknowledges, he has been raised in Angola. And although he is nothing like the man who was convicted of murder in 1959, as the film closes we learn that his petition for a pardon is still on the governor's desk. The governor has never signed such a pardon, and in all likelihood the Bishop will join the statistics of those who never leave Angola.

George Ashanti Witherspoon is serving a seventy-five-year sentence for armed robbery. At the time of filming, Witherspoon had served twenty-five years, which means that he has "only" a half-century left to go. Unlike most of the other inmates, Witherspoon has gotten out of Angola for short trips to teach CPR classes. In many ways, Witherspoon is a model prisoner. Yet, as the film closes we learn that, once more, he has been turned down for parole.

Vincent Simmons is serving a hundred-year sentence for raping a white woman. Simmons maintains that he is innocent. For one thing, in a police lineup Simmons was the only person in handcuffs, which would certainly seem to bias anyone. Added to that, at that time the victim was quoted as saying "all niggers look alike," which would most certainly call into question her positive identification of Simmons. In one of the most startling and depressing scenes, the viewer gets to see Simmons's parole hearing. The victim tells the parole board that she has "problems" with black people. When the only black board member asks her if she has problems with him, she says that she does not—but then goes on to say that she would never be in a room alone with him. Simmons then comes in, and he presents newly discovered evidence that a medical exam taken at the time of the alleged incident shows that the victim was still a virgin and thus could not have been raped. The parole board dismisses this evidence without attempting to even look at it, and it denies parole.

Bones Theriot is a white prisoner who killed his wife for abusing their child. Angola has made Bones a philosophical man. As he puts it, you might be dead to the outside world, but that does not mean that you are dead inside. Bones is in the last stages of life, and one of the most moving scenes occurs when some of his fellow inmates visit him to say their last goodbyes. He decides to be buried inside the prison, among his friends, as he puts it. His blood relatives object to this, but it is perfectly understandable to the viewer.

Finally, there is John Brown, another white inmate, who is sentenced to death for murder. The film shows us what death row and the procedure for killing a man are like. There is actually a kind of execution rehearsal where prison authorities walk through how the body will be positioned (for maximum viewing opportunities for the victim's family) and how many men it will take to tie the prisoner down. In the early morning hours near the end of the film, Brown's soul was sent out of the prison for final judgment. Prior to this, Brown had been asked if he believes in God and heaven and he says that he does. He is then asked what it takes to get to heaven, and he says that one must be Christlike, but that he does not believe that he has gotten there yet.

Certainly the same could be said of many of the prison authorities and parole board members who are shown in this film. The warden, who is interviewed throughout, maintains that the job of prison is to keep hope alive, but there does not seem to be any reason why anyone would have even a scent of hope in Angola. In one of the more pathetic scenes, on Christmas Eve a clown (yes, a clown) goes to visit the death row prisoners. There is some banal discussion about God and all that, and perhaps the visit breaks up the undying monotony of the prisoners' existence. But another way of interpreting this is as some kind of cosmic joke that we have visited on the Angola inmates.

50

The Dictator Hunter
(Klaartje Quirijns, 2007)

As mentioned before, the Pinochet principle provides that violations of certain international human rights standards are so egregious that any country in the world is lawfully able to prosecute those who directed or carried them out, through the exercise of what is known as universal jurisdiction. More than that, under the Torture Convention, state parties obligate themselves to either prosecute or extradite any torturers who are within a country's territorial borders. Similarly, the Genocide Convention obligates state parties to "punish" those who are responsible for carrying out genocide. On the basis of this law, one might conclude that dictators and torturers would simply have no place to hide. Think again.

✳ ✳ ✳

Reed Brody of Human Rights Watch is the dictator hunter in the title of this moving documentary—an Inspector Javert of sorts in terms of his doggedness and determination. But rather than seeking to arrest a petty thief who has already done years in prison, Brody wants to bring Hissène Habré, the former dictator of Chad, to justice. The problem is that Habré, whose brutal rule finally ended in 1990, is living the good life in Senegal, surrounded by the riches he has accumulated and bodyguards to protect him, and under the security provided by the Senegalese government—but truthfully the entire international community.

As Brody tells the interviewer at the outset of the film, if you kill a person you are sent to prison; if you kill forty people you are sent to an asylum; but if you kill 40,000 people, as Habré did, nothing happens to you. The prosecution of Augusto Pinochet was supposed to change all that, but this has not been the case. The film shows Brody and his associate, Souleymane Guengueng, a former political prisoner from Chad now living in New York, pursuing Habré any way they can. The problem is that they are up against an international system that finds it easier to maintain dictators in power, and then to provide them refuge if and when they are removed from office, than it is to do what international law demands: prosecute or extradite.

The single most moving scene in this film does not take place in New York or Geneva or the various other places that the camera takes us to. Instead, it takes place at the site of a mass grave in Chad where a small group of those who suffered under Habré's rule surround Brody, in part for solace but also as a way of providing him much needed support in his fight against overwhelming odds and international inertia and blindness.

51

The Emperor's Naked Army Marches On

(Kazuo Hara, 1987)

International human rights law is sweeping in its coverage and intended to prevent viola-
tions. The problem has always been enforcement and, failing that, formulating a proper
response. One response has been to hold individuals accountable. This was the approach taken
at the Nuremberg trials following World War II but also the motive behind the creation of
the International Criminal Court. A slightly different approach involves state responsibility,
as evidenced by the establishment of human rights tribunals such as the European Court of
Human Rights, where states can be challenged on the basis that their actions violate inter-
national human rights standards. But in most cases there has been little accountability for
those who have violated international human rights standards. To many, this best describes
Japan, which has refused to sufficiently acknowledge and apologize for its actions in World
War II. Into the breach steps Kenzo Okuzaki.

✳ ✳ ✳

Kenzo Okuzaki is certifiably crazy—yet he might also be the sanest person in all of Japan. Kenzo is a World War II veteran who was one of the few survivors of the military campaign in New Guinea, and he has now dedicated his life to holding Japanese military and political leaders accountable for war crimes. Kenzo makes everyone around him extraordinarily uncomfortable and with good reason. He wants to confront head on what the rest of Japan would like to avoid at all costs. So he ends up doing things that perhaps he ought not to do, such as shooting a slingshot at the emperor or plotting the murder of a former prime minister. That is the kind of thing that will get you sent to jail, and Kenzo makes note of the fact that he has spent thirteen years and nine months in jail for these and other acts. But he is not going to let something like jail stop him.

The tone of the film is set early on as we see Kenzo in his car, which is a veritable billboard with signs about Japanese war crimes plastered all over it. And if this is not enough to get the attention of pedestrians and other drivers, he also makes good use of a loud microphone. A short time later, Kenzo goes to the hospital bearing a gift for a patient lying in bed who is in obvious distress. But Kenzo is not there to soothe this person but to confront him, and since the patient cannot get out of bed, let alone leave, he is subject to Kenzo's angry diatribe. Kenzo's real concern is the murder of two soldiers from his unit, Yoshizawa and Nomura, who were executed after the fighting had ended. It is not clear why they were killed. The families of these two individuals believe it was because they threatened to report that Japanese soldiers had engaged in cannibalism, while their former commanders maintain that they were shot because of desertion. Of course, they tell Kenzo that all this happened decades ago in a different time and setting. But he will have none of this. So what he does is to arrive unannounced at peoples' homes and demand that they atone for their crimes. None are willing to do so, at least initially, but Kenzo has a unique way of making people speak, and if this doesn't work, he resorts to physically attacking them, which seems to do the trick.

It is an odd sight to see two elderly Japanese men wrestling on the ground, but Kenzo has a point. Japan has engaged in virtually no critical self-examination for its role in initiating World War II or for the behavior of Japanese troops in the conduct of the war itself. And if government officials are not going to take up such matters, Kenzo will. As the film closes, the viewer learns that Kenzo has shot at one of his former commanding officers. Although he missed his intended target, he hit his son and Kenzo then spends some time on the lam before he is arrested and sentenced to hard labor where he eventually dies. But perhaps this really did not change his life all that much. Before all this, Kenzo had built a prison cell in his own home as a means of his own atonement. And his hard labor came in the form of getting the Japanese people to make their own atonement.

Appendix

Films and the Universal Declaration of Human Rights

The Universal Declaration of Human Rights (UDHR) was adopted by the UN General Assembly on December 10, 1948. It is a direct result of the atrocities committed during World War II and the international community's commitment to avert such violations in the future. It may be viewed as an international bill of rights, with thirty different Articles enumerating both general and specific rights the international community affirms. The films in this book do not cover every single right enumerated in the UDHR, but they do span a broad spectrum. This appendix shows how the films included in the book may be categorized according to the key Articles in the UDHR. For the complete listing of UDHR articles, go to: http://www.un.org/en/documents/udhr/

This UN site is linked on the website for this book:
http://www.paradigmpublishers.com/Books/BookDetail.aspx?productID=298816

Articles 1 and 2

These are general statements of rights to which many films could be related; therefore, we have not specified them here.

Article 3: The Right to Life, Liberty and Security of the Person

Genocide

The Holocaust

Schindler's List (FF-1)

The Pianist (FF-12)

Sophie's Choice (FF-27)

Au Revoir, Les Enfants (FF-42)

Cambodia

The Killing Fields (FF-5)

Enemies of the People (D-21)

Rwanda

Sometimes in April (FF-9)

Hotel Rwanda (FF-9)

The Sudan

The Devil Came on Horseback (D-42)

Government Oppression

Burma

Burma VJ (D-46)

Burma Soldier (D-46)

Israel

One Day in September (D-48)

Arna's Children (D-7)

Paradise Now (FF-30)

Budrus (D-28)

South Africa

A Dry White Season (FF-21)

Amandla! A Revolution in Four Part Harmony (D-41)

Long Night's Journey into Day (D-9)

Northern Ireland

Hunger (FF-7)

Bloody Sunday (FF-28)

Omagh (FF-29)

Latin America

Missing (FF-3)

The Official Story (FF-4)

When the Mountains Tremble (D-43)

Granito: How to Nail a Dictator (D-43)

Men with Guns (FF-40)

War Crimes

City of Life and Death (FF-49)

White Light/Black Rain: The Destruction of Hiroshima and Nagasaki (D-12)

Waltz with Bashir (FF-32)

Lord of War (FF-46)

Pray the Devil Back to Hell (D-20)

Non-State Actors

Crude (D-25)

The Constant Gardener (FF-44)

The Insider (FF-19)

The Interrupters (D-39)

Article 5: Freedom from Torture

The Battle of Algiers (FF-41)

The Road to Guantanamo (FF-48)

Taxi to the Dark Side (D-23)

Ghosts of Abu Ghraib (D-23)

You Don't Like the Truth: 4 Days Inside Guantanamo (D-15)

Article 7: Equal Protection and Nondiscrimination

Sexual Minorities

Milk (FF-17)

We Were Here (D-8)

Philadelphia (FF-22)

Out in the Silence (D-34)

Gender Discrimination

The Circle (FF-35)

Persepolis (FF-31)

Moolaadé (FF-43)

4 Months, 3 Weeks and 2 Days (FF-37)

Vera Drake (FF-38)

Lilya 4-Ever (FF-39)

Racial Discrimination

Amazing Grace (FF-33)

Mississippi Burning (FF-34)

4 Little Girls (D-6)

Once Were Warriors (FF-6)

Rabbit-Proof Fence (FF-50)

Ethnic and Caste Discrimination

Days of Glory (Indigènes) (FF-25)

Even the Rain (FF-45)

Gandhi (FF-15)

Slumdog Millionaire (FF-16)

District 9 (F-26)

Children

Children Underground (D-31)

Article 8: The Right to an Effective Remedy

Judgment at Nuremberg (FF-47)

The Pinochet Case (D-27)

The Dictator Hunter (D-50)

Article 9: Freedom from Arbitrary Arrest/Article 10: Right to a Fair Trial

Presumed Guilty (D-22)

To Kill a Mockingbird (FF-24)

In the Land of the Free (D-14)

The Farm: Angola, USA (D-49)

USA vs. Al-Arian (D-4)

Dead Man Walking (FF-11)

Petition (The Court of Complaints) (D-45)

Bamako (FF-36)

Article 13: Freedom of Movement/Article 14: The Right to Apply for Asylum

Journey of Hope (FF-13)
Well-Founded Fear (D-30)
Pushing the Elephant (D-19)

Article 18: Freedom of Thought/Article 19: Freedom of Opinion and Expression

The Lives of Others (FF-2)
Good Night, and Good Luck (FF-23)
Fahrenheit 9/11 (D-44)
V for Vendetta (FF-20)
The Agronomist (D-5)

Article 22: The Right to Social Security/Article 25: The Realization of ESCR

Precious: Based on the Novel "Push" by Sapphire (F-8)
Midnight Cowboy (F-14)
Roger & Me (D-11)
Hoop Dreams (D-3)
Public Housing (D-35)
When the Levees Broke: A Requiem in Four Acts (D-29)

Article 23: The Right to Work and the Right to Form and Join Trade Unions

Norma Rae (FF-18)
Harlan County, USA (D-36)
American Dream (D-36)
Last Train Home (D-17)
Mardi Gras: Made in China (D-38)
The Inheritors (D-33)

The Shipbreakers (D-37)

Article 26: The Right to Education

Waiting for "Superman" (D-10)
Where Soldiers Come From (D-13)

Article 28: The Right to a Social and International Order to Promote and Protect Human Rights

Darwin's Nightmare (D-1)
Nero's Guests (D-2)
An Inconvenient Truth (D-16)
The Age of Stupid (D-40)

Index

About the Author

Mark Gibney is the Belk Distinguished Professor at the University of North Carolina–Asheville. He is one of the film editors for *Human Rights Quarterly* and since 1984 has directed the Political Terror Scale (PTS), which measures levels of physical integrity violations in more than 185 countries (www.politicalterrorscale .org).

He has worked at several human rights institutions in Scandinavia: the Norwegian Institute of Human Rights, the Christian Michelsen Institute (Bergen), and the Danish Institute for Human Rights. He is currently a Distinguished Visiting Faculty Member at the Lancaster University School of Law. He is one of the founding members of the Extraterritorial Obligations Consortium, and this work puts him in almost daily contact with human rights scholars, NGOs, and activists all over the world.

Gibney is the author of numerous books and scholarly articles including, most recently, *The Handbook of Human Rights* (edited volume with Anja Mihr) (Sage Publications, forthcoming); *The Politics of Human Rights: The Quest for Dignity* (with Sabine Carey and Steven Poe) (Cambridge University Press, 2010); *Universal Human Rights and Extraterritorial Obligations* (edited volume with Sigrun Skogly) (University of Pennsylvania Press, 2010); and *The Global Refugee Crisis* (ABC-CLIO, 2010).

He has received several awards for teaching and scholarship.